UNION WITH CHRIST

Union with Christ

The New
Finnish Interpretation
of Luther

Edited by

Carl E. Braaten *and* Robert W. Jenson

William B. Eerdmans Publishing Company
Grand Rapids, Michigan / Cambridge, U.K.

© 1998 Wm. B. Eerdmans Publishing Co.

255 Jefferson Ave. S.E., Grand Rapids, Michigan 49503 /

P.O. Box 163, Cambridge CB3 9PU U.K.

Printed in the United States of America

03 02 01 00 99 98   7 6 5 4 3 2 1

Library of Congress Cataloging-in-Publication Data

Union with Christ: the new Finnish interpretation of Luther /
edited by Carl E. Braaten and Robert W. Jenson
p.   cm.
Includes bibliographical references.
ISBN 0-8028-4442-1 (pbk.: alk. paper)
1. Luther, Martin, 1483-1546.
2. Justification — History of doctrines — 16th century.
3. Lutheran Church — Relations — Orthodox Eastern Church.
4. Orthodox Eastern Church — Relations — Lutheran Church.
5. Theology, Doctrinal — Finland.
6. Deification (Christianity).
I. Braaten, Carl E., 1929-
II. Jenson, Robert W.
BR333.5.J8U55 1998
230'.41'092 — dc21   98-28328
                                                         CIP

Contents

CONTENTS

Preface: The Finnish Breakthrough in Luther Research

CARL E. BRAATEN *and* ROBERT W. JENSON

We first met Professor Tuomo Mannermaa at the 1993 Luther Congress held at Luther Seminary, St. Paul, Minnesota. He was accompanied by an entourage of disciples representing the new "Finnish school," which is radically revising our understanding of Luther. The Finnish delegation was by far the most impressive and interesting new voice in the various seminars. Dr. Eero Huovinen, Bishop of Helsinki and a member of the Mannermaa circle, rented a van and drove a dozen of the Helsinki group to visit the Center for Catholic and Evangelical Theology in Northfield, Minnesota.

From that encounter came the idea to co-sponsor a theological conference on "salvation," featuring the new Finnish understanding of Luther's teaching on justification and its convergence with the Orthodox view of salvation as *theosis*. On June 1, 1996, Professor Tuomo Mannermaa and three of his younger colleagues from the Finnish Academy for Luther Studies led a seminar at St. Olaf College that was attended by one hundred people. The first four papers in this volume were seminar presentations, each of which is followed by a response by an American theologian. The additional chapters by Tuomo Mannermaa, Simo Peura, and Risto Saarinen have appeared as articles in *Pro Ecclesia: A Journal of Catholic and Evangelical Theology*.

Tuomo Mannermaa is the creative spirit leading the Finnish

breakthrough in Luther research. At its heart lies the theme of salvation, not surprisingly because soteriology has always been the deepest passion of Lutheran theology and the source of its never-ending internal turmoil. Mannermaa's key idea is that "in faith itself Christ is really present,"[1] a literal translation of Luther's *"in ipsa fide Christus adest."* This idea is played off against a purely forensic concept of justification, in which the *Christus pro nobis* (Christ for us) is separated from the *Christus in nobis* (Christ within us).

Mannermaa and his colleagues went behind the disputatious history of the Lutheran doctrine of justification and reread Luther's texts. There they found that for Luther faith is a real participation in Christ, that in faith a believer receives the righteousness of God in Christ, not only in a nominal and external way, but really and inwardly. According to the forensic model of justification, it is *as though* we are righteous, while in reality we are not. But if through faith we really participate in Christ, we participate in the whole Christ, who in his divine person communicates the righteousness of God. Here lies the bridge to the Orthodox idea of salvation as deification or *theosis.*

Righteousness as an attribute of God in Christ cannot be separated from his divine being. Thus Luther found it appropriate to say that through faith in Christ a real exchange occurs, the righteousness of God in exchange for the sinfulness of human beings. The righteousness of God that is ours by faith is therefore a real participation in the life of God. This seems to come close to what the Orthodox understand by deification and *theosis.* It is, in any case, what the Finnish theologians are saying, and understandably some of the language falls like a thud on Lutheran ears accustomed to hearing from Luther chiefly what echoes their Lutheran tradition.

The Mannermaa school is revising a century of Luther interpretation dominated by German Protestant theologians, who notoriously read Luther under the spell of neo-Kantian presuppositions. This is true of a long line of German Luther scholarship from Albrecht Ritschl to Gerhard Ebeling. On this basis one should ignore all ontology found in Luther; faith is purely an act of the will with no

---

1. Cf. Tuomo Mannermaa's book, *Der im Glauben gegenwärtige Christus* (Hannover, 1989).

ontological implications. Faith as volitional obedience rather than as ontological participation is all that a neo-Kantianized Luther could allow. The Finns have found that Luther's texts, when read critically against the background of late medieval philosophy and theology, speak to the contrary.

Professor Tuomo Mannermaa

Why Is Luther So Fascinating?
Modern Finnish Luther Research

TUOMO MANNERMAA

1. Introduction

I call "modern" the Finnish Luther research that has been done since about the mid-seventies at the Department of Systematic Theology of the University of Helsinki. Luther studies have flourished in Helsinki since the twenties, and an almost unbroken tradition of Luther research has been handed down since then. But the studies that have been done since the mid-seventies have actually promulgated a new beginning, a new way of putting the fundamental questions in Luther research. Luther has also become more interesting than before.

The external impulse for this new wave of Luther studies in Helsinki came surprisingly from outside the boundaries of Luther research. It came from the ecumenical dialogue between the Evangelical Lutheran Church of Finland and the Russian Orthodox Church that was initiated by Archbishop Martti Simojoki at the beginning of the seventies. Archbishop Simojoki asked some younger members of the theological faculty at the University of Helsinki to participate in a preparatory group, which had the task of finding a firm point of departure for the Lutheran-Orthodox dialogue that was just beginning at that time. We decided to seek a methodologically secure common standpoint from which we could in time systematically and safely proceed toward further topics.

1

The invitation from the archbishop, then, was the external impulse to the latest phase of Finnish Luther research. Following this invitation began the labor of quite ordinary academic Luther studies. For even though the outer impulse for this work came from the ecumenical situation, it still had to be carried out with academic rigor. In the course of this research Luther once again became fascinating for us.

2. The Course and Publications of the Research Program

At the very beginning of our studies we came to the conclusion that Luther's idea of the presence of Christ in faith could form a basis for the Lutheran-Orthodox dialogue.[1] The indwelling of Christ as grasped in the Lutheran tradition implies a real participation in God, and it corresponds in a special way to the Orthodox doctrine of participation in God, namely the doctrine of *theosis*. This conclusion was not a commonly accepted understanding of how one might find the point of contact that we were seeking.

According to Luther, Christ (in both his person and his work) is present in faith and is through this presence identical with the righteousness of faith. Thus, the notion that Christ is present in the Christian occupies a much more central place in the theology of Luther than in the Lutheranism subsequent to him. The idea of a divine life in Christ who is really present in faith lies at the very center of the theology of the Reformer.

Having published these initial insights for the purposes of the Lutheran-Orthodox dialogue, a long-range research into Luther's thought began. Finland's Academy of Sciences has financed this work since 1984. The first task of this project was to analyze the philosophical (i.e., the epistemological and/or ontological) assumptions of modern Luther research concerning the idea of the presence of Christ in faith. The question was, How do modern Luther scholars

1. T. Mannermaa, *In ipsa fide Christus adest* (Finnish ed. 1978); German ed.: *Der im Glauben gegenwärtige Christus. Rechtfertigung und Vergottung. Zum ökumenischen Dialog. Arbeiten zur Geschichte und Theologie des Luthertum, Neue folge Bd. 8* (Hannover, 1989), pp. 11-93.

understand this presence(Being)-of-Christ? What does "Being" mean here?

The dissertation addressing this task, written by Risto Saarinen and published in 1989, was entitled *The Transcendental Interpretation of the Presence-of-Christ Motif in Luther Research.*[2] Saarinen's study treats the philosophical assumptions of traditional Luther research, which made it impossible to view Luther's doctrine of justification as a doctrine of real participation or divinization.

The second task of the project was to analyze Luther's own understanding of the participation in God as realized in faith. Simo Peura's dissertation, *Theosis in the Theology of Martin Luther 1510-1519,*[3] addressed this issue. Peura's dissertation, complementing Saarinen's book on Luther research by studying the concept of participation in Luther's theology itself, demonstrates that the motif of participation in God *(theosis)* is inherent in Luther's theology. And this insight is important because it highlights an idea that has been neglected in modern Luther research.

The third study contributing to this work is Antti Raunio's dissertation, *Die Summe des christlichen Lebens. Die "Goldene Regel" als Gesetz der Liebe in der Theologie Martin Luthers von 1510 bis 1527.*[4] This analysis attempts to portray Luther's theology as a theology of love. The Golden Rule is for Luther not only an "ethical" but also an eminently "dogmatic" rule of his doctrine of faith. God himself follows the Golden Rule, which describes the essential dynamic of God's Being. Thus, the Golden Rule is the *summa* of the Christian faith and life. Luther's entire theology thereby takes on the character of a consistent theology of love. It is at same time completely a theology of faith and a theology of love.

---

2. In German: *Gottes Wirken auf uns. Die transzendentale Deutung des Gegenwart-Christi-Motivs in der Lutherforschung.* Veröffentlichungen des Institut für Europäische Geschichte Mainz, Abteilung Religionsgeschichte, ed. Peter Manns. Bd. 137.

3. In German: *Mehr als ein Mensch? Die Vergöttlichung als Thema der Theologie Martin Luthers von 1513-1519,* Veröffentlichungen des Instituts für Europäische Geschichte Mainz, Bd. 152 (Stuttgart, 1994).

4. Systemaattisen teologian laitoksen julkaisuja 13, Universität Helsinki, 1993. It will be published in Germany by Veröffentlichungen des Instituts für Europäische Geschichte, Mainz.

The fourth dissertation in this project is Sammeli Juntunen's *The Concept of Nothing in the Theology of Martin Luther.*[5] In classical ontology "nothing" is a central complementary notion to that of "Being." By analyzing the notion of "nothing" that Luther frequently uses, Juntunen has been able to sketch out some interesting insights into Luther's underlying concept of Being.

Actually the first dissertation in this new Finnish Luther project was Juhani Forsberg's *Das Abrahambild in der Theologie Luthers. Pater fidei Sanctissimus.*[6] The study treats most of the central themes of our Luther interpretation. Several other dissertations are currently being prepared.

The Finnish Luther project has been carried on in cooperation with the Luther-Akademie Ratzeburg, with the Institut für Europäische Geschichte in Mainz, and with the Ecumenical Institute of Strasbourg. Five symposia have been arranged and, correspondingly, five volumes from these symposia have been published.

3. Epistemological and Ontological Presuppositions of Luther Research

Since certain philosophical assumptions have influenced Luther research so decisively, I will deal with some fundamental philosophical questions in respect to this research. It will be useful to deal first of all with Risto Saarinen's thesis.

Saarinen investigates the philosophical and/or ontological assumptions of Luther studies by analyzing how the presence-of-Christ motif has been interpreted in that research. As is well known, Luther emphasizes vigorously that Christ is *really present* in faith. What is the ontological status, then, of this "being" of Christ and/or the "being" of God in the Christian faith? What philosophical assumptions have been employed in defining more precisely the sense of God's "being present"?

---

5. *Der Begriff des Nichts bei Luther in den Jahren 1510 bis 1523*, Schriften der Luther-Agricola-Gesellschaft 36 (Helsinki, 1996).

6. Veröffentlichungen des Instituts für Europäische Geschichte, Mainz, Bd. 117 (Stuttgart, 1984).

Saarinen shows in his dissertation that the ontology of the German philosopher Hermann Lotze (1817-1881) has exerted a decisive influence on the explication of the presence-of-Christ motif. The initial assumption of Lotze's ontology is that the everyday conception of reality, according to which things first must exist in themselves in order subsequently to be able to stand in relationship to other things, is false. There is no being in itself. The only sense of "being" is "standing in relationship." The world is not properly to be conceived as a space filled with things that, with their own being already assured, then take up relationship to other beings. Rather, standing in a mutually affecting relationship to other beings is the primary sense of what it means for a thing to *be*. Being is what happens in reciprocal affectings. Saarinen writes: "Thus Lotze wants to replace static thinking about being, which views the world as a totality of isolated things existing in themselves, with 'effect thinking' (Wirkungsdenken), in which the 'affecting relationships' caused by constant reciprocal action engender the order of the world" (Saarinen, p. 12).

Lotze's epistemology runs parallel to this ontology. The world of substances existing in themselves remains beyond the scope of human knowledge. Things in themselves cannot be objects of human understanding, but only their effects. We can achieve no certainty about the "being-in-itself" of the assumed causes of our knowledge. Nor can their nonexistence be given a philosophical proof. Even if things actually do exist "in themselves," we must "content ourselves in our epistemology with their effects on us, because we cannot arrive at their being-in-itself" (p. 12).

The import of Lotze is a crucial epistemological determination: our knowledge does not consist in the intelligible forms of things *entering into us* themselves, but only in *their affect upon us (dass die Dinge auf uns wirken)*. The result of this affecting upon us is that, in the epistemological context, things receive their form *from our nature*. Lotze writes: "For even if things are, our *'knowledge'* of them nevertheless cannot consist in their entering into us themselves, but only in their affects upon us. The products of this affecting, however, as effects in *our* being, can only receive their form from *our* nature."

In my opinion, a profound change takes place at this point: according to classical realist epistemology, human understanding originates with the entrance of the intelligible epistemic form *(forma,*

Erkenntnisform) into the intellect via the senses. The Being *(= forma = Seinswirklichkeit)* of the known thing itself is present in the knower. *"Species cogniti est in cognoscenti,"* says Thomas Aquinas, and *"Idem est intellectus et intellectum,"* "knowing and that which *is* known are identical."

Whatever Luther's stance on nominalism may be, in his theology, at least, he follows this classical epistemology quite explicitly from beginning to end. Luther says, for example, in his early Christmas sermon (1514): "It is no wonder that I said that we must become word, because the philosophers, too, say that the intellect, through the act of intellectual knowing, is the known object, and that sensuality, through the act of sensual perception, is the sensual object; how much more is this true of the spirit and of the word!"[7]

The unity of the intellect and its object is expressed perhaps even more strongly in a passage immediately after the above quotation, where Luther says that the objects of the intellect and of sense *are* the *being* and *act* of intellect and sense: *"ita obiecta sunt eorum esse et actus, sine quibus nihil essent, sicut materia sine formas nihil esset."*[8] He follows this with a statement concerning the *status gloriae:* "God as the object of blessedness is the essence itself of the blessed" *(Deus Obiectum beatitudinis est ipsa essentia beatorum).* In like manner, he says later in the longer *Commentary on the Epistle to the Galatians* that Christ is not only the object of faith but is himself present in faith.

An analogous pattern appears when Luther says that man has in faith the righteousness of Christ; for example, in *Sermo de duplici iustitiae* (1518): "Thus the righteousness of Christ becomes our righteousness through faith in Christ, and everything that is his, even he [be]comes ours . . . and he who believes in Christ clings to [is] one with Christ and has the same righteousness with [him]. Luther expresses a realist conception of knowledge ac[cording to] which knowledge brings about a real participation in the [being] known. Thus Luther teaches by means of philosophical [that] the essence of the relationship to God is a community

29, 15-18.
29, 26-27.

The situation is different in the case of Lotze and the theologians who have taken up Lotze's epistemology and/or ontology. In their view, the *intelligible form* that knowledge grasps in the object is not conceived of as real. Rather, the effects that flow from the unknown "being-in-itself" of the object of knowledge receive their form only from the nature of a person, that is, from one's *a priori* constitution.

Instead of presenting a detailed analysis of Hermann Lotze's epistemology and philosophy of religion, I will limit myself to a few brief remarks. According to Lotze, religious effects belong not to the realm of the knowledge of "nature" but to the realm of the "person." That is, they pertain to the area of "values" and ethics. Ethical and aesthetic values belong, according to Lotze, to the "worldview of the soul" *(Weltansicht des Gemüthes)*. And this worldview can involve a broader conception of reality than that of the mere "sum of the pieces of knowledge" of which our scientific consciousness treats. The highest, infinite value of the cosmos is in its effect present in the soul *(Gemüth)*. And Lotze understands the effect of this Infinite value *(das Unendliche)* on the soul *(Gemüth)* as a special kind of holistic experience, *Erlebnis,* as distinguished from rational knowledge.

Now comes the crucial determination that has functioned as a model for many subsequent theological solutions to the problem of Christ's presence. Saarinen writes, after establishing that for Lotze the effects of the Infinite on the soul *(Gemüth)* are effects of the *will* of God: "In the unity of the will of God and its effects on the soul 'the living penetration of the creature by the creator takes place.'" Lotze does not mean that a unity of being is achieved but rather a unity of the will and its effects: "When God affects upon us as an immediately affecting will *(als unmitelbar wirkender Wille),* thus causing our actions, He is present as this will in us" (p. 24). The presence of God is, according to Lotze, a community of willing and of affecting *(gemeinschaft des Wollens und des Wirkens),* but not a union of being *(unio).*

The influential Protestant theologian Albrecht Ritschl (1822-1889) takes up the central content of Lotze's philosophy directly. "In theology, we cannot assume the isolated existence of things. Right theological knowledge is . . . transcendental, in the sense that only effects of God's action in the world, not his being in itself, is accessible to us" (Saarinen, p. 31.) According to Ritschl, Luther supported in

7

principle this "correct" epistemology, even though he occasionally used the inappropriate expressions and forms of thought of metaphysical scholasticism.

According to the genuine, "religious" epistemology of Luther, Ritschl maintains, what is called Christ's presence in faith is an effect of the will of God. The anthropological point of contact of this effect of the will of God on humans is human will. God himself remains outside of human reality so that only the impulse of God's will reaches us. Logically, then, Christ in us means that God affects the human will through an external causal impulse. The impulse does not have any being in itself, because "being-in-itself" and "effect" have been ontologically separated from each other. Saarinen succinctly formulates Ritschl's view: "Christ in us means therefore that we ourselves live a moral life for him (i.e. Christ)."

Ritschl claims, however, that along with this "correct" epistemology, Luther retained vestiges of the old, metaphysical view. Luther speaks contrary to such "proper" statements, for example, of justification as a real impartation of the being of God to the believer. Thus, Luther's "correct" epistemology struggles against its foundation and falls back to the false Osiandrian line that was dependent on the old substance-orientation. According to a "correct" epistemology, Christ's presence in faith is not a reality in itself, neither a substantial nor an ontological reality, but rather a kind of community of action (affecting) of the divine and human will.

I cannot examine in detail here the history of how the motif of Christ's presence has been interpreted. But I can note the astonishingly great influence of Lotze and Ritschl on Wilhelm Herrmann and his interpretation of Luther. And the entire structure of Karl Holl's interpretation of Luther as well is permeated and determined by this transcendental effect orientation. Saarinen writes about the great initiator of the Luther renaissance:

> Karl Holl also understands the manner of being of the present Christ in Luther's writings as God's "effect power" *(Wirkungsmacht)*, which was conceived of in opposition to metaphysical substance-orientation. According to Holl, Christ is for Luther God's "tool" *(Werkzeug)*, with whose help God exercises his power in man. Thus in Holl's Luther interpretation Christ has on the one hand a significance subordinate to God; on the other hand, however, the pres-

ence-of-Christ motif is especially important to Holl, because with it he can conceptually determine effective justification as God's unique effective power using Christ as his "tool." The "presence" expressed in this conception is in its essence neither a mystical nor a substantial union, but rather a "union of wills" that is carried out in the consciousness of the believer. (Saarinen, pp. 227-28)

It is perhaps surprising that the transcendental effect orientation that Lotze originated determines not only the understanding of revelation in "Neoprotestant" theology and in the Luther renaissance but also the interpretation of Luther in dialectical theology. Saarinen demonstrates this influence, for example, in the interpretations of Luther found in Karl Barth and Ernst Wolf: "The continuity between Neoprotestantism and the Luther Renaissance on the one hand and dialectical theology on the other can likewise be found in the emphasis on theocentric 'action', which, in opposition to metaphysical substance-orientation, determines the nature of the revelation. Karl Barth and Ernst Wolf conceive of the union of Christ with man in Luther's writings as a 'community of deed' *(Tatgemeinschaft)* conditioned by God's action. This analysis, however, bears a great similarity to the 'sharing in the effects of God and/or Christ' as taught by the Luther Renaissance. Thus Barth's and Wolf's view of Luther is not as distant from that of the Luther Renaissance as its authors themselves seem to think" (Saarinen, p. 231).

In Luther research a long tradition to this day stands in solving the problem of the presence-of-Christ motif with the help of this notion of transcendental effect. Many contemporary German Luther scholars, for example, owe a great deal to this concept. On the basis of this tradition, however, one can make hardly anything of those passages in Luther that speak of real participation in God.

Clearly, the concept of real participation in God is fundamental for Luther's theology. Luther employs other terms as well to describe this idea of participation, such as "unification with God" or the "transformation of man." The concept of participation reaches its peak expression in the notion of *theosis,* or "divinization." Since Simo Peura has published his dissertation on the theme *Theosis in the Theology of Martin Luther 1513-1519,* I will report only briefly on Finnish studies of Luther's notion of *theosis.*

9

4. Luther's Concept of Participation and/or Divinization

Theosis is based causally on the divinity of God. According to Luther, the divinity of the triune God consists in that "He gives." And what he gives, ultimately, is himself. The essence of God, then, is identical with the essential divine properties in which he gives of himself, called the "names" of God: Word, justice, truth, wisdom, love, goodness, eternal life, and so forth. The *theosis* of the believer is initiated when God bestows on the believer God's essential properties; that is, what God gives of himself to humans is nothing separate from God himself.[9]

Before God gives himself to a person in his Word (which is God himself), he performs his "nihilizing work" — he makes the person "empty" and "nothing." This *reductio in nihilum,* of course, does not imply a total annihilation of the person. It refers only to the destruction of the individual's constant effort to make himself god and to justify himself.

One must pass through this agony and, ultimately, through the cross in order to achieve a true *cognitio sui.* Only in this way is one made *vacuum* and *capax Dei.* And this doctrine implies that, according to Luther, the modus of a Christian is always *passio:* a person is neither inwardly nor outwardly active; one experiences only what God affects in him or her.

Luther's concept of *theosis,* then, is understood correctly only in connection with his theology of the cross. The participation that is a real part of his theology is hidden under its opposite, the *passio* through which one is emptied. It is not grasped in rational knowledge but only in faith, and the grasp that faith has of it in this life is still only the beginning of a much greater participation that awaits in eschatological fulfillment.

God gives himself as the Word in the historical birth of Christ and in the spiritual birth of Christ in the faith of the believer. Luther's Christmas sermon of 1514 serves well as a point of departure for treating his understanding of the connection between the coming of the Word and *theosis.*[10] In this sermon Luther elucidates the core of

9. WA 3, 303, 20-21.
10. I am familiar with the objection that this sermon is pre-Reformation

his doctrine of participation with the help of the classical formulations of the doctrine of *theosis:* "Just as the word of God became flesh, so it is certainly also necessary that the flesh may become word. In other words: God becomes man so that man may become God. Thus power becomes powerless so that weakness may become powerful. The *Logos* puts on our form and pattern, our image and likeness, so that it may clothe us with its image, its pattern, and its likeness. Thus wisdom becomes foolish so that foolishness may become wisdom, and so it is in all other things that are in God and in us, to the extent that in all these things he takes what is ours to himself in order to impart what is his to us."[11]

Thus, in this text, divinization *(Vergöttlichung)* is understood by the help of the formulations of Athanasius and Irenaeus as a union *(unio)* of Logos and flesh, of Word and man. As Luther says later in the text, this *unio* does not signify any change of substance. God does not stop being God, and man does not stop being man. Both retain the substances proper to them; that is, they remain throughout such union realities that exist in themselves *(ens in se),* a phrase that defines precisely the notion of a substance.

The fact that the union of God and man does not signify a change of substance does not allow us to infer, though, that the *unio* does not signify a community of being. Just as, according to the Christmas sermon, the Logos not only "took on our flesh" in the incarnation but "really *is* flesh," so "we not only *have* the word in faith," but we "*are* it as well." Shortly after this statement Luther further substantiates the real character of the union by employing analogies from Aristotelian philosophy. According to these, the objects of intellect and of love are the being and act *(esse et actus)* of the intellect and love itself.

Thus arises a radically different concept of the relationship between God and man than had been previously described in the interpretative traditions of the Luther Renaissance and of dialectical

---

and therefore cannot be used as a direct source for Luther's theology. Without being able here to substantiate my claim, I only answer that the theological construct I am noting permeates every aspect of the Reformer's thinking from its beginning all the way to his final commentary on Genesis.

11. WA 1, 28, 25-32.

theology. Luther's concept concerns more than the notion of the union of the will of God with that of man (Luther Renaissance). And it also goes beyond the concept of a community of deed or of act in revelation (dialectical theology). Rather, it refers to a community of being of God and man.

One should nevertheless take note that thus far nothing has been said concerning *how* we are precisely to understand and to define this being. And important restrictions govern what we can say about it: we cannot describe it appropriately by means of the concepts of an "effect" ontology, the concepts of a static substantial ontology, or the concepts of other forms of philosophical ontology. For Luther's understanding of the being of Christ in faith is theological in its nature. That is, his ontology is a theological one, even though he uses philosophical terminology in expressing what he intends to say. Since Sammeli Juntunen has addressed the structure of being in Luther's theology (see "Luther and Metaphysics: What Is the Structure of Being according to Luther?"), I will confine myself to a few brief remarks.

In my article "Has Luther a Trinitarian Ontology?"[12] I have tried to outline some of the elements of Luther's ontology. God is in *relation* to himself in the movement of Word *(Deum Patrem sibi suum apud se verbum proferre)* at the same time that he *is* this movement of the Word. The being of God is relational, and as such has the character of *esse*. This understanding of the being of God is the basis for understanding the being-present-of-Christ in faith. In Christ the inner-trinitarian Word, which is the being of God, becomes incarnate. The presence of Christ's word and the word about Christ in faith are the presence of God himself.

This ontological basis has its epistemological side as well: the act of knowing and the object of knowledge are identical. God who illuminates and the illuminated heart, the present God and the God seen by us, are identical *(Idem enim est et utrumque simul est; deus illuminans et cor illuminatum, deus visus a nobis et deus presens)*.[13] God is both the object and subject, the actor and act, of faith.

12. *Hat Luther eine trinitarische Ontologie? Luther und die trinitarische Tradition. Ökumenische und philosophische Perspektiven. Veröffentlichung der Luther-Akademie Ratzeburg* Bd. 23 (Erlangen, 1994), pp. 43-60.
13. WA 2, 201, 20-21.

5. Participation and Love

The idea of participation and/or *theosis* is fundamental for one's understanding of various *loci* in Luther's theology. One of these *loci,* which can be understood more fully on the basis of participation, is Luther's theology of love. Luther's concept of love in connection with the idea of participation is an important focal point in Finnish Luther research. Here I will treat the notion of love only in its relation to participation. Luther's understanding of the relationship between participation and love will be fruitfully analyzed on the basis of a text that provides a paradigmatic model of the Reformer's understanding of participation *(theosis)* and love.

> Once again the example of love is prefigured here in Christ with the leper. For here you see how love makes him a servant, so that he helps the poor man freely and for nothing, seeks neither pleasure, favor, nor honor thereby, but only the good of the poor man and the honor of God the father. For which reason he also forbids him to tell anyone, so that it be absolutely pure work of free, kindly love. That is how, as I have said often enough, faith makes us lords; through faith we even become gods and partake of the divine nature and name, as Psalm 81 says: "I have said, you are gods and children all together of the highest of the high." But through love we become like the poorest of the poor. According to the faith we need nothing and yet have complete abundance. Through faith we receive good from above from God. Through love we release them from below to our neighbor. Just as Christ according to his deity needed nothing, but in his humanity served everyone who needed him.
>
> We have said often enough that through faith we must be born God's children and gods, lords and kings, just as Christ is born in eternity a true God of the Father. And we must once again break out through love to help our neighbor with good deeds, just as Christ became man to help us all. And just as Christ did not earn his divinity beforehand through works or achieve it by becoming man, but rather had this divinity from birth without any works and before he became man, so also we have not through works of love earned being God's children, by which our sins are forgiven and death and hell cannot harm us, but rather have received this out of grace through faith in the gospel, without works and before

love. And as Christ did not become man to serve us until after he had been God eternally, so also we do good and love our neighbor only after we have previously become pious, without sin, living, blessed, and God's children through faith.[14]

The relation between faith and love in this text is determined christologically. Christ and the Christian are portrayed as having exactly parallel characteristics. They seem to have analogous constitutions. First, Christ is begotten by the Father continuously in eternity as true God. In like manner, Christians are born in faith as "God's children and gods, lords and kings." Second, Christ has "broken out" through pure love and stepped into the position of man in all his misery. In like manner a Christian, who in faith participates in the divine and human nature of Christ, must step into the position of the neighbor and become "like the poorest of the poor." Third, just as Christ did not earn his divinity through his loving deed, so the Christian, even before stepping into the position of the neighbor out of pure love, is by faith alone "pious, without sin, living, and blessed."

In this passage faith is understood as an analogue to the divine Logos before his incarnation. As the Logos is continuously born of the Father, so Christians are born continuously in their faith as "God's children." As the Logos takes on human nature and becomes incarnate out of pure love, so Christians out of love step into the position of their neighbors and become "like the poorest of the poor." And as Logos does not need to be incarnated in order to be God, so the Christian does not need to step loving into the position of his neighbor before he is by faith alone "pious, without sin, living, and blessed."

Let me recapitulate the underlying concept of participation that makes it possible for Luther to determine the relation between faith and love with the christological analogy. The basis for understanding this analogy is as follows. Luther does not distinguish between the person and the work of Christ. Christ himself, both his person and his work, is the righteousness of man before God. Christ is both *favor* of God (forgiveness of sins, atonement, abolition of wrath) and gift *(donum)*, God himself present. Faith means justification precisely on the basis of Christ's person being present in it as favor and gift. *In*

14. WA 17 II, 74, 20–75, 11.

ipsa fide Christus adest: in faith itself Christ is present, and so the whole of salvation.

The idea of participation does not mean that Luther had given up the notion of love as *agape.* In order to understand this it is useful to keep in mind that the presence of Christ in Luther's theology of faith finds its theoretical expression in the notion of Christ as the form (= *Seinswirklichkeit,* Being) of faith *(Christus forma fidei). Christ himself,* as incarnated *agape,* and not the striving *caritas*-love *("eros")* of the scholastic theology that Luther criticized, is the divine reality of being, the *forma,* that makes faith "real." The right relationship of faith is not a striving, dynamic movement of love toward the transcendent. God cannot be found "above" by means of striving love. Rather, he is "below" in faith, present in the sinful human: "An excellent, beautiful, and (as St. Peter says) one of the cherished and greatest promises of all has been given to us poor, miserable sinners: that we, too, are to partake of the divine nature and be so highly ennobled so that we are not only to be loved by God through Christ, possessing his favor and grace as the highest, most cherished sanctuary, but are to have him, the Lord himself, dwelling in us entirely. . . . For the two things that Christians receive from God (as mentioned by St. Paul in Romans and elsewhere) are grace and gift."[15]

When Luther portrays God's essential presence in faith, he often refers to the "Hebrew manner of speaking" (cf., e.g., WA 10 I, 1, 157, 14). According to this way of speaking, the properties of God constitute the essence of God, as we have already seen. Consequently, "the righteousness of God" is identical to the Hebrew expression "God the righteousness"; "the wisdom of God" in its turn is equally "God the wisdom"; and "the power of God" is "God the power." The properties of God, which at the same time form the essence of God, are, for example, righteousness, wisdom, power, holiness, joy, peace, eternal life — and especially love. All of these properties of God, which are at the same time the essence of God, are present in their abundance in the person of Christ. Luther says, "Christ is God's grace, mercy, righteousness, truth, wisdom, power, comfort, and salvation, given to us by God without any merit on our part. Christ, I say, not as some express it in blind words, 'causally,' so that he grants righ-

15. WA 21, 458, 11-24.

teousness and remains absent himself, for that would be dead. Yes, it is not given at all unless Christ himself is present, just as the radiance of the sun and the heat of fire are not present if there is no sun and no fire."[16]

The believer, having on the basis of God's *agape*-love a share in Christ, also thereby partakes of the properties of God's being. Expressed differently, the believer partakes of the "names" of God. Luther says:

> . . . and we are so filled "with all sorts of God's abundance," which is in the Hebrew manner as much as saying that we are filled in all ways in which he makes full, and, full of God we are showered with all gifts and grace and filled with his Spirit, so that it makes us courageous and illuminated by his light, and his life lives in us, his beatitude makes us blessed, his love awakens love in us. In short, that everything he is and can do be in us fully and affect vigorously, so that we become completely divine, not having a piece or even a few pieces of God, but all abundance. Much has been written about how man is to become divine; they have made ladders on which one might climb up to heaven and many such things. But this is all vain beggar's work *(Parthekenwerk)*; here the right and closest way to get there is shown so that you may become full of God, that you may not be lacking any piece, but have everything all together, that everything you say or think, everywhere you go, in sum: that your whole life be completely divine.[17]

This text clearly expresses the relationship between participation and love. Faith means participation in the being and thus in the properties of God. And one of the properties of which the Christian in his faith partakes is love. Christ, who is present in faith as *donum*, brings love with him, because Christ is in his divine nature God, and God is love.

This understanding of faith as partaker of divine properties was essential for Luther. When he describes his reform-engendering discovery in the famous passage of the preface of volume one of his Latin works (1545), participation in the properties of God has the

16. LW 14, 204, The Seven Penitential Psalms 1525 edition.
17. WA 17 I, 438, 14-28.

decisive role: Luther says that he began to understand that the justice of God means the justice "through which the just lives through the gift of God" *("qua iustus dono Dei vivit, nempe ex fide").* This discovery consists clearly in the insight that the justice of God is *donum,* gift, through which the just live. This insight, Luther says, opened to him the gateway of heaven, and he was enabled to see the Holy Scripture in quite a new way. Thereafter, Luther continues, he went through the Scriptures and collected analogical words. The list of these words proves that the reformatory discovery denotes understanding of participation in the properties of God: "Work of God, i.e., which God works in us, power of God, through which he makes us powerful, wisdom of God, through which God makes us wise, courage of God, salvation of God, glory of God, etc."[18] The idea of participation in Christ and in his divine properties was thus the content of his so-called reformatory insight and at the same time the foundation of his criticism of scholastic theology.

It is necessary here to make a brief comment on Anders Nygren's famous theory of Christian love. Nygren conceives of the union between God and man always in connection with the *eros*-motif. *Unio* takes place as the culmination point of the ascending movement of man to God. Nygren does not know the union on the foundation of the *agape*-motif as the culmination point of God's descending to humanity in incarnation and in faith. The idea of participation in God does not mean that Luther had given up the notion of Christian love as *agape.* According to Luther, Christ himself, not the striving elevated love of humans, is the divine reality, the *forma* of faith. The right relationship of faith is not a striving movement of love toward the transcendent God. God cannot be found "above" by means of elevated and striving love. Rather, God is "below" in faith, present in sinful human beings. *Unio* between God and humans takes place on the foundation of *agape*-love.

Now I can return to my main theme. The relationship between

18. *"Discurrebam deinde per scripturas, ut habebat memoria, et colligebam etiam in aliis vocabulis analogian, ut opus Dei, i.e. quod operatur in nobis Deus, virtus Dei, qua potentes facit, sapientia Dei, qua nos sapientes facit, fortitudo Dei, salus Dei, gloria Dei"* (WA 54, 185, 13–186, 22).

faith and love can be very precisely defined as follows from the perspective of Luther's doctrine of participation and/or *theosis*.

Faith in itself is not the fulfillment of the law, that is, of the commandment to love. On the other hand, *love is* the fulfillment of the law. But even if faith is not the fulfillment of the law, it nevertheless *imports* love along with it, and love *is* the fulfillment of the law. Luther describes in pertinent terms the relationship between faith and love:

> Although faith does not fulfill the law, it does have that through which it is fulfilled, for it acquires the Spirit and love so that it be fulfilled. And in turn, though love does not justify, it does give evidence of that through which the person is justified, namely faith. In sum, as St. Paul himself speaks about this: "Love is the fulfillment of the law," as if he were saying: it is two different things, to be the fulfillment of the law and to make or give the fulfillment of law. Love fulfills the law in such a way that it itself is the fulfillment. But faith fulfills the law in offering that with which it is fulfilled. For faith loves and acts, as Galatians 5 says: "Faith is active through love." Water fills the pitcher, the person pouring also fills the pitcher; the water with itself, the person pouring the water. The sophists called this in their language *effective et formaliter implere*.[19]

Clearly, Luther's understanding of the relation between faith and love is grounded on his concept of participation and/or *theosis*. And such a notion is the fundamental idea that gives the underlying structure to his work *De libertate christiana*, which he himself calls the compendium of his theology. In this work Luther says that a Christian is through faith free and lord over all, but is bound by love and is everyone's servant. The theological ground of this double characterization of the Christian is revealed in the concept of participation and/or *theosis*. Since Christ is truly present in faith, the Christian has in a certain manner "two natures," though the term "nature" here is understood in the theological sense. The "divine nature" of the believer is Christ himself. The Christian himself no longer lives, but rather Christ lives in him or her. Luther says, "Christ remains in

19. WA 17 II, 98, 13-14.

me, and that life lives in me, and the life through which I live is Christ."[20]

In Christ the Christian possesses all of the names, treasures, and goods of the divine nature. He is free and "rich," needing nothing to be saved. He participates in the kingship and the priesthood of Christ. He has in a real sense become "rapt above himself in God."

In love, however, believers give themselves freely to their neighbors and take upon themselves their neighbors' burden, misery, sins, poverty, and weakness as if these were their own burdens, their own misery, their own sin, poverty, and weakness. Like Christ, then, Christians take upon themselves "human nature," that is, the misery and burden of the neighbor. Luther concludes his theological summation, the treatise on the freedom of a Christian, with the idea that Christians live not in themselves but in Christ and in their neighbors.

These remarks display Luther's doctrine of divinization in its final intention. The Christian has become Christ to the neighbor: *Christianus Christus proximi.* The conclusion of the tractate "The Freedom of a Christian" summarizes Luther's doctrine of participation and love: "But alas in our day this life is unknown throughout the world; it is neither preached about nor sought after; we are altogether ignorant of our own name and do not know why we are Christians or bear the name of Christians. Surely we are named after Christ, not because he is absent from us, but because he dwells in us, that is, because we believe in him and are Christs one to another and do to our neighbors as Christ does to us."[21]

"We conclude, therefore, that a Christian lives not in himself, but in Christ and his neighbor. Otherwise he is not a Christian. He lives in Christ through faith, in his neighbor through love. By faith he is caught up beyond himself into God. By love he descends beneath himself into his neighbor. Yet he always remains in God and in his love."[22]

---

20. *"Christus manet in me et ista vita vivit in me, et vita quo vivo, est Christus"* (WA 40 I, 283, 7-9).

21. LW 31, 368.

22. LW 31, 371.

6. Why Is Luther So Fascinating?

Luther is fascinating as an object of research. One always finds something new in him, and he often surprises the reader with revealing insights. One can read the tractate "The Freedom of a Christian" many times and each time find something previously unknown or inadequately understood.

Second, although the outer appearance of Luther's writings do not give the impression of being very systematic, the result of the whole is nevertheless a systematic structure that lurks in the background. This system is, of course, difficult to uncover, because one must bore through scattered remarks, statements, and arguments into the core of a matter before being able to view the systematic character of his thought. But the effort to get at his system rewards the researcher with the disclosure of a very stringent systematic thinker.

Another reason for finding Luther fascinating is that he joins the Lutheran tradition to the common classical Christian heritage. The bridge to this heritage from the Augustana and from the Formula of Concord is too weak to stand up to the traffic of the whole Lutheran tradition. But Luther himself forges a serviceable passage for dialogue. Luther's theology is ecumenically fruitful.

Fourth, although Luther's theology is based on the classical doctrinal heritage of the church, it is existentially relevant. Despite being extremely complicated, it discloses our faith with utmost simplicity. Luther combines theology of the cross, theology of participation, and theology of love in such a way that Christian faith and life become existentially highly understandable and realizable.

Finally, the existential relevance of Luther's theology derives from the central content of his thinking: God comes near and gives himself to us in the mode of favor and gift. *In ipsa fide Christus adest.*

Response to Tuomo Mannermaa, "Why Is Luther So Fascinating?"

ROBERT W. JENSON

Introduction

I cannot respond to Tuomo Mannermaa's paper in the usual fashion: by first expressing appreciation and then registering reservations. For I have none of the latter. Since my attention was first called to the contemporary Finnish school, I have thought that Professor Mannermaa and his associates were simply and wholly right in their chief contentions, which are what appear in the paper. I agree: leading scholars have distorted Luther's theology by presuming he must have been a proper Kantian like themselves; and the surprising system and teachings the Finns find in Luther are plainly there.

Now of course the Finnish theses may seem so evident to me because I so want them to be true. My interest in Luther is not that of a *Lutherforscher*, but that of a systematic theologian and ecumenist. As a systematician, I have found I can *do* very little with Luther as usually interpreted. And the sort of Lutheranism that constantly appeals to that Luther has been an ecumenical disaster. With Luther according to the Finns, on the other hand, there can be much systematically and ecumenically fruitful conversation.

So all I will do is attach two excursuses to the paper.

Excursus 1

Much of the dispute between Finnish and other Luther scholars has not in fact been about the texts but about the theological legitimacy of the concept of being. Leading German scholars have thought it antecedently established that ontology has no place in theology, and therefore have not wished to find their hero seriously involved in it. The Finns have said, "But he nevertheless is."

The concept of being is undoubtedly a difficult one for Christian thinking. It is neither biblical nor humanly inevitable, but the product of a historically specific group of pagan thinkers, those notorious Greeks who were the conceptual preceptors of our civilization. "What is it to be?" is not a question everyone has asked or that the Bible asks.

With the concept of being, the Greeks attributed two things above all: something "has being" insofar as it perdures, insofar as it is immune to time's slings and arrows; and something "has being" insofar as it can be the object of knowledge, of the kind that protects the knower against surprises. "Being" was a name for what the Greeks sought in their gods.

The problem is plain: Does the Christian God, or his followers, want to be immune to time's slings and arrows? To, for example, sorrows and crucifixions? And is the Christian God so transparent to knowledge as to harbor no surprises? Do we have the same thing to seek in the Lord as in, say, Aristotle's Unmoved Mover?

As the gospel penetrated the Greek-instructed world, the question about being could not be ignored. Converted Hellenists inevitably asked themselves: "Can a God who gets involved with a crucifixion be the source of being?" "How reliably can we know this biblical God? Who seems to repent and change his mind and make fresh starts?" Three tactics are possible and have been followed in the history of theology.

We can apply the concept of being to God and ourselves, and then just deny some of its implications: "God is being — but remains free and mysterious because he is also above being." This has doubtless been the most common move. Or we can try to dehellenize theology, to exclude the concept of being. This has been the typical modern move. One form is the Kantian scheme that has, as the Finns have shown, shaped the minds of German Luther researchers: the notion of "beings as such" is retained as a limiting concept, but the world of human experience is said to consist only in their effects.

But there has always been a tradition of those who have taken a third way, accepting the Greeks' question about being but proposing new and specifically Christian answers. Great figures of this sort include Gregory of Nyssa, Maximus, Aquinas, Edwards, Hegel, and Barth. Some may recognize these as my heroes. Mannermaa and his students have rescued Luther for this company, and I thank them for it.

To be, according to Luther according to Mannermaa, is to give oneself to an other, by speaking. Note the subtle but vital difference between this and Kantianism. According to the Kantians, we cannot deal with being but only with relations. According to Luther according to Mannermaa, a certain mode of relation *is* being.

Excursus 2

Then there is justification versus(?) deification. Let us consider the tract on *Christian Liberty,* reference to which makes an internal conclusion in Professor Mannermaa's paper.

This work is puzzling to Lutherans. On the one hand it seems very familiar, being all about forgiveness and righteousness and how these are obtained by faith and not by works. But already the relation between these contents and the title and stated thesis of the tract seems problematic: How do we become free universal lords — surely a divine title? — simply by being made righteous?

And then there is the question central to the tract: *How* does faith make us righteous? Luther gives at least three explanations. These are not on their surface connected to each other, and none of them says anything about imputation or unconditional acceptance of the unacceptable or the other "Lutheran" items. Faith makes righteous (1) because believing what God says fulfills the first and great commandment; (2) because the soul that hearkens to the word becomes what the word is, holy and right; and (3) because in faith the soul is united with Christ as a bride with the groom, to be "one body" with him and so possess his righteousness.

23

One sees how all this works together only when one notices the astonishing switch that Luther has pulled on the Greeks' ontology and epistemology. In their doctrine, the specific character of personal beings, "souls," is that their being is determined by what they, as perfect eyes, *see*. Luther switched that; for him the specific character of personal being is that we are what, as perfect ears, we *hear*. Moreover, if for the Greeks "to be" generally is to perdure, to hang on to oneself, for Luther "to be" is to share oneself by speaking: thus for Christ "to be" is to share himself in his word.

Therefore to hear Christ's word in the church is to become one being with Christ; thus two of Luther's three explanations fit together. And what Christ does is fulfill the first and great commandment. Thus an ontological identification with the Son's inner-trinitarian obedience to the Father is what Luther means by "becoming righteous," being "justified." Luther's is indeed a doctrine more accessible to Orthodoxy than to any Lutheranism most of us know.

Justification and Theosis *in Lutheran-Orthodox Perspective*

TUOMO MANNERMAA

1. The Lutheran-Orthodox Perspective: Introduction

In the ecumenical dialogue between the Evangelical Lutheran Church of Finland and the Russian Orthodox Church it has come out that the idea of *theosis* can be found at the core of the theology of Martin Luther himself. My task here is to expound this idea of *theosis* in Luther's theology and its relationship to his doctrine of justification.

Finnish Luther research has come to the conclusion that Luther's idea of the presence of Christ in faith can form a basis for treating the question of divinization. The Lutheran understanding of the indwelling of Christ implies a real participation in God and is analogous to the Orthodox doctrine of participation in God, or *theosis*. When seen in the light of the doctrine of *theosis*, the Lutheran tradition is born anew and becomes once again interesting.

This thesis, that Luther's doctrine of justification can be seen in the perspective of *theosis*, has not always been commonly accepted. Protestant scholarship has long been marked by the notion that a mutual point of contact between the Orthodox and the Lutheran concepts of salvation was, in fact, impossible to find. The patristic-Orthodox doctrine of "divinization" and the Lutheran doctrine of "justification" have been considered mutually contradictory. One of the most important reasons for this view is the widely held belief that

25

the doctrine of divinization is based on an "ontological" or "metaphysical" and therefore "physical" way of thinking, which is diametrically opposed to the "personal-ethical" and "relational" way of thinking that Protestants find in the Bible and proclaim in the Reformation. Ontological thinking does not belong to the Christian faith, they claimed, because it is based on statements concerning Being *(Seinsaussagen),* and such statements refer meaningfully only to nature as it is grasped in the natural sciences. Statements about Being can never be used in respect to persons, because in the realm of persons only statements about values *(Werturteile)* or personal existence are valid. The idea of divinization, therefore, belongs to an inappropriate and false way of speaking about God, since it employs precisely such statements concerning Being in respect to God. These critical arguments were typically "modern."

From within its own standpoint, however, the core of the often misunderstood patristic doctrine of *theosis* can be briefly formulated as follows. Divine life has manifested itself in Christ. In the church, understood as the body of Christ, human beings participate in this life and thereby partake of "the divine nature" (2 Pet. 1:4). This "nature," or divine life, permeates the being of humans like leaven permeates bread, in order to restore it to its original condition as *imago Dei.*

Two classical formulations express appropriately the fundamental meaning of the doctrine of *theosis.* Irenaeus says succinctly: "Because of his great love (Jesus Christ) was made into that which we are, so that he might bring about that we be what he is" (Haer. V, praef.). The other formulation comes from Athanasius: "He [Christ] became man so that we might become divine."

The different variations of the doctrine of *theosis* cannot here be examined in detail. But we can at least state that the doctrine of the participation of the believer in the divine life of Christ is the core of the doctrine of *theosis,* or divinization.

In patristic thought the idea of *theosis* was often expressed by the help of concepts derived from Greek ontology. This does not mean, however, that the doctrine itself should be labeled as an entirely Hellenistic one, as was suggested by the Ritschlian and many other schools of Protestant theology in our century. As mentioned, the Ritschlian theses relied essentially on the philosophical premise that a "physical" relationship with God, based on the notion of a union of "being" with God, must be sharply distinguished from the notion of a "personal-ethical" relationship with God. So the presence of Christ in faith has been understood in the category of outward causality. God himself remains outside the person and is only acting upon him. The resulting effect on man's will (or existence) is conceived as the presence of God. There is, however, no communion of being between God and man, but only causal affecting and being affected. This affect-orientation has been common in Luther-research, at least in Germany.

In patristic thought itself the "ethical" and the "ontic" were never actually separated from each other in the modern way. Thus, the doctrine of divinization rests more profoundly on the presupposition that a human being can participate in the fullness of life that is in God. It is precisely this participation that is called *theosis* in the tradition of the early church and in the Orthodox Church. And it remains an often misunderstood term in Protestantism.

Contrary to the assumptions of modern Protestant thought, classic Lutheranism is undoubtedly familiar with the notion of God's essential indwelling in the believer *(inhabitatio Dei)*. The classic text dealing with God's indwelling is found in the Formula of Concord (FC). According to this text, God, in the very fullness of his essence, is present in the believer. Important here is to recognize that any notion that God himself does not "dwell" in the Christian and that only his "gifts" are present in the believer is explicitly rejected.

A difficult problem for Lutheran self-understanding arises, however, from the Formula of Concord's definition of the relation between "justification" and "divine indwelling"; this is different from that found in Luther's theology, at least insofar as terminology is concerned. Thus, in the Formula of Concord, "justification by faith" merely denotes the forgiveness of sins that is "imputed" to a human being on the basis of the perfect obedience and complete merit of Christ. But the *inhabitatio Dei* is distinguished conceptually as a separate phenomenon that is logically subsequent to justification. The classic *inhabitatio* text of the Formula of Concord reads as follows:

> We must also explain correctly the discussion concerning the indwelling of God's essential righteousness in us. On the one hand,

27

it is true indeed that God the Father, Son, and Holy Spirit, who is the eternal and essential righteousness, dwells by faith in the elect who have been justified through Christ and reconciled with God, since all Christians are temples of God the Father, Son and Holy Spirit, who impels them to do rightly. But, on the other hand, this indwelling of God is not the righteousness of faith of which St. Paul speaks and which he calls the righteousness of God, on account of which we are declared just before God. This indwelling follows the preceding righteousness of faith, which is precisely the forgiveness of sins and the gracious acceptance of poor sinners on account of the obedience and merit of Christ.

In presenting the notion that the presence of the Trinity in faith is not the same phenomenon as the "righteousness of faith," the Formula of Concord draws on the later theology of Lutheranism, upon which practically all subsequent Lutheran theology after Luther relies. Justification is understood here in a totally forensic manner; that is, it is regarded as a reception of the forgiveness that is "imputed" to a human being because of the obedience and merit of Christ. The *inhabitatio Dei* is considered merely a consequence of this "righteousness of faith."

In Luther's theology, however, the relation between justification and the divine indwelling in the believer is, undoubtedly, defined differently from the formulation of the Formula of Concord. The Reformer's notion of the "righteousness of faith" is permeated by christological thinking. Luther does not separate the person of Christ from his work. Rather, Christ himself, both his person and his work, is the ground of Christian righteousness. Christ is, in this unity of person and work, really present in the faith of the Christian *(in ipsa fide Christus adest)*. The favor *(favor)* of God (i.e., the forgiveness of sins and the removal of God's wrath) and the "gift" of God *(donum,* God himself, present in the fullness of his essence) are united in the person of Christ. In contrast to Luther's theology, forgiveness *(favor)* justification and the real presence of God *(donum)* in faith are in danger of being separated by the one-sidedly forensic doctrine of justification adopted by the Formula of Concord and by subsequent Lutheranism. In Luther's theology, however, both of these motifs are closely united in his understanding of the person of Christ. Christ is both the *favor* and the *donum.* And this unity is, to use Chalcedonian expressions, both inseparable and unconfused.

One can characterize Luther's position in contrast to the position of the Formula of Concord also as follows: For Luther *evangelium* is not proclamation of the cross and/or of the forgiveness of sins only, but the proclamation of the crucified *and* risen Christ himself. It is one of the main themes of Luther's theology that only the crucified *and* risen Christ himself as present can mediate salvation. Thus, we must clearly note the organic connection between the doctrine of justification and christological themes in the theology of Luther.

2. The Basis of the Doctrine of Justification in the Christology of the Early Church

Christ as the "Greatest Sinner" (maximus peccator)

Luther's concept of Christian faith is based on the christological thinking of the early church. But he accents these doctrines in a specific manner. The second person of the Trinity did not take upon himself merely human nature as such, in a "neutral" form, but precisely *sinful* human nature. This means that Christ has and bears the sins of all human beings *in a real manner* in the human nature he has assumed. The sins of humankind are not only imputed to Christ; he *"has"* the sins in his human nature. Therefore Christ is the greatest sinner *(maximus peccator, peccator peccatorum)*. The Reformer says:

> And all the prophets saw this, that Christ was to become the greatest thief, murderer, adulterer, robber, desecrator, blasphemer, etc., there has ever been anywhere in the world. He is not acting in His own Person now. Now he is not the Son of God, born of the Virgin. But he is a sinner, who has and bears the sin of Paul, the former blasphemer, persecutor, and assaulter; of Peter, who denied Christ; of David, who was an adulterer and a murderer, and who caused the Gentiles to blaspheme the name of the Lord (Rom. 2:24). In short, He has and bears all the sins of all men in His body — not in the sense that He has committed them but in the sense that He

took these sins, committed by us, upon His own body, in order to make satisfaction for them with his own blood.[1]

The text of the lecture notes continues in words not found in the printed text of the commentary, making apparent the realistic way in which Luther thinks of Christ's union with sinners. The Logos communicates himself to the human nature of "thieves and sinners"; moreover, he is said even to be "immersed" in it: "And so He is regarded as someone who is among thieves — even though He is innocent Himself, and even more so, because of His own free will and by the will of the Father He wanted to communicate Himself to the body and blood of those who were thieves and sinners. Therefore He is immersed in all."[2]

The special emphasis in Luther's theology of incarnation is found precisely in the notion that Christ became, in the human nature assumed by him, the greatest sinner of all.

Christ as the "Greatest Person" (maxima persona)

Luther's concept of Christ as the "greatest sinner" discloses a premise that is of central importance for his theology of incarnation and his doctrine of atonement. According to this premise, Christ is a kind of "collective person," or, as the Reformer formulates it himself, the "greatest person" (maxima persona), in whom the persons of all human beings are united in a real manner. Christ is every sinner:

> This is the most joyous of all doctrines and the one that contains the most comfort. It teaches that we have the indescribable and inestimable mercy and love of God. When the merciful Father saw that we were being oppressed through the Law, that we were being held under a curse, and that we could not be liberated from it by anything, He sent His Son into the world, heaped all the sins of all men upon Him, and said to Him: "Be Peter the denier; Paul the persecutor, blasphemer, and assaulter; David the adulterer; the sinner who ate the apple in paradise; the thief on the cross. In short,

1. *Lectures on Galatians* 1535. LW 25, 277. WA 40 I, 433,26–434,12.
2. WA 40 I, 434, 1-4. Lecture notes.

be the person of all men, the one who has committed the sins of all men.[3]

The idea of Christ as the "greatest person" *(maxima persona)* culminates in the notion of Christ as the "only sinner" *(solus peccator)*. After the Logos has become flesh and is immersed *(submersus)* in all sins, all sins are immersed in him, and there is no sin anywhere else that is not in his person. This idea is the beginning point for Luther's doctrine of the atonement. Without going into detail, let me present here briefly the aim of this doctrine, which has not yet been sufficiently studied.

As a human being, Christ is the "greatest sinner of all"; at the same time, as the Logos, he is God himself, that is, "perfect righteousness and life." Therefore, his person is marked by an extreme tension and a most profound contradiction. By his divine nature Christ is the "divine Power, Righteousness, Blessing, Grace, and Life."[4] These divine attributes fight against sin, death, and curse — which also culminate in his person — and overcome them. Hence, there is no sin or death or curse any more, because "all sin is gathered together" in Christ, making him the "only sinner." Luther unites, then, the Latin and the Classic theories of reconciliation. In his theology, Christ's expiatory work as such is at the same time victory over the Powers.

It is important to appreciate that the conquest of the forces of sin and destruction takes place within Christ's own person — and, in a sense, in his faith. He won the battle between righteousness and sin "in himself" *(triumphans in seipso)*. Sin, death, and curse are first conquered in the person of Christ; "thereafter," the whole of creation is to be transformed through his person. And this brings us to a most important insight: salvation is participation in the person of Christ.[5]

---

3. *Lectures on Galatians* 1535. LW 26, 280.
4. *Lectures on Galatians* 1535, LW 26, 282. WA 40 A, 440, 21.
5. *Lectures on Galatians* 1535, LW 26, 282; WA 40 I, 26-30.

Faith as Participation in the Person of Christ

Central in Luther's theology is that in faith the human being *really* participates by faith in the person of Christ and in the divine life and the victory that is in it. Or, to say it the other way around: Christ gives his person to the human being through the faith by which we grasp it. "Faith" involves participation in Christ, in whom there is no sin, death, or curse. Luther quotes John: " 'For this,' as John says, 'is our victory, faith.' " And, from Luther's point of view, faith is a victory precisely because it unites the believer with the person of Christ, who *is* in himself the victory.

According to the Reformer, justifying faith does not merely signify a reception of the forgiveness imputed to a human being for the sake of the merit of Christ, which is the aspect emphasized by the Formula of Concord. Being a real sharing (participation) in Christ, "faith" stands also for participation in the institution of "blessing, righteousness and life" that has taken place in Christ. Christ himself *is* life, righteousness, and blessing, because God is all of this "by nature and in substance" *(naturaliter et substantialiter)*. Therefore, justifying faith means participation in God in Christ's person.

The core of Luther's concept of participation finds expression in the notion of the "happy exchange," according to which Christ takes upon himself the sinful person of the human being and bestows his own righteous person upon that humanity. What takes place here between Christ and the believer is a communication of attributes or properties: Christ, the divine righteousness, truth, peace, joy, love, power, and life gives himself to the believer. At the same time, Christ "absorbs" the sin, death, and curse of the believer into himself.[6] Because faith involves a real union with Christ and because Christ is the divine person, the believer does indeed participate in God. That is what Luther means when he speaks of Christ as a "gift." Christ is not only the favor of God, that is, forgiveness, but also a "gift" *(donum),* God himself as present.

---

6. *Lectures on Romans* 1515-1516. LW 25, 332. WA 56, 343, 16-21.

Christ as a "Gift" (donum)

The idea that Christ is both God's favor *(favor)* and his gift *(donum)* permeates Luther's entire theology. "Favor" signifies God's forgiveness and the removal of his wrath. And Christ is a "gift" in that the real self-giving of God comes through him to the human person. The presence of Christ in faith is real, and he is present in it with all of his properties, such as righteousness, understanding, blessing, life, power, peace, and so forth. Thus, the notion of Christ as a "gift" means that the believing subject becomes a participant in the "divine nature." Indeed, the Reformer often refers to the same passage in 2 Peter on which also the patristic doctrine of *theosis* is based. He uses other expressions quite freely, too. In the following extract he says that the Christian is "greater than the world," because the gift in his heart, Christ, is greater:

> Therefore a Christian, properly defined, is free of all laws and is subject to nothing, internally or externally. But I purposely said, "to the extent that he is a Christian" (not "to the extent that he is a man or a woman"); that is, to the extent that he has his conscience consecrated, adorned, and enriched by this faith, this great and inestimable treasure, or, as Paul calls it, "this inexpressible gift" (2 Cor. 9:15), which cannot be exalted and praised enough, since it makes men sons and heirs of God. Thus a Christian is greater than the entire world. For in his heart he has this seemingly small gift; yet the smallness of this gift and treasure, which he holds in faith, is greater than heaven and earth, because Christ, who is this gift, is greater.[7]

This text reveals how real (indeed, ontologically real) Luther supposes the presence of the "gift," that is, Christ, to be. In the following extract, taken from a sermon in the so-called Church Postil, Luther expresses his thoughts concerning "favor," "gift," and "participation in the divine nature" with particular clarity:

> This is one of those apposite, beautiful, and (as St. Peter says in 2 Pet. 1) precious and very great promises given to us, poor mis-

---

7. *Letter on Galatians* 1535. LW 26, 134; WA 40 I, 235,26–236,16.

erable sinners: that we are to become participants of the divine
nature and be exalted so high in nobility that we are not only to
become loved by God through Christ, and have His favor and grace
as the highest and most precious shrine, but also to have Him, the
Lord Himself, dwelling in us in His fullness. Namely (he wants to
say), His love is not to be limited only to the removal of His wrath
from upon us, and to having the fatherly heart which is merciful
to us, but we are also to enjoy this love (otherwise it would be
wasted and lost love, as it is said: "to love and not to enjoy . . ."),
and gain great benefit and riches from it.[8]

Thus, in addition to being "favor" (forgiveness), Christ is also
"gift." In other words, the presence of Christ means that the believer
participates in the "divine nature."[9] And when participating in God's
essence, the Christian also becomes a partaker of the properties of
this essence.

8. Cruciger's *Summer Postil* 1544. WA 21, 458, 11-22.
9. The deeper Christ indwells the heart of the believer, the deeper the
Christian is under the favor of God: "Also sihestu, das Got mit diesen worten
Christum ynn sich zeucht und sich ynn Christum mit dem, das seyn wolgefallen
sey ynn allem, was Christus thut, und widderumb mit den selbigen worten beyde
sich selbs und Christum seynen lieben son ausschuttet uber uns und sich ynn uns
geust und uns ynn sich zeucht, das er gantz und gar vermenschet wird und wyr
gantz und gar vergottet werden. Wie so? Also, weyl Gott spricht, Es gefalle yhm
wol, was Christus ist und thut. So furen dich die wort dahyn, das du Gotts
wolgefallen und seyn gantz hertz ynn Christo sihest ynn allen seynen worten und
wercken, und widderumb Christum sihest, ym hertzen und wolgefallen Gottes,
und sind die beyde ynn eynander auffs aller tieffest und hohest, und kan dyr des
keyns feylen, weyl Gott nicht liegen kan. Weytter, weyl denn Christus das liebe
und angeneme kind ynn solchem wolgefallen und ym hertzen Gottes gefasset mit
all seym reden und thun deyn ist und dyr damit dienet, wie er selbst sagt, So
bistu gewisslich auch ynn dem selbigen wolgefallen und eben so tieff ym hertzen
Gotts als Christus und widderumb Gotts wolgefallen und hertz eben so tieff ynn
dyr, als ynn Christo, das nu du und Gott sampt seynem lieben sone ynn dyr gantz
und gar ist, un du gantz und gar ynn yhm bist, und alles mit eynander eyn ding
ist, Gott, Christus und du." WA 20,229,28–230,10.

Faith and the Divine Properties

The notion that Christians are partakers of the "divine nature" means that they are also partakers of the properties of God, that is, "filled with all the fullness of God." God's righteousness makes Christians righteous; God's "life lives in them." God's love effects in them the capacity to love, and so forth. Luther says, "And so we are filled with 'all the fullness of God'. This phrase, which follows a Hebrew manner of speaking, means that we are filled in all the ways in which God fills a man. We are filled with God, and He pours into us all His gifts and grace and fills us with His spirit, who makes us courageous. He enlightens us with His light, His life lives in us, His beatitude makes us blessed, and His love causes love to arise in us. Put briefly, He fills us in order that everything that He is and everything He can do might be in us in all its fullness, and work powerfully."[10]

According to the "Hebrew manner of speaking," the properties of God constitute the essence of God. Consequently, "the righteousness of God" is identical to the Hebrew expression "God the righteousness"; "the wisdom of God" in its turn is equally "God the wisdom"; and "the power of God" is "God the power."[11] The properties of God, which at the same time form the essence of God, are, for example, righteousness, wisdom, power, holiness, joy, peace, eternal life — and especially love. All of these properties of God, which are at the same time the essence of God, are present in their abundance in the person of Christ. The believer, having on the basis of God's *agape*-love a share in Christ, also thereby partakes of the properties of God's being.

In his early Christmas sermon Luther elucidates the core of his doctrine of participation in the properties of God with the help of the classical formulations of the doctrine of *theosis*:

> Just as the word of God became flesh, so it is certainly also necessary that the flesh may become word. In other words: God becomes man so that man may become God. Thus power becomes powerless so that weakness may become powerful. The *Logos* puts on our

10. Sermon 1525. WA 17 I, 438, 14-28.
11. WA 10 I,1, 157, 1-4.

35

form and gestalt *(Form und Gestalt)*, our image and likeness, so that it may clothe us with its image, its gestalt, and its likeness. Thus wisdom becomes foolish so that foolishness may become wisdom, and so it is in all other things that are in God and in us, to the extent that in all these things he takes what is ours to himself in order to impart what is his to us.[12]

3. *Fides charitate formata — fides Christo formata*

Christ as the Form of Faith (Christus forma fidei)

Luther's criticism of the scholastic *fides charitate formata* program and the core of his program of Reformation itself can be formulated by saying that the form (i.e., the living reality) of faith is not divinely elevated human love, as in the scholastic program of *fides charitate formata,* but is in reality Christ himself. Luther does, indeed, use the slogan *Christus forma fidei* (Christ as the reality of faith). From Luther's standpoint, the difference between the scholastic view and his view lies precisely in that, according to scholastic teaching, the *fides charitae formata* is valid, whereas the Reformer maintains that it is *fides Christo formata* that describes what happens in faith.

According to the scholastic doctrine, as Luther criticized it, faith was only an uncertain knowledge, a kind of supposition. It could not mediate salvation, which takes place only as God infuses love and thus supernaturally elevates a person's own capacity to love. According to Luther, faith is not such a "dead quality" in the soul, but rather contains the divine reality *(forma)*, which is Christ himself, who is present in faith. He is the only way to salvation, which excludes this role for the human's supernaturally elevated love.

We do not understand Luther's concept of faith correctly if we regard Christ merely as an object of faith. Rather, Christ, as the object of faith, is present himself; thus, he is, in fact, also the "subject" of faith. Luther says that Christ is the object of faith, but not merely the object; rather, "Christ is present in the faith itself" *(in ipsa fide Christus adest)*. Faith is knowledge that "sees nothing." Thus, accord-

12. WA 1, 28, 25-32.

ing to the Reformer's description, faith is like the cloud in the most holy place of the Temple of the Old Covenant in which God wanted to dwell (cf. 1 Kings 8:12: "Then Solomon said, 'The Lord has said that he would dwell in thick darkness' "). It is in the darkness of faith that Christ sits on his throne in all his reality and reigns, just as God did in the darkness and cloud in the most holy place of the Temple. In the following quotation, which is a passage central to Luther's theology as a whole, the Reformer crystallizes his idea of *Christus forma fidei:*

> We substitute that love with faith. And while they say that faith is the mere monogram (= ornamental letters), but love is its living colors and fullness itself, we say in opposition that faith takes hold of Christ and that He is the form that adorns and informs faith as color does the wall. Therefore Christian faith is not an idle quality or an empty husk in the heart, which may exist in a state of mortal sin until love comes along to make it alive. But if it is true faith, it is a sure trust of the heart and firm assent through which Christ is taken hold of. Christ is the object of faith, or rather not the object but, so to speak, in the faith itself Christ is present. Thus faith is a sort of knowledge or darkness that nothing can see. Yet the Christ of whom faith takes hold is sitting in this darkness as God sat in the midst of darkness on Sinai and in the temple. Therefore our formal (= real) righteousness is not love that informs faith; but it is faith itself and the cloud of our hearts, that is, trust in a thing we do not see, in Christ, who cannot in any way be seen *(ut maxime non videatur),* but, nevertheless, is present.
>
> Therefore, faith justifies because it takes hold of and possesses this treasure, the present Christ. But the mode in which He is present cannot be thought, for there is darkness, as I have said. Therefore, where true confidence of the heart is present, there Christ is present, in that very cloud and faith. This is the formal (= real) righteousness on account of which a man is justified; it is not on account of love, as the sophists say. In short, just as the sophists say that love forms and makes faith perfect, so we say that it is Christ who forms and fulfils faith or who is the form (= reality) of faith *(formam esse fidei).* Therefore the Christ who is grasped by faith and who lives in the heart is the Christian righteousness, on account of which God counts us righteous and gives us eternal life as gift. Here there

37

is no work of the Law, no love; but there is an entirely different kind of righteousness, a new world above and beyond the Law. For Christ or faith is neither the Law nor the work of the Law.[13]

This extract shows that Luther's idea of Christ as the form of faith and his doctrine of justification are inseparable. The Reformer says, "Christ who is grasped by faith and who lives in the heart is the Christian righteousness, on account of which God counts us righteous and gives us eternal life as gift." He says further, "Therefore faith justifies because it takes hold of and possesses this treasure, the present Christ." The notion of the presence of Christ as favor and gift in faith is the essence of Luther's concept of justification. At least on the level of terminology, the distinction, drawn in later Lutheranism, between justification as forgiveness and sanctification as divine indwelling, is alien to the Reformer. Forgiveness and indwelling of God are inseparable in the person of Christ, who is present in faith. In that sense, in Luther's theology, justification and *theosis* as participation in God are also inseparable.

The Reformer claims that if the person of Christ and that of the believer are separated from each other in the *locus* of justification, salvation is still within the framework of the order of the law, where such separation means being dead in the sight of God: "It is unprecedented and insolent to say: 'I live, I do not live; I am dead, I am not dead; I am a sinner, I am not a sinner; I have the Law, I do not have the Law.' But this phrase is true in Christ and through Christ. *When it comes to justification (in causa iustificationis), therefore, if you divide Christ's person from your own, you are in the Law;* you remain in it and live in yourself, which means that you are dead in the sight of God and damned by the Law."[14]

In contrast to Luther, justification and the indwelling of God in the believer are conceptually separated from each other in the Formula of Concord. Justification is only the forgiveness of sins. The indwelling of God follows in a logical sense after justification. One must ask here whether what Luther considers damning for the believer to think is exactly what the Formula of Concord calls sound doctrine: in the

13. *Lectures on Galatians* 1535. LW 26, 29-130.
14. *Lectures on Galatians* LW 26, 168.

locus of justification the divine person of Christ is separated from the person of the believer, because justification is only a forensic imputation and does not presuppose the divine presence of Christ in faith.

Theosis *and the Theology of the Cross*

I must emphasize that *theosis* and the theology of the cross do not exclude each other. On the contrary, they belong inseparably together. The theology of the cross is the necessary context of the idea of participation in God.

The decisive insight is that a human does not make himself empty and *"in nihilum."* It is God who effects this. Before God gives himself to a person, he performs his "nihilizing work" on human beings. He makes them "empty" and "nothing." This *reductio in nihilum,* of course, does not imply a total annihilation. It refers only to the destruction of the person's constant effort to make himself god and to justify himself.

One must pass through this agony and, ultimately, through the cross in order to achieve a true *cognitio sui.* Only in this way is one made *vacuum* and *capax Dei.* And this doctrine implies that, according to Luther, the modus of the existence of a Christian is always *passio (Gewirktwerden):* a person is neither inwardly nor outwardly active; one experiences only what God affects in oneself.

We correctly understand Luther's concept of *theosis,* then, only in connection with his theology of the cross. The participation that is a real part of his theology is hidden under its opposite, the *passio* through which a human is emptied. It is not grasped in rational knowledge but only in faith, and the grasp that faith has of it in this life is still only the beginning of a much greater participation that awaits in the eschatological fulfillment. But — and this is often forgotten — the goal of the *theologia crucis* is precisely *theosis:* "*Id enim facit beneficium Crucis mortificans nos et nostra omnia, ut consortes efficiamur divinae naturae, ut ij. Petri i. dicitur.*"[15]

15. WA 5, 445, 36-38.

4. Participation and/or *Theosis* and Love

The idea of participation and/or *theosis* is fundamental to understanding *locus iustificationis* and *theologia crucis* in Luther's thinking. One further *locus* that can be understood more fully on the basis of participation is Luther's theology of love.

The relationship between participation and love can be fruitfully analyzed on the basis of a text that provides a paradigmatic model of the Reformer's understanding of participation *(theosis)* and love.

> Once again the example of love is prefigured here in Christ with the leper. For here you see how love makes him a servant, so that he helps the poor man freely and for nothing, seeks neither pleasure, favor, nor honor thereby, but only the good of the poor man and the honor of God the father. For which reason he also forbids him to tell anyone, so that it be absolutely pure work of free, kindly love. That is how, as I have said often enough, faith makes us lords; through faith we even become gods and partake of the divine natureand name, as Psalm 81 says: "I have said, you are gods and children all together of the highest of the high." But through love we become like the poorest of the poor. According to the faith we need nothing and yet have complete abundance. Through faith we receive good from above from God. Through love we release them from below to our neighbor. Just as Christ according to his deity needed nothing, but in his humanity served everyone who needed him.
>
> We have said often enough that through faith we must be born God's children and gods, lords and kings, just as Christ is born in eternity a true God of the Father. And we must once again break out through love to help our neighbor with good deeds, just as Christ became man to help us all. And just as Christ did not earn his divinity beforehand through works or achieve it by becoming man, but rather had this divinity from birth without any works and before he became man, so also we have not through works of love earned being God's children, by which our sins are forgiven and death and hell cannot harm us, but rather have received this out of grace through faith in the gospel, without works and before love. And as Christ did not become man to serve us until after he had been God eternally, so also we do good and love our neighbor

40

only after we have previously become pious, without sin, living, blessed, and God's children through faith.[16]

In this passage faith has been understood as an analogue to the being of the divine Logos before his incarnation. Love, in its turn, has been understood as an analogue to the incarnation of God.

As the Logos is continuously born of the Father, so Christians are born continuously in their faith as "gods and children." As the Logos takes on human nature and becomes incarnate out of pure love, so Christians out of love step into the position of their neighbor and become "like the poorest of the poor." And just as the Logos does not need to be incarnated in order to be God, so the Christian does not need to step by love into the position of his neighbor before he is by faith alone "pious, without sin, living, and blessed."

16. WA 17 II, 74, 20–75, 11.

Christ as Favor and Gift (donum): The Challenge of Luther's Understanding of Justification

SIMO PEURA

1. Justification as Both Grace and Gift

One of the most difficult problems to be solved in Lutheran theology concerns the relation between the forensic and the effective aspects of justification. The question is crucial above all for Lutheran identity. Lutheran theologians today encounter this question particularly in the ecumenical context as they discuss the understanding of salvation with the Roman Catholic and the Orthodox churches.[1]

The two aspects of justification are expressed in Luther's theology in his conceptions of grace *(gratia, favor)* and gift *(donum)*. One indicates that a sinner is forensically declared righteous, and the other that he is made effectively righteous. Luther grasps this understanding of justification in the beginning of his theological career, not later than in his *Lecture on Romans* (1515/1516). The conceptions of grace and gift rest on Romans 5:15 *(gratia Dei et donum in gratia)*. Luther

---

1. In the Lutheran-Catholic dialogue some have insisted that the forensic aspect of justification is characteristic of the Lutheran way of understanding it, and the effective aspect is typical of the Catholic understanding. And when Lutherans discuss the notion of salvation with Orthodox Christians, they seek to relate justification and *theosis* to each other. We Lutherans will encounter great difficulties if we try to represent only the forensic aspect of justification.

found it most important already in these years to relate grace and gift closely to each other, and to understand them both as given to a Christian through Christ: "But 'the grace of God' and 'the gift' are the same thing, namely, the very righteousness which is freely given to us through Christ."[2] Thus we can see that grace and gift together constitute the donated righteousness of a Christian.

Furthermore, grace and gift are given not only through Christ, but in Christ and with Christ. For whatever distinction Luther makes between them, he also always keeps them together. In his foreword to the German translation of Romans (1522) Luther points out that grace and gift are in Christ and they become ours when Christ is "poured" into us. "Between grace and gift there is this difference. Grace actually means God's favor, or the good will which in himself he bears toward us, by which he is disposed to pour Christ and the Holy Spirit with his gifts into us. This is clear from chapter 5, where St. Paul speaks of 'the grace and gift in Christ' etc."[3]

Luther explains the relation between grace and gift most thoroughly in his writing against the Catholic theologian Latomus (1521).[4] According to Luther the gospel proclaims and teaches that God gives a sinner two goods *(bona)* to oppose his two evils, the wrath of God and the corruption of the Christian. These two goods of the gospel are grace and gift.[5]

2. " 'Gratia Dei' autem et 'donum' idem sunt sc. ipsa Iustitia gratis donata per Christum." WA 56, 318, 28-29; Am 25, 306.

3. "Gnade und Gabe sind des Unterschieds: daß Gnade eigentlich heißet Gottes Huld oder Gunst, die er zu uns trägt bei sich selbst, aus welcher er geneigt wird, Christum und den Geist mit seinen Gaben in uns zu gießen, wie das aus dem 5. Kapitel (15) klar wird, wo er spricht: 'Gnade und Gabe in Christo' etc." WA DB 7, 9, 10-14. (Cf. with the translation in Am with its intention to separate Christ and the Holy Spirit with his gift from each other: "by which he is disposed to give us Christ and to pour into us the Holy Spirit with his gifts." Am 35, 369.)

4. StA 2, 491, 19-503, 17 (= Am 32, 226-41).

5. "Nam Euangelium etiam duo praedicat et docet, Iustitiam et gratiam dei. Per iustitiam sanat corruptionem naturae, Iustitiam vero quae sit donum dei, fides scilicet Christi, sicut Ro. iij. dicit. . . . Huic fidei et iustitiae comes est gratia seu misericordia, fauor dei, contra iram, quae peccati comes est, vt omnis qui credit in Christum, habeat deum propitium." StA 2, 491, 21-30 (= Am 32, 227). (The description of grace and gift based here mainly on StA 2, 491, 22-492, 13; 493, 9-10 [= Am 32, 227, 228]).

Grace is the external good that opposes the greater evil, God's wrath. Grace is God's mercy *(misericordia Dei)* and favor *(favor Dei)*. This favorable and friendly attitude toward a sinner is an attitude that God has in himself. When God shows his grace, a sinner encounters not a hostile God but a merciful and favorable God. God's favor effects in the sinner a conviction that God is gracious, and his conscience becomes joyful, secure, and fearless. According to Luther, then, grace is God's favorable mood effecting in a sinner confidence in God's forgiveness and benevolence. Furthermore, grace is by its nature always comprehensive: either God is favorable toward a sinner or he is not.

Gift, however, constitutes the Christian's internal good, and it opposes his internal evil, that is, the corruption of human nature. Gift means righteousness *(iustitia)* and faith of/in Christ *(fides Christi)*. It is donated with the purpose of conquering the sin *(concupiscentia)* that remains as a corruption of the Christian's human nature. Gift effects in a sinner his real renewal *(renovatio)*, because it replaces sin with the righteousness of Christ and purifies a sinner from sin *(sanitas iustitiae)*. And though this renewal, according to its nature, has a beginning point and affects us partially, it also proceeds to greater effectiveness. Luther describes this renewal with the help of metaphors (e.g., leaven, Matt. 13:33). One should also notice that the good deeds of a Christian are good "fruits" provided by gift; that is, they are consequences of receiving the gift.

Thus far there is little difficulty in understanding Luther's meaning. But as soon as one wants to know more about the relation between these two goods of the gospel, problems arise. Luther insists, on the one hand, that a Christian must have both grace and gift. And he is convinced that grace and gift belong closely together. On the other hand, Luther says that Scripture distinguishes grace and gift from each other. In the history of Lutheran theology the relation between grace and gift usually has been explained according to the interpretation in the Formula of Concord. This interpretation followed Luther's demand to discern grace and gift in a special way, but it also diminished gift to its minimum *in loco iustificationis*.

2. The Common Interpretation of Grace and Gift in the Lutheran Tradition — and Its Corrective

According to the Formula of Concord (FC) the doctrine of justification *(iustitia fidei coram Deo)* includes only God's favor, that is, imputed righteousness. Justification is the same as absolution, the declared forgiveness of sins. The imputation of Christ's obedience to us has the effect of changing the position of the sinner *coram Deo*. One is accepted as a child of God and as an inheritor of eternal life.

Contrary to Luther, however, the FC excludes gift, the renewal of a Christian and the removal of sin, from the doctrine *(locus)* of justification. The FC indeed mentions gift, but at the same time it defines the gift in a radically limited sense compared with Luther. The gift is faith: the right knowledge of Christ, confidence in him, and the security that God the Father considers us righteous because of the obedience of Christ. So, gift means in the FC only the reception of forgiveness, knowledge of faith, and confidence *(fiducia)*, a gift that I would call a *donum minimum*.[6]

The FC then excludes from gift everything else that according to Luther is included in it. Regeneration, renewal *(renovatio)*, vivification *(vivificatio)*, and God's presence in the sinner *(inhabitatio Dei)* do not belong to the doctrine of justification but are consequences of God's declarative act (imputed righteousness).[7] According to the FC, the indwelling of God is not that righteousness by which we are declared righteous. The indwelling of God follows the antecedent of justification by faith. This means that God is not really present in a Christian when declaring him or her righteous through faith for Christ's sake.

6. "Haec bona nobis in promissione evangelii per spiritum sanctum offeruntur. Fides autem unicum est medium illud, quo illa apprehendimus, accipimus nobisque applicamus. Ea fides donum Dei est, per quod Christum redemptorem nostrum in verbo evangelii recte agnoscimus et ipsi confidimus, quod videlicet tantum propter ipsius obedientiam, ex gratia, remissionem peccatorum habeamus et iusti a Deo reputemur et in aeternum salvemur." SD III, 10-11. (See also Epit. III, 3-4; SD III, 9.)

7. See Epit. III, 5; SD III, 17-21, 28, 39, 54. (Cf., e.g., this quotation by Luther: "Ecce haec fides est donum dei, quae gratiam Dei nobis obtinet, et peccatum illud expurgat, et saluos certosque facit, non nostris sed Christi operibus . . ." StA 2, 499, 31-32.)

The FC came to this conclusion mainly because of its aim to reject Andreas Osiander, who emphasized the indwelling of the divine nature in his doctrine of justification. However, the problem of Osiander's doctrine was not actually his claim that justification was based on God's indwelling in a Christian, but the christological presuppositions of this claim. Osiander (in opposition to Luther) separated Christ's human nature and divine nature from each other and broke the *unio personalis* in Christ. Therefore Christ's human nature and everything that he did as a human being on the cross had only an instrumental and subsidiary role in redemption as well as in justification.[8]

Lutheran theologians have since repeated in general outline the interpretation of grace and gift and their relation given in the FC. The domination of the FC and its interpretation of grace and gift were guaranteed in Lutheranism since the end of the nineteenth century above all through neo-Kantian theology and philosophy. Characteristic of neo-Kantian theology is the radical separation of God's being *(esse)* and his effects *(Wirkungen)* from each other. This means either that only certain effects (of God) exist or that God is in no way present in the effects he produces. Because of this separation, such theological ideas as the union of God and the Christian *(unio cum Deo)* become impossible. The neo-Kantian theological school has had a wide and comprehensive influence on Luther research until now.[9]

Because of the FC and the neo-Kantian interpretation, gift and the effective aspect of justification have lost their ontological content in Lutheran theology. Gift *(donum)* has taken on the meaning of a new relation to God, a change in one's self-understanding or existential confidence in God's mercy. The content of gift is actually reduced to the Christian's insight that he has a new position *coram Deo.* Even

---

8. See my *Gott und Mensch in der Unio. Die Unterschiede im Rechtfertigungsverständnis bei Osiander und Luther. Unio: Gott und Mensch in der nachreformatorischen Theologie,* ed. Matti Repo and Rainer Vinke (Helsinki: Luther-Agricola-Gesellschaft 35, 1996), pp. 33-61.

9. See Risto Saarinen, "Gottes Wirken auf uns. Die transzendentale Deutung des Gegenwart-Christi-Motivs in der Lutherforschung," *VIEG* 137 (1989).

if this conviction is the most important existentially for a Christian, since he can then trust in God's favor, it actually means that the effective aspect of justification is reduced to something that happens only intrinsically in the human mind, in awareness, and in knowledge. The renewal of the sinner is a consequence of one's new relation to God. When a Christian has become aware of forgiveness and finds himself freed from the punishment for sin, his mood changes and he begins to do good works toward others.[10]

To reduce the gift to the Christian's *coram*-relation to God and to a change of self-understanding lets Lutherans argue that the Lutheran understanding of justification is something profoundly different from the Catholic doctrine of justification. For example, in Rudolf Herrmann's analysis of Luther's concept of gift *(donum)* he worries about the possibility that Luther's view might correspond to an Augustinian-Roman view, that the renewed Christian is covered by a supranatural gift *(donum)* and can therefore come before the merciful God. Herrmann works out "the problem" by first separating grace and gift from each other and then reducing the gift of faith to a mere relation. Faith in God's grace and favor means that a Christian is always placed directly opposite to God. And sanctification is for Herrmann an effect of forgiveness.[11] Herrmann thus succeeds in excluding the gift as a real renewal of the Christian from the doctrine *(locus)* of justification.

In my opinion, the FC and modern Lutheran theology have not correctly communicated Luther's view of grace and gift. I have argued from the very beginning of this article that justification includes gift in its broader sense, that is, in its effective aspect as the renewal of the sinner *(renovatio)*. This aspect belongs integrally to Luther's view of justification, and it is not a mere consequence of forensic imputa-

---

10. The interpretation of gift as a change of self-understanding through faith is not sufficient to explain Luther's view of faith. E.g., Luther's concept of illumination presupposes the real presence of God. God effects the illumination through his own presence. Luther says: "Idem enim est et utrumque simul est: deus illuminans et cor illuminatum, deus visus a nobis et deus praesens." WA 5, 201, 20-21 (Operationes in psalmos, 1519).

11. See Rudolf Herrmann, *Luthers These "Gerecht und Sünder zugleich"* (1930; Gütersloh, 1960), pp. 108-9, 280.

tion. Justification is not only a change of self-understanding, a new relation to God, or a new ethos of love. God changes the sinner ontologically in the sense that he or she participates in God and in his divine nature, being made righteous and "a god."

This interpretation is based on the thesis that both grace and gift are a righteousness given in Christ to a Christian. This donation presupposes that Christ is really present and that he indwells the Christian. Christ on the one hand is the grace that is given to the sinner that protects him against the wrath of God (the forensic aspect), and on the other hand he is the gift that renews and makes the sinner righteous (the effective aspect). All this is possible only if Christ is united with the sinner through the sinner's faith. So, the crucial point of this interpretation rests in the notion of *unio cum Christo*.

It is my aim in the following sections to show that this corrective interpretation holds its ground and explains Luther's view of grace and gift. But first we must turn to a discussion of some basic elements of Luther's doctrine of salvation.

3. Some Basic Theological Decisions

Grace Is Not a Quality of the Christian

In his controversy with the late scholastic theology of his own time Luther abandons the concept of created grace. The scholastic understanding of grace as created held that habitual grace was, according to its ontological status, a quality, an accident adhering to the human being considered as substance. This doctrine did not go far enough to stress the ontological points that Luther wished to maintain. He preferred the interpretation of Peter of Lombard, who claimed that the Holy Ghost himself is the love *(charitas)* of a Christian. This standpoint was very important for Luther's view of justification.

Luther points out in his *Lecture on Romans* that love has an exceptional position among the gifts given to a Christian. This position is based on the fact that love is donated as a gift only under the condition that its donator is present. So, if a Christian is supposed to have love and to become loving he must first have Christ and the

Spirit of Christ, the Holy Ghost. When Christ is present and gives his Spirit, the Christian receives as well the gift of love.[12]

Luther's view of love as the Spirit of the real present Christ leads us to another matter important for his understanding of salvation. Love is not the only essential divine attribute that a Christian receives as a gift of God. Luther holds all saving divine attributes in the same way: he does not separate God's essential nature ontologically from the divine attributes effecting salvation.

3.2. God Is Identical to His Attributes and Names

According to Luther the divine nature of the trinitarian God is the same as God's characteristic attributes. Luther argues already in his *Lecture on Psalms* that all attributes of God, such as truth, wisdom, and goodness, are identical to God. Divinity is for Luther the same as wisdom, light, virtue, glory, truthfulness, holiness, goodness, salvation, and all kinds of good of eternal life.[13]

Luther also calls these divine attributes spiritual goods *(bona spiritualia)* or God's names *(nomen Dei)*. They have no independence from God nor any being of their own, but on the contrary are what they

---

12. "Quia non satis est habere donum, nisi sit et donator presens. . . . Immo proprie soli Charitati tribuit Apostolus presentiam simul et donationem spiritus cum ipsa. Quia Cetera omnia dona 1. Corinth. 12. ab eodem spiritu dari dicit, Sed non ipsum spiritum. Sicut hic de Charitate dicit, Quod non detur nisi prius dato ipso spiritu, qui eam diffundat in cordibus nostris." WA 56, 308, 27-309, 2.

"Sed per Christum solum legem impleri, qui diffundit spiritum in cordibus nostris. Hec est rata differentia veteris et noue legis, Quod vetus dicit superbis in sua Iustitia: tu debes habere Christum et spiritum eius; Noua dicit humiliatis in sua eiusmodi paupertate et Christum petentibus: Ecce hic est Christus et spiritus eius." WA 56, 338, 25-30.

13. "Unde nota, quod sicut sub carne abscondita fuit benedicta divinitas, id est sapientia, lux, virtus, gloria, veritas, bonitas, salus, vita et omne bonum . . ." WA 4, 82, 32-33.

"In hiis laudatur Deus, ut quando veritatem, sapientiam, bonitatem loquimur, quia hec omnia est deus. Unde dicit ad Mosen 'Ego ero in ore tuo': quia os iusti meditabitur sapientiam, que est Deus ipse." WA 3, 189, 13-15.

are only in God and through God. Correspondingly, Luther identifies God and God's names with each other. According to him, God's name is Christ, the Word by which God named himself in eternity.[14]

A Christian is saved when the spiritual goods or the names of God are given to him. God is, as Luther says, the whole beatitude *(beatitudo)* of his saints; the name of God donates God's goodness, God himself, to the Christian; the spiritual goods are God's gifts in the Christian.[15] The divine attributes exist, then, not only in God and in his intra-trinitarian being, but are given to the Christian as well. God can be identified with the goodness and the beatitude of which Christians become the partakers. The donation of these spiritual goods, such as grace and gift, means that God gives himself in them to us.

God Gives Himself in His Goods — Theosis

Luther's view of God reveals another standpoint important for our topic: God gives himself to the one who needs him. According to Luther, the triune God proves to be the real God when he donates his own being to humanity. Thus, God realizes himself and his own nature when he gives his wisdom, goodness, virtue, beatitude, and all of his riches to the Christian, and when a Christian receives all that he gives.[16]

---

14. ". . . quia bona spiritualia non persistunt in se, sed in deo sine intermissione ex eo scaturientia. . . . Esto mihi in deum protectorem: quia firmamentum meum es tu. Esto mihi in locum munitum: quia refugium meum es tu. Protector et firmamentum conservando tua dona in me." WA 3, 454, 4-10.

" 'Nomen' est divinitas, maxime autem in persona filii. Quia ipse est nomen et verbum patris." WA 3, 158, 18-19.

"Nomen domini non dat sanctis bonum aliud quam est ipsummet: sed ipsummet est bonum eorum. Et sic dat seipsum et ita non dat, sed est bonum et tota beatitudo sanctorum. Nam sicut dicitur 'deus dat sanctis seipsum', quod valet 'Deus est bonum sanctorum suorum', ita etiam nomen eius dat seipsum illis, i.e. est bonum eorum. Est autem nomen dei ipse Christus filius dei, verbum quo se dicit et nomen quo se nominat ipsum in eternitate." WA 3, 303, 20-26.

15. See n. 14.

16. "Utique optimus, quia hoc ipso, ut dixi, se verum deum probat, qui vult sua dare nobis et noster deus esse, nobis benefacere, nos ipsius egere, et non nostra accipere, non nos habere suos benefactores et velut deos ac nostri

50

The self-giving of God is realized when Christ indwells the sinner through faith and thus unites himself with the sinner. This means that the Christian receives salvation *per Christum* only under the condition of *unio cum Christo*. Luther's conviction on this point leads to the conclusion that a Christian becomes a partaker of Christ and that a Christian is in this sense also deified.

Luther is well aware of the concept of participation as well as divinization. God, he says, lets a human being receive faith and truth so that he is truthful in front of God, and not as a mere human being, but as God's child and a god.[17] This deification is based on God's indwelling, or inhabitation: a Christian is a god, God's child and infinite, because God indwells in him.[18] Deification means for the Christian participation in God and in his divine nature: *"pars Christi vel sors Christi in terris fuit deus, sed partialiter."*[19] *Theosis* is a culmination of the train of Luther's thought as he claims the effective aspect of justification.

It is my aim in the next section to argue in detail for the thesis that *unio cum Christo* is the necessary prerequisite for the Christian to receive the two divine goods, grace and gift. Luther affirms that grace and gift do not exist separated from their giver. They are, as we have noted, ultimately received only in Christ. Because grace and gift are present only in Christ, and also because they constitute a donated righteousness, participation in Christ means that a Christian receives both grace and gift.

---

indigere. Benefacere enim alteri divinum est. . . . Nunc autem vult, quod nos tantummodo accipiamus, et ipse solus det, et ita sit vere deus." WA 4, 278, 24-35.

"Ideo confiteor domino, quoniam bonus est, et invoco eum de tribulatione tali, et exaudit me dans suam bonitatem, sapientiam, virtutem, beatitudinem, divitias mihi." WA 4, 279, 12-14.

17. "Sed hoc est esse deum: non accipere bona, sed dare, ergo pro malis bona retribuere. Quia enim prius dona dat quam accipit, quid aliud facit quam reddit bona pro malis? siquidem bona antequam daret, non erant ibi, ergo tantummodo mala. Quid ergo retribuam ego, quia retribuit mihi fidem et veritatem, qua coram ipso sum verax, ac sic iam non homo, sed deus ac dei filius et similis patri proles?" WA 4, 269, 25-30.

18. "Eodem modo quilibet Christianus debet se agnoscere magnum esse, quia propter fidem Christi, qui habitat in ipso, est deus, dei filius et infinitus, eo quod iam deus in ipso sit." WA 4, 280, 2-5.

19. WA 3, 106, 14-15.

4. Grace and Gift in Christ

As I have already stated, Luther's view of the relation between grace and gift is based on his interpretation of Romans 5:15 *(gratia Dei et donum in gratia unius hominis Iesu Christi in plures abundavit)*.[20] His argumentation proceeds in two phases.

Luther emphasizes first the importance of Christ's person for our salvation. The concept of *gratia Christi* refers to Christ's personal grace, because he is among all people the only one who is in God's judgment favorable and acceptable. While Christ's person is acceptable for God, the merciful God manifests his favor to Christ. This means that God favors all of Christ's deeds as well. So, everything that Christ has done for our salvation is good and favorable in God's judgment. Therefore Christ is also able to merit both grace and gift for sinners for the sake of their justification. We can note that the concept of Christ's personal grace reveals here a fact that is in general central for Luther's doctrine of justification, namely, that God judges deeds in accordance with the quality of the acting person.

Second, Luther points out that Christ's person on the one hand and the grace and gift that is merited on the cross on the other hand belong inseparably together. With the help of John 1:17 he insists that grace and gift are performed *(facta)* through Christ. Christ is not only the necessary means *(per Christum)*, however, by which grace and gift are caused or produced. Christ is in himself full of grace and gift (John 1:14). Thus, it is Christ himself who has become grace and

---

20. "Haec duo sic Ro. v. distinguit, Si enim vnius delicto mortui multi sunt, multo magis gratia dei et donum in gratia vnius hominis Iesu Christi in plures abundauit. Donum in gratia vnius hominis, fidem Christi vocat [quam et saepius donum vocat] quae nobis data est, in gratia Christi, id est, quia ille solus gratus et acceptus inter omnes homines, propitium et clementem deum haberet, vt nobis hoc donum et etiam hanc gratiam mereretur. Iohannes .i. Iohan. sic. Lex per Mosen data est. Gratia vero et veritas per Ihesum Christum facta est. Et infra, Plenum gratia et veritate. Ita veritas ex Christo in nos fluens fides est, gratia fidem comitatur ob gratiam Christi, sicut ibidem praemisit, de plenitudine eius omnes accepimus, gratiam pro gratia. Quam gratiam, pro qua gratia? gratiam nostram vt nobis faueret deus, pro gratia Christi, qua illi fauet deus." StA 2, 492, 13-493, 8 (= Am 32, 227-28).

gift for sinners. We might say as well that grace and gift exist for us only in Christ.

Thus, the basic starting point of Luther's interpretation of Romans 5:15 *(gratia Dei et donum in gratia)* is as follows: Christ himself is grace and gift. Christ himself is the grace that covers a sinner and hides him from God's wrath, and Christ himself is the gift that renews the sinner internally and makes him righteous. This occurs, then, when Christ unites himself with a sinner.

5. *Unio cum Christo* —
The Necessary Condition of the Gift

According to Luther, union with Christ is effected in baptism. The necessary precondition of baptism is always the preaching of God's word. The sacrament of baptism achieves validity when the Word of God, that is, Christ, joins himself to natural water.[21] When the sacrament is employed according to its purpose, baptism effects that the sins immersed into baptismal water are "swallowed up," the baptized dies in relation to sin, and a newborn Christian is raised up from the water. Even the external performance of baptism points out its meaning.[22]

It is Luther's conviction that everything which comes into existence through baptism is totally God's work. Christ is given to the baptized as well as the personal faith through which she receives Christ. Both are God's gratuitous gifts.[23]

The essential idea in Luther's theology of baptism is that baptism is a merciful and consoling union in which God joins himself with the sinner and becomes one with him or her. Thus, baptism is not

21. Cf. Luther's *Great Catechism* and his baptismal sermons in the 1530s (WA 37, 627-72). The *unio cum Deo* comes into being when Christ is proclaimed. Luther's view of the word of God is a sacramental one. The words of Christ or the words preached by Christ do not refer only to their object, which is external to the words, but they also include the object. This is why the words are able to give in themselves the Christ proclaimed. See WA 9, 439-42. (The sacrament of eucharist is in a specific sense *unio cum Christo*. See WA 33, 181-242.)

22. StA 1, 259, 5-260, 20 (= Am 35, 29-30).

23. See in detail Eero Huovinen, *Fides infantium* (Helsinki, 1991).

just a covenant or an agreement between two partners bound together to function or act for the same purpose, the salvation of the baptized. It is much more: through the sacramental act of baptism God binds himself ontologically to a sinner and is one with him through his whole earthly life, if he adheres to Christ in faith.[24]

Since the idea that baptism means union with Christ is not commonly accepted in Luther research, we should note another passage in which Luther points to the role of union for his understanding of baptism. According to Luther, baptism does not just guarantee the death of sin and the Christian's resurrection on the first day of eternal life *(der Jüngste Tag)*. Its meaning is realized through a firm faith already in this life. Baptism initiates through faith the realization of death and resurrection, joins us with God, and empowers us to struggle against sin.[25]

The core of the matter is that the *meaning* of baptism, the death of sin and the resurrection of the new person, becomes effective in the baptized person because God unites himself with the sinner both through the sacramental act and through faith. This most important standpoint of Luther must be brought into the discussion, since his view of grace and gift in his *Antilatomus* relies on it. Luther explains his understanding of the relation between grace and gift from the point of view that even though all sins are forgiven in baptism *(favor)*, real sin must be expelled by gift in the baptized person. Therefore the real presence of Christ and union with God are necessary for the Christian.

In his *Antilatomus* Luther unfolds the idea of *unio cum Christo*

24. "Das hilfft dir das hochwirdig sacrament der tauff/das sich gott daselbs mit dyr vorpindet vnd mit dyr eyns wird eyns gnedigen trostlichens bunds." StA 1, 262, 27-29 (= Am 35, 33). Hans-Ulrich Delius, the editor of the sermon, makes the following note to the concept of *vorpindet:* "Für Luther war das Verbinden gleich Einswerden wie etwa WA 37, 642, 22-30." See also StA 1, 266, 18-20; 269, 1-3 (= Am 35, 38-39, 42).

25. "Hie ist nu das dritte stuck/des sacraments zu handeln/das ist der glaub/das ist/das man diß alles festiglich glaub/das das sacrament/nit allein bedeut/den todt vnnd auffersteeung am Jungsten tag/durch wilche der mensch new werd ewiglich an sund zu leben/ßondern das es auch gewißlich dasselb anhebe vnd wirck/vnd vnß mitt gott vorpyndet/das wir wollen biß ynn den tod/die sund todten vnd widder sie streyten." StA 1, 264, 12-17 (= Am 35, 35).

with the help of different metaphors.[26] In each of these we see Luther's characteristic emphasis that grace and gift belong to each other. But at the same time he underlines that the Christian, though favored by God, can be renewed (gift) only on the condition that he "is in Christ" and that he "is with Christ."

The most important metaphor is that of the mother hen who protects her baby chicks and lets them get well or recover under her wing. According to Luther, faith hides the Christian under the protection of Christ (Mal. 4:2). The Christian then hangs onto Christ and trusts him to be righteous in respect to him. This union with Christ is the basis of the Christian's salvation. As Luther says, it is the gift of faith that acquires God's mercy *(favor)* as well as expels sin from him.[27] This sequence of claims is understandable only on the basis of real union with Christ. Christ is on the one hand the favor that protects the sinner against the wrath of God, and on the other hand he is the gift who begins to drive sin away and make a sinner truly righteous.

Moreover, Luther argues that the metaphor of the mother hen describes our being in Christ *(esse in Christo)*. For those who are in Christ, there is no damnation despite the fact that they still are more or less sinful (Rom. 8:1). Luther says: "The reason why there is no condemnation is not that men do not sin, as Latomus in lying fashion suggests, but because — as Paul says — they are in Jesus Christ; that

---

26. E.g., leaven and three measures of meal (StA 2, 496, 11-14; 493, 33-494, 2), the good Samaritan and the half-dead wayfarer (StA 2, 496, 16-20; see also WA 56, 272, 11-273, 2 and WA 2, 413, 30-36), Christ washing the feet of his disciples (StA 2, 496, 20-22; 430, 5-18), the vine and its branches (StA 2, 496, 22-27), and the occupation of Canaan and the Jebusites (StA 2, 497, 7-12; 470, 17). See for all Am 32, 232-33.

27. "Quid istis vult Apostolus, nisi quod non satis est illa fides vaga sophistarum, quae accepto dono putatur operari? sed ea demum fides est, quae te pullastrum Christum gallinam facit, vt sub pennis eius speres. Nam salus in pennis eius, ait Malachias, vt scilicet non in fide accepta nitaris, hoc est enim fornicari, sed fidem esse scias, si ei adhaereris, de ipso praesumpseris, quod tibi sanctus iustusque sit. Ecce haec fides est donum dei, quae gratiam dei nobis obtinet, et peccatum illud expurgat, et saluos certosque facit, non nostris sed Christi operibus, vt subsistere et permanere inaeternum possimus, sicut scriptum est, Iustitia eius manet in seculum seculi." StA 2, 499, 25-34 (= Am 32, 236).

is, they repose under the shadow of his righteousness as do chicks under a hen. Or as is said more clearly in Rom. 5, they have grace and the gift through his grace."[28]

This quotation shows that our being in Christ *(esse in Christo)* means that a Christian has become one with Christ, and that Christ's righteousness protects him. Therefore Luther goes on to argue that a Christian is provided with two firm and immensely strong foundations or supports, namely grace and gift. Because of them the still remaining and real sin is not able to bring damnation to a Christian.[29]

In sum, Luther's understanding that God the Father is favorable to a sinner *(favor Dei)* and that Christ renews a sinner *(donum Dei)* is based on the idea of *unio cum Christo*. This same idea explains why grace and gift are necessary to each other. Gift is not only a consequence of grace, as is usually emphasized in Lutheran theology, but it is in a certain sense a condition for grace as well.

6. Grace and Gift Presuppose Each Other

The mutual conditioning of grace and gift appears in Luther's more detailed explanation of how the two firm supports given to a Christian shelter him from damnation. Luther illustrates his thought again with the help of the mother hen metaphor. Thus, we must acknowledge his presupposition that a Christian is in Christ and one with him.

The first of the two supports is Christ as the throne of grace. Christ is for Luther the grace that protects Christians at all times in spite of their sin. This protection has its foundation not in the Christian's faith or any possession of the gift of faith or because of the struggle against sin. On the contrary, the Christian can have the gift

28. "Nihil esse damnationis, licet nonnihil sit peccati, quia tot de peccato praemiserat, sed ideo nihil est damnationis, non quia non sit ibi peccatum, vt Latomus mentitur, sed quia sunt in Christo Ihesu, dicit Paulus, id est pullastri sub gallina et sub vmbra iustitiae illius pausant, seu vt Ro. v. clarius dicit. Gratiam et donum in gratia illius habent." StA 2, 502, 2-7; Am 32, 239.

29. "Deinde non ambulant secundum peccatum seu carnem peccati, id est, non consentiunt peccato, quod reuera habent. Deus enim eis prouidit duo robustissima munitissimaque firmamenta, ne hoc peccatum eis sit in damnationem." StA 2, 502, 7-10 (= Am 32, 239).

of faith only on condition that he is in Christ's grace. According to Luther, no Christian could hold on to his faith without basing it on Christ's own righteousness and without being protected by Christ. Because of residual sin a Christian can stand before God's judgment only if he puts the righteousness of the innocent Christ against his own condemnation.[30]

Thus, according to Luther, one who is in Christ is also perfect and protected by the complete righteousness of Christ. Covered by the protecting Christ, the Christian gains the possibility of believing and living as a Christian. Because of its completeness the first foundation, grace, is the strongest one; it is called the main foundation of the Christian. Because of its completeness grace is also the necessary condition of the gift; that is, the Christian's renewal, which is by nature always partial and imperfect. Thus, it is only because of grace that the gift has an objective reality for us *(aliquid)*.[31] We can say in this sense that grace is the necessary condition of gift.

The second support of the Christian is the gift, with the help of which he can fight against sin. When those who are in Christ have received the gift, they no longer live according to the flesh and obey sin. Luther's emphasis here reminds us that God enters into a (baptismal) union only with those who in Christ fight against sin. This means that a Christian is protected by Christ's grace insofar as the gift (i.e., renewal) is realized in his life.[32] In this sense we could say

30. "Primum, ipsum Christum propitiatorium vt Ro. iij. vt sub huius gratia tuti sint, non quia credunt et fidem aut donum habent, sed quia in gratia Christi habent. Nullius enim fides subsisteret, nisi in Christi propria iustitia niteretur, et illius protectione seruaretur. Haec est enim fidem vt dixi vera, non absoluta immo obsoleta illa qualitas in anima, vt illi fingunt, sed quae se a gratia Christi non patitur auelli, nec alio nititur, quam quod scit, illum esse in gratia dei nec posse damnari, nec aliquem, qui sic in eum se proiecerit. Scilicet tam magna res est hoc peccatum reliquum, sic intolerabile iudicium dei, vt nisi eum pro te opponas, quem sine omni peccato esse nosti, subsistere nequeas, id quod facit fides vera." StA 2, 502, 10-20 (= Am 32, 239).

31. See n. 32.

32. "Alterum est, quod dono accepto non ambulat secundum carnem, nec obediunt peccato, sed prius illud principale et robustissimum est, licet et alterum sit aliquid, sed in virtute prioris. Quia pepigit deus pactum iis qui sunt hoc modo in Christo, vt si pugnent contra seipsos et peccatum suum, nihil sit dam-

that the Christian's renewal is the necessary condition for grace and for staying under Christ's protection. Moreover, we can note that this emphasis leads Luther unavoidably to synergism unless we take account of his view on *unio cum Christo*. For this view is the basic presupposition of his claim. Gift, the expulsion of sin and the renewal of the Christian, is realized in a Christian only as a work of the real presence of Christ.

Luther's idea that gift is a condition for grace has usually been passed over in Luther research. We should therefore refer to another quotation that lends clarity to his standpoint. He says: "To be sure, for grace there is no sin, because the whole person pleases; yet for the gift there is sin which it purges away and overcomes. A person neither pleases, nor has grace, except on account of the gift which labors in this way to cleanse from sin."[33]

This quotation shows without doubt that the whole person of the Christian is favored by God, since the gift purifies the Christian from sin and opposes it. Unless the gift continuously labors to expel sin, the Christian cannot receive favor in God's judgment. In this sense Luther can also state "that this faith is the gift of God, which obtains the grace of God for us."[34] Thus, the gift also is always a permanent condition of grace and of God's favorable intention.

As we can see, Luther's interpretation of the relation between grace and gift becomes understandable only from the point of view that a Christian is in Christ and one with Christ. It is the idea of *unio*

---

nationis. Non ergo nihil est damnationis, vt Latomus delyrat, quia non peccant, aut non sit peccatum in opere bono. Hoc fingit sophista, extra et contra apertum textum pauli e proprio capite. Sed quia sunt inquit in Christo Ihesu, et non ambulant secundum carnem, manifeste de mortali peccato loquens." StA 2, 502, 21-29 (= Am 32, 239-40).

33. "Gratia quidem nullum ibi peccatum habet, quia persona tota placet. Donum autem peccatum habet quod expurget et expugnet, sed et persona non placet nec habet gratiam, nisi ob donum hoc modo peccatum expurgare laborans." StA 2, 494, 9-12; Am 32, 229.

34. "Ecce haec fides est donum dei, quae gratiam dei nobis obtinet, et peccatum illud expurgat, et saluos certosque facit . . ." StA 2, 499, 31-32. (Cf. the translation in Am 32, 236: "Observe that this faith is the gift of God, which the grace of God obtains for us, and which, purging away sin, makes us saved and certain. . . .")

cum Christo that secures for Luther the principle of *sola gratia* in his doctrine of salvation. That a Christian is really made righteous, although only partially so, is not his own achievement but is effected by Christ who indwells the Christian. This means that the presence of Christ is the permanent condition of the Christian's effective righteousness.

Luther insists again and again that the Christian's righteousness must be continuously connected with the origin of the gift. Even if the gift of righteousness is really given to a Christian, and he has it as his own (*eigene Gerechtigkeit* does not mean the *"Selbstgerechtigkeit"!*), no Christian should either trust in himself or steal the gifts that belong to God and make them his own. A Christian must always be aware that salvation is based on Christ. The Christian's own righteousness is sufficient for salvation only when it is linked to the righteousness of Christ and flows as a continuous stream from it.[35]

Thus, the firmness of salvation can by no means be based on a Christian's own righteousness, even though God has given it to him and made him righteous and even when the gift has already to some extent expelled residual sin. Rather, the Christian must direct his confidence away from himself toward Christ. This Christ-centered reliance is important because of the possibility that a Christian might become "saturated" or self-confident when he has received the gift.[36] We cannot speak about Luther's notion of false security (*securitas*) in its full meaning until we understand that for him the gift of righteousness is really donated to a Christian.

If residual sin leads a Christian to begin trusting in his own righteousness instead of that of its giver, the idea of *unio cum Christo* proves to be a valuable antidote. Luther can emphasize in its terms on the one hand the real and effective character of justification in which Christ who has joined with the sinner begins to renew him and make him righteous, and on the other hand guard a Christian from disastrous

---

35. "Nam quamuis per donum fidei nos iustificarit, et per gratiam suam nobis factus sit propitius, tamen ne vagaremur in nobis ipsis, et in his donis suis, voluit vt in Christum niteremur, vt nec iustitia illa cepta nobis satis sit, nisi in Christi iustitia haereat et ex ipso fluat, ne quis insipiens, semel accepto dono, iam satur et securus sibi videatur . . ." StA 2, 499, 7-12 (= Am 32, 235).

36. See n. 35.

self-confidence through the idea of *unio cum Christo*. The donated righteousness and the effected renewal are not a Christian's "own" in the sense that he can keep them in his possession or because they constitute permanent qualities in him. He is renewed and made righteous only on condition that he is one with Christ, that he remains in Christ, and that his righteousness permanently flows from Christ.[37]

The mode *(modus)* of having this donated righteousness, through a union with Christ and not by means of one's own permanent quality of righteousness, demands that a Christian direct his attention away from himself and toward Christ. He can be continuously righteous only if he continually reasserts his trust in Christ. Thus does this confidence lead to an ever deeper union with Christ.

Luther's view of justification includes one other important matter worthy of discussion. It contains, as we have seen, the concepts of participation, change, and deification. The aim of justification is actually a complete transformation in Christ. This view might easily be confused with a pantheistic one: the difference between God and human beings disappears; they melt into each other and reach a total identity. But this conclusion is too rash in respect to Luther's real meaning. Actually, he avoids pantheism, basing his idea of *conformitas Christi* on the notion of union with Christ.

7. Conformitas Christi

Luther's doctrine of justification contains a conception originating in the mystical tradition that a Christian might be caught up *(raptus)* in Christ. It means not only that a Christian is joined with Christ but that he is in this union transformed into a likeness of Christ. This change is a process, and it creates in the Christian the same form *(forma)* as Christ *(plane in Christum transformari)*.

Luther explains his understanding of transformation in this passage: ". . . so that no fool, having once accepted the gift, will think himself already contented and secure. But he does not want us to halt in what has been received, but rather to draw near from day to day so that we may be fully transformed into Christ. His righteousness

37. See n. 35.

is perpetual and sure; there is no change, there is there no lack, for he himself is the Lord of all. Therefore, whenever Paul preached faith in Christ, he did so with the utmost care to proclaim that righteousness is not only through him or from him, but even that it is in him. He therefore draws us into himself, and transforms us, and places us as if in hiding 'until the wrath passes away.' "[38]

Rudolf Herrmann found it difficult to take seriously Luther's view of transformation. He writes: "God's will for us is that we be 'fully transformed' into him. . . ? Can that really be Luther's meaning? His words cannot be taken to mean quite what they say."[39]

Clearly on the grounds of an exclusively forensic understanding of justification and a so-called relational ontology, this passage from Luther is either incomprehensible or reveals a pantheism. But we can discount the possibility of pantheism if we acknowledge the presupposition of Luther's understanding of transformation, *unio cum Christo,* where Luther's view of justification appears in its fullness.

The passage informs us that the Christian's righteousness is completely dependent on Christ. A Christian is righteous only through Christ *(per Christum),* his righteousness comes from Christ *(ab Christo),* and it always turns toward Christ *(in Christum).* The last phrase means that a Christian cannot be satisfied with the righteousness already given to him or with the renewal already effected in him by the gift. He must direct his attention ever more deeply toward the origin of the gift, Christ.

The *sine qua non* of the transformation is, as we have claimed,

---

38. ". . . ne quis insipiens, semel accepto dono, iam satur et securus sibi videatur, sed in illum nos rapi de die in diem magis voluit non in acceptis consistere, sed in Christum plane transformari. Illius enim iustitia certa et perpetua est, ibi non est nutare, ibi non est deficere, ipse dominus omnium. Ideo Paulus mira diligentia quoties fidem Christi praedicat, sic praedicat, vt non tantum per illum aut ab illo sit iustitia, sed etiam in illum, vt nos in ipsum referat et transformet, et velut in absconsum ponat, donec transeat ira." StA 2, 499, 11-18; Am 32, 235.

39. Herrmann solves his problem by emphasizing God's favor and reducing God's gift to its minimum, i.e., to a relation to God. "Und wenn wir aus unseren früheren Erwägungen über gratia und donum wissen, daß donum den glaubenden Menschen bedeutet, wie er vor den gnädigen Gott (dank der gratia) gestellt und zu Leben und Dasein aufgerufen wird, so. . . ." Herrmann, *Luthers These "Gerecht und Sünder zugleich,"* p. 280.

unio cum Christo. Christ is the one who transfers a sinner to Christ himself and who changes the sinner. The transformation also means that Christ hides the Christian from God's wrath until it has passed. But we are hid in Christ throughout our earthly life, because sin is always present in a Christian. A Christian can be saved only under the condition that he or she has the gift of faith, through which one can be hidden under the protection of Christ.

Thus, we note that Luther's understanding of transformation contains two aspects. On one hand our transformation in Christ involves a continuous change into the form of Christ *(conformitas Christi).* Its purpose is complete conformity with Christ, which occurs in the resurrection. On the other hand the transformation involves an ever deepening enclosure in Christ and in his righteousness. Faith makes us like those chicks whom Christ the mother hen protects under his wing so that we can be healed and trained to full conformity with our Protector. When joined together with Christ, a Christian trusts not in himself, but in the complete righteousness of Christ.[40]

The complete righteousness of a Christian — God's favor as well as God's gift — depends permanently and throughout one's life on Christ and Christ's own righteousness. A Christian participates in Christ's righteousness on the condition that he has become one with Christ. Grace and gift presuppose each other, but both of them come to existence only because of the union with Christ.[41]

---

40. "Ecce fides non satis, sed fides quae se sub alas Christi recondat, et in illius iustitia glorietur. Et iterum, Per quem habemus accessum ad deum, per fidem in gratiam istam. Iterum fidem sic docet, vt eam sub alas Christi proiiciat. Et Colos. i. Et per eum placuit reconciliari omnia in ipsum. Ecce per eum in ipsum, Et vltra, Pacificans per sanguinem crucis eius, per ipsum. Ecce per sanguinem crucis eius per ipsum. Quid istis vult Apostolus, nisi quod non satis est illa fides vaga sophistarum, quae accepto dono putatur operari? sed ea demum fides est, quae te pullastrum Christum gallinam facit, vt sub pennis eius prosperes. nam salus in pennis eius, ait Malachias, vt scilicet non in fide accepta nitaris, hoc est enim fornicari, sed fidem esse scias, si ei adheseris, de ipso praesumpseris, quod tibi sanctus iustusque sit." StA 2, 499, 19-31 (= Am 32, 235-36).

41. "Ecce haec fides est donum dei, quae gratiam dei nobis obtinet, et peccatum illud expurgat, et saluos certosque facit, non nostris sed Christi operibus, vt substistere et permanere inaeternum possimus, sicut scriptum est, Iustitia eius manet in seculum seculi." StA 2, 499, 31-34 (= Am 32, 236).

The main purpose of Luther's critique of Latomus was to defend the notion of residual sin in the Christian after baptism. Luther's argumentation is based on his view that justification includes the forensic aspect as well as the effective aspect. Therefore, the issue for Luther is primarily the difference between his view of effective justification and that of Latomus. His issue with Latomus, then, is quite different from what it is commonly thought to be, namely that Luther emphasizes forensic justification while Latomus emphasizes effective justification.[42]

Luther's conviction that residual sin is according to its nature real sin also requires as its counterweight the effective aspect of justification. The purpose of justification is that a Christian be made righteous, be completely transformed in Christ. Thus, the main difference between Luther and Latomus concerns the ontological basis of justification. Luther points to the real presence of Christ, whereas Latomus explains the transformative aspect of justification with the help of Aristotelian-scholastic metaphysics (the doctrine of *fides charitate formata*). The ecumenical issues now culminate in the question concerning how to fit together these two views of justification and the different interpretations of residual sin.

8. The Real Present Christ — Challenge for the Lutheran-Catholic Ecumenical Approach

The Lutheran-Catholic ecumenical commission has published a "Joint Declaration on the Doctrine of Justification." The partners state in Article 26, "And yet concupiscence no longer separates the justified from God. Properly speaking, it therefore is not sin."[43]

In my opinion this statement is inconsistent with the view represented by Luther and the Lutherans in common. Sin after baptism

---

42. It is in a sense easy to relate the forensic understanding of justification to the view of sin in Latomus. According to Latomus the sin of a Christian after baptism is not sin in the true sense of the word but only its punishment or guilt. The absolution, i.e., declaration of forgiveness, could discharge this kind of sin.

43. *Joint Declaration on the Doctrine of Justification* (Geneva: LWF and PCPCU, 1995), p. 26.

is real sin. This article is important for Catholics, however, because they want to emphasize the reality of the effective aspect of justification. Thus, it appears that the Catholic partner as well as perhaps most Lutherans is claiming that the notion of the real character of sin *post baptismum* is in contradiction to the view that a Christian is made righteous.

This is obviously a false conclusion in the light of the interpretation of Luther presented here. The reality of residual sin and the truth that a Christian is also really made righteous can be integrated through the medium of the indwelling Christ who effects unity with the Christian. Because of Luther's view of the real union with Christ, we can connect the effective aspect of justification to the forensic aspect. But this argument has not informed the method of the Joint Declaration. That document lacks totally the idea of union with Christ.

According to the document the forensic aspect seems to characterize especially the Lutheran way of understanding justification, and the effective aspect explains specifically the Catholic point of view. The document indicates that the two aspects describe two different sides of the same thing. But actually the two aspects are connected to each other so that we might properly say that they coexist side by side.

This is not the first time that this "method" has been relied on in the history of the Lutheran-Catholic dialogue. The most obvious example is the discussion in Regensburg in 1541 between Lutherans (Melanchthon, Bucer, and Pistorius) and Catholics (Eck, Pflug, Gropper, and Contarini). The result of these negotiations was the so-called *Book of Regensburg*, the fifth article of which contains the convergence in the doctrine of justification.[44] The aim was to interrelate the forensic view of justification *(iustitia imputata)* represented by Melanchthon, and the Catholic concept of *fides charitate formata*,

44. To the discussion on the *Book of Regensburg* (CR IV, 190-238), see in detail *Justification by Faith: Lutherans and Catholics in Dialogue VII* (Minneapolis, 1985), pp. 32-33; Karl-Heinz zur Mühlen, "Die Einigung über den Rechtfertigungsartikel auf dem Regensburger Religionsgespräch von 1541 — eine verpaßte Chance?" *ZThK* 76:331-59; and Walther von Loewenich, "Duplex iustitia. Luthers Stellung zu einer Unionsformel des 16. Jahrhunderts," *VIEG* 68 (1972): 23-55.

based on Galatians 5:6 *(fides quae est efficax per charitatem)*. In spite of a serious attempt no consensus could be reached. Rome as well as Wittenberg rejected the result, the "double justification formula," because it was unsatisfying and because of its ambiguity.

Most important ecumenically, however, is not the fifth article of the *Book of Regensburg,* but Luther's reaction. Neither research nor the modern dialogue has taken the challenge of Luther's response seriously enough or made good use of it. Luther did not accept the convergence, because he found that it did not represent a true and real consensus. According to him the convergence was reached by "glueing together" the scholastic doctrine of *fides charitate formata* and the biblical understanding of justification. He claims that the problems with this position become obvious when one properly interprets Galatians 5:6.

According to Luther this biblical passage does not explain how someone becomes righteous but argues something about one who is already righteous. So, Luther finds it necessary to distinguish between two concepts: becoming something and acting; that is, between being something and doing something. The question concerning how to become righteous before God differs from the question concerning what righteous Christians do. It is one thing to become a good tree and another to produce fruit. Galatians 5:6 does not speak about how to become righteous, which is possible only through faith and not through works. It argues instead for a quality of Christian life that includes self-evidently good deeds as well. The good tree does not exist without producing good fruit. Action is always in accordance with being *(agere sequitur esse).*[45]

After Luther had paid attention to the misinterpretation of Galatians 5:6, he gave his own answer to the question that was most important for him: how to become righteous. Righteousness is not achieved by the help of works, of inherent habitual love, or of inherent grace.[46] The righteousness valid in God's judgment is not an inherent quality of the Christian, that is, a substantially inherent quality of habitual grace in the Christian. Therefore, according to Luther, the doctrine of *fides charitate formata* is wrong.

45. WA Br. 9, Nr. 3616, 40-50.
46. WA Br. 9, Nr. 3616, 51-55.

Luther replaces the scholastic understanding with his own view of justification. He says, "For nothing counts with God, except his beloved Son Jesus Christ, who is completely pure and holy before him. Where he is, there God looks and has his pleasure. . . . Now the Son is not grasped and held in the heart by works but only by faith, without works. So God says: 'This heart is holy on account of my Son, who lives within it through faith.' "[47] Only Christ can be the righteousness that stands through God's judgment. Christ is completely holy and pure in the eyes of God. Where Christ is, there God directs his favor. Moreover, Christ indwells in the Christian's heart through faith. So, according to Luther, the righteousness that stands in front of God is based on the indwelling of Christ. The indwelling Christ in the heart of the Christian is the necessary condition for God's favor as well as for the renewing gift. The heart of the Christian is holy because of the indwelling of Christ.

Luther's explanation is not a haphazard but an exact and carefully considered one. To be sure that his point of view will be understood, he repeats his position: "Love and works are not and cannot be the Son of God or such righteousness as is pure and holy before God as the Son is. Therefore they cannot in themselves stand before God as pure righteousness, as the Son does. That they nevertheless count as right and holy happens from sheer grace and not from merit. For God will not regard them as he does his Son. Rather he takes them in good part and does not count their impurity for the sake of his Son, and indeed also crowns and rewards them — but all for the sake of the Son, who dwells in the heart by faith."[48] So, according to Luther, God is not only favorable toward a sinner because of the indwelling of Christ, but he also adorns *(kronen)* and rewards *(belohnen)* a sinner through the real present Christ. The idea of adornment means here as well as in Luther's first *Lecture on Psalms* the effective aspect of justification, the gift renewing a sinner. It is Luther's firm conviction that the Christian needs always both grace *and* gift. Notice that Luther argues in this same way in his *Preface to the Romans* (1546). He insists that a sinner is accounted completely righteous before God because of Christ, our Mediator, *and* because

47. WA Br. 9, Nr. 3616, 55-61.
48. WA Br. 9, Nr. 3616, 62-69.

of the fact that the gifts are begun in us. There is no condemnation for the one who is in Christ, "simply because of the incompleteness of the gifts and of the Spirit."[49]

As we have seen, according to Luther it is possible to connect the forensic aspect and the effective aspect of justification to each other with the help of the concepts of *unio cum Christo* and *inhabitatio Christi.* If these ideas are taken into account, Lutherans can without difficulty argue that a Christian is both made righteous and also deified as a partaker of divine nature. Most important, though, is that this affirmation can be made on the grounds of genuine Lutheran tradition.[50]

Even if the Lutheran understanding of effective righteousness is not the same as the Catholic doctrine of *fides charitate formata,* we can in any case more easily reach a real consensus on justification with the Catholics with the help of Luther's central ideas. At least it becomes easier with the help of Luther than on the basis of the common Lutheran view of justification as a one-sided, declarative, imputative act or judgment of God. We should make good use of Luther's ideas concerning grace and gift and their mutual relation in the modern Lutheran-Catholic dialogue, too.

In my point of view Luther's understanding of justification offers many challenges for recent ecumenical discussions. For example, con-

49. "So thut doch die Gnade so viel, das wir gantz und fur vol gerecht fur Gott gerechnet werden. Denn seine gnade teilet und stücket sich nicht, wie die gaben thun, sondern nimpt uns gantz und gar auff in die hulde, umb Christus unsers Fursprechers und Mittlers willen, und umb das in uns die Gaben angefangen sind. . . . Es sey nichts verdamlichs an denen, die in Christo sind, der unuolkomenen Gaben und des Geistes halben." WADB 7, 9, 18-25. (Cf. the translation in Am: ". . . we are accounted completely righteous before God. For his grace is not divided or parceled out, as are the gifts, but takes us compeletely into favor for the sake of Christ our Intercessor and Mediator. And because of this, the gifts are begun in us." Am 35, 370.)

50. The *Book of Regensburg* includes the idea of participation in the divine nature: "Item, nulli Christiano ambigendum est, nullum hominem posse Deo reconciliari, itemque liberari a servitute peccati, nisi per Christum unum mediatorem Dei et hominum, per cuius gratiam, ut inquit Apostolus ad Romanos, non tantum reconciliamus Deo, et liberamur a servitute peccati, sed etiam efficimur consortes divinae naturae et filii Dei." CR IV, 198-99. (Here Luther by no means criticizes the participative motive of justification.)

sider the so-called *communio* ecclesiology of the Faith and Order Conference in Santiago de Compostela (1993), or the panlutheran-panorthodox dialogue (1995) with its convergence on justification and *theosis,* or the discussions with the evangelicals, who emphasize the reality and importance of spiritual life, Christ living in us. And if we take seriously Luther's idea of Christ's real presence through faith and his notion of cooperation, we can bridge the gorge between faith and love in ecumenical ethics.

The content of Luther's theology makes him a Catholic teacher in the primary sense of the word and not a denominational one. He can, therefore, be a common teacher for Lutherans, Catholics, and other Christians. That is why Luther is so inspiring as well as fascinating.

Bibliography of Sources and Reference Works

Luther, Martin

WA 3-4	Dictata super Psalterium. 1513-1516.
WA 56	Divi Pauli apostoli ad Romanos epistola. 1515/1516.
Am 25	
WA 2, 391-435	Resolutiones Lutherianae super propositionibus suis Lipsiae disputatis. 1519.
StA 1, 258-69	Eyn Sermon von dem heyligen Hochwirdigen Sacra-
Am 35, 29-43	ment der Tauffe. 1519.
WA 5	Operationes in Psalmos. 1519.
WA 9, 439-42	Sermon to Matthew 1,1-. 1519.
StA 2, 405-519	Rationis Latomianae. 1521.
Am 32, 137-260	
WA 33, 181-242	Sermons to John 6,51-58. 1531.
WA 37, 627-72	Sermons to the holy Baptism. 1535.
WABr. 9, Nr. 3616	Luther and Bugenhagen to Kurfürst Johann Friedrich. 10./11.5.1541.
WADB 7, 2-27	Vorrede auf die Epistel S. Pauli an die Römer.
Am 35, 365-80	1522/1546.
CR IV, 190-238	Liber Ratisbonensis (The Book of Regensburg). 1541.
Epit.	Formula Concordiae. 1577.
SD	

Herrmann, Rudolf

1960   Luthers These "Gerecht und Sünder zugleich." Gütersloh.

Huovinen, Eero

1991   Fides infantium (in Finnish; in German 1996 or 1997). Helsinki.

Joint Declaration

Joint Declaration on the Doctrine of Justification. LWF and PCPCU. Geneva 1995.

Justification by Faith

1985   Justification by Faith. Lutherans and Catholics in Dialogue VII. Minneapolis.

von Loewenich, Walther

1972   Duplex iustitia. Luthers Stellung zu einer Unionsformel des 16. Jahrhunderts. VIEG 68. Wiesbaden.

Peura, Simo

1996   Gott und Mensch in der Unio. Die Unterschiede im Rechtfertigungs-verständnis bei Osiander und Luther. Unio. Gott und Mensch in der nachreformatorischen Theologie. Hrsg. von Matti Repo und Rainer Vinke. Luther-Agricola-Gesellschaft 35. Helsinki. S. 33-61.

Saarinen, Risto

1989   Gottes Wirken auf uns. Die transzendentale Deutung des Gegen-wart-Christi-Motivs in der Lutherforschung. VIEG 137. Mainz.

zur Mühlen, Karl-Heinz

1979   Die Einigung über den Rechtfertigungsartikel auf dem Regensburger Religionsgespräch von 1541 — eine verpaßte Chance? (ZThK 76, 331-59.

Response to Simo Peura,
"Christ as Favor and Gift"

CARL E. BRAATEN

1. Preliminary Considerations

Dr. Simo Peura's paper is an exciting one; it confronts us with a number of challenges.

Luther challenged the church and theology of his day with the gospel of justification derived from his study of the apostle Paul's letters. That is a complex challenge that entails the entire history of the Reformation. Certainly, anyone wishing to evaluate the volume of the Ecumenical Study Group of Protestant and Catholic Theologians titled *The Condemnations of the Reformation Era, Do They Still Divide?* will want to take into account the significance of Dr. Simo Peura's interpretation of Luther. My view is that the work of the Ecumenical Study Group would have welcomed the input of the new Finnish approach, because it underlines elements of basic continuity of Luther with the Catholic tradition. Peura says: "The content of Luther's theology makes him a Catholic teacher in the primary sense of the word and not a denominational one."

Dr. Simo Peura's challenge is an important part of the current Finnish Luther-interpretation that calls into question the adequacy of the predominantly German reading of Luther's theology, which, of course, has influenced American Luther-scholars and Lutheran systematic theologians. The Finnish scholars allege that the German reading of Luther is biased; modern Luther-research has been reading Luther's texts through the lens of neo-Kantian epistemology, which was blind to the ontological concepts in Luther's thought.

The churches that are affected by the ecumenical dialogues on justification, particularly the Lutheran-Catholic dialogue, are challenged to consider whether their "consensus" would not be more solidly grounded in light of the key Finnish insight into Luther's theology, namely, the idea of the real presence of Christ in the faith that justifies, *"in ipsa fide Christus adest."* These dialogues do acknowledge that there are two aspects of justification, the forensic and the effective, but they do not grasp how closely the two are related as functions of the "union with Christ," who is simultaneously both the grace *(favor)* and the gift *(donum)* of justification. For example, the "Joint Declaration on the Doctrine of Justification" between the Lutheran World Federation and the Pontifical Council for Promoting Christian Unity strongly emphasizes the forensic aspect of justification but lacks the explicit christological basis to speak of the effective aspect as a real participation of the Christian in the righteousness of God.

Ecclesiastically, Lutherans are indirectly challenged to consider what sense it makes continually to hold up justification formally as the chief dogma of the Christian faith if they are so unclear and in fact in wide disagreement about its material content. Lutherans are better at stressing its importance than at articulating its basis, contents, and implications. Recall the whole series of exclamatory statements about justification from Luther, the Confessional Writings, and the Lutheran dogmatic tradition. Justification is

- "the proposition of primary importance"
- "the true and chief article of Christian doctrine"
- "the head and cornerstone which alone begets, nourishes, builds, preserves, and protects the church"
- *"the articulus stantis et cadentis ecclesiae"*

Also recall how Lutherans failed at Helsinki in 1963 to develop a common statement on justification but concluded their assembly on a defeatist note, acknowledging that people today no longer ask Luther's question, "How can I find a gracious God?" but ask the supposedly more radical question whether God exists at all. I like

Karl Barth's comment, which he wrote prior to the Helsinki assembly: "Of all the superficial catchwords of our age, surely one of the most superficial is that, whereas 16th century man was occupied with the grace of God, modern man is much more radically concerned about God Himself and as such. . . . As though the Christian community and Christian faith had any interest in the existence or nonexistence of this God Himself and as such!"[1] What if our partners in ecumenical dialogue call the Lutheran bluff and announce that "the emperor has no clothes"?

Confessional Lutherans are presented with a challenge bearing on the normative sources of theology. In case of fundamental disagreement between Luther's theology and the Lutheran Confessions on an issue so crucial as justification, which is normative? Is Luther normative for Lutheran churches today? When does an interesting historical finding (regarding Luther's theology) become theologically binding? What is the doctrinal relevance in general of the results of historical research? Lutheran churches and pastors subscribe to the Ecumenical Creeds and the *Lutheran Confessional Writings,* starting with the *Augsburg Confession,* although quoting Luther has in fact functioned as an appeal to authority. It would seem that, when push comes to shove, many Lutheran dogmaticians would rather have Luther on their side than the Formula of Concord. Recently Lutheran churches have issued statements repenting of things that Luther said. If they keep doing this, what with all of Luther's thundering denunciations, the list could get pretty long. So what is Luther's ecclesiastical status within the hierarchy of authorities in matters of faith and doctrine?

It occurred to me to raise this question in view of the rather sharp distinction drawn between Luther and the Formula of Concord on the doctrine of justification.

2. Propositional Contents

Dr. Simo Peura does introduce a new perspective on Luther's doctrine of justification, one that dropped out of sight in the Lutheran tradition

1. Karl Barth, *Church Dogmatics* IV/1, p. 530.

because of an over-reaction to Osiandrianism. Melanchthon's forensic view of justification prevailed over Osiander's view of the essential indwelling of the righteousness of Christ in the believer. Peura makes clear that he is not repeating the part of Osiander's doctrine that was condemned in Article III of the Formula of Concord, namely, "that Christ is our righteousness only according to the divine nature." Whether the latest Osiander-research supports this characterization of Osiander's teaching is something I do not know. If Nestorius was not a Nestorian, perhaps Osiander was not an Osiandrian. The point here is that Dr. Peura is not repeating what Osiander is alleged to have taught, and agrees with the Formula that "the entire Christ according to both natures is our righteousness."

Peura renders a real service to the Lutheran tradition by integrating the doctrine of justification into Christology. The justifying act of God by grace alone through faith alone means nothing apart from Christ alone. The Christ by whom those who have faith are justified is not only *extra nos* but also *in nobis,* not only an external cause of a change in God's *attitude* toward sinners, but an internal condition of the possibility of a sinner being changed from a state of unbelief *(sine fide)* to one of faith. In the words Peura takes from Luther, the righteousness of God in Christ is both "grace" and "gift," that is, not only forensically imputed to sinners but also a Real Presence in whom sinners participate through faith empowered by the Holy Spirit. (Cf. Luther's "I believe that by my own reason or strength I cannot believe in Jesus Christ, my Lord, or come to him. But the Holy Spirit has called me through the Gospel. . . .")

According to Luther, so Peura says, grace and gift must be properly distinguished, but neither separated nor identified. This is perhaps a typically Lutheran principle, that theology is the fine art of drawing proper distinctions, for example, between the two natures of Christ, the water and the Word, law and gospel, the two kingdoms, and so forth. What is the distinction to be drawn between grace and gift? Both communicate the righteousness of Christ; they occur simultaneously. Where Christ is, there is both *favor dei* and *donum.* Then what is the relation between them? The gift, namely, the effective aspect of justification as the renewal of the sinner *(renovatio),* is not a mere consequence of the grace, namely, the forensic aspect as the forgiveness of sins. They presuppose and mutually condition each other. As grace is a necessary condition for gift, so gift is a necessary condition for grace. The latter is the aspect that "has usually been passed over in Luther research." Luther can hold this idea without slipping into synergism, because the Christian's ongoing renewal in the struggle against sin is a work of Christ who indwells the Christian, and not the result of the Christian's independent effort. The difference between grace and gift, forgiveness and renewal, is that the one is total and complete, the other is partial and continuing. Both aspects direct Christians to place their entire confidence and hope of salvation in Christ and not to trust in themselves or anything else.

How does justification as union with Christ come about? It happens through baptism when Christ the Word unites himself with water, the baptized person dies to sin and is raised to newness of life. Baptism means union with Christ, participation through faith in the death and resurrection of Christ, an aspect that Simo Peura observes has not been commonly noted in Luther research.

When Christians receive the righteousness of God in Christ, they receive God himself, because the attributes of God are ontologically identical with the being of God. The doctrine of the Trinity is clearly the presupposed framework of these ideas. Insofar as Christians partake of Christ, they are being transformed into a likeness of Christ, they are being divinized because the person of Christ is God incarnate. Simo Peura states: "*Theosis* is a culmination of the train of Luther's thought as he claims the effective aspect of justification."

3. Conclusion

This in sum is what I take to be the bare bones of Simo Peura's daring proposal for a new look at Luther's doctrine of justification. He has based his own systematic reconstruction on a close reading of Luther's texts. For me reading what the Finnish scholars are writing about Luther is like going back to school again. What they find missing in modern Luther-research is a lack for which Lutherans have undoubtedly paid a price. I am not a Luther-scholar, but I have read enough of them to become suspicious of endeavors that overly harmonize and systematize Luther, that subject him to the tyranny of a single category. That is the complaint of the Finnish scholars against the Kant-Ritschl-Herrmann line of Luther-interpretation, and I think it is apropos. This is partly due to the relentless pressure to modernize Luther for contemporary application. The Finnish scholars discovered their Luther-insight in the context of their ecumenical dialogue with theologians of the Russian Orthodox Church. I am immensely interested in what they have found of ecumenical relevance in Luther. That leads me to want to place the most favorable construction on what they are teaching us. In the future Luther-scholarship around the world will have to be in dialogue with the Finnish picture of Luther to determine whether, like the standard neo-Kantian German picture, it is in part a *tour de force*.

Finally, I am convinced that the christological *(unio cum Christo)* treatment of justification is essential, and that only on its basis is it possible to stress both aspects of justification, while observing the proper distinction between the gracious mercy of God as the forgiveness of sins for Christ's sake, on the one hand, and the lifelong process of renewal and sanctification in the Holy Spirit, on the other hand. Both are necessary; they belong together and must not be separated, neither should they be confused. We have reason to hope that there can now be sufficient consensus on "justification by Christ alone" with our major ecumenical partners that holds promise for the continuing quest for visible church unity.

What God Gives Man Receives: Luther on Salvation

SIMO PEURA

1. Luther's Question: The Problem of Pure Love

Many have claimed, and far too often, that the question "How can I find the merciful God?" is the primary issue for Luther and is the one that generates his theological work. The answer that scholars have often given to this question, of course, is to be found in the Reformer's doctrine of the justification of the sinner.

In my opinion this answer, insofar as it involves Luther's doctrine of justification, is at least partially correct. But the question formulated above is not precise enough to catch the issue that accounts for Luther's theological efforts. Luther's work cannot be understood properly as deriving from the existential anguish of a monk who became freed from his distress only when he discovered that God in his grace had declared him righteous. Rather, the question challenging Luther was simply the classic problem that has exercised all Christians throughout the history of the church. He was trying to work out a solid answer to the great commandment of Scripture: "You shall love the Lord your God with all your heart, and with all your soul, and with all your strength, and with all your mind; and your neighbor as yourself" (Luke 10:27). Thus the doctrine of justification understood as declared righteousness does not grasp the whole intent of Luther's doctrine of justification.

This commandment of love is a twofold commandment: we must love God with our whole heart and our neighbor as ourselves; these belong to each other and cannot be separated from each other. Furthermore, this great commandment is "written in the human heart." And Luther insists that God did not write it into the human heart only for the pedagogical purpose of revealing to us our inability to fulfill the commandment of love. Nor did he wish only to bring us into the depths of despair. The preaching of the law might affect us in this way, but Luther says that the intention of the law is that it be fulfilled through the pure, unselfish love of God and neighbor.

Our desperation is, as a matter of fact, the result of our conviction that we are not able to live according to this commandment. When we realize on one hand that we cannot live according to God's will, that we cannot love purely, and on the other hand that God punishes all sinners, we naturally become desperate.

Our love is impure when we love in order to use or in order to promote our own ends. And what shall we say about our love of God? Do we love God only for the sake of our own happiness? We tend easily to think either that belief in God is useful because God may reward it and make our earthly life better, or else that our faith has the rational aim of at least avoiding hell or eternal punishment. In both cases faith appears to have a use. But such faith is not in accordance with pure love. It signifies that our love of God actually is directed toward the *good* that God is able to give us and not toward the *triune God himself*.

This problem of self-serving love concerns our ordinary life as well. We tend to love those who have achieved something in life, who offer us such advantages as a greater sense of self-worth, wealth, beauty, power, or a higher social position. And we all know that it is much more difficult to love poor, ugly, worthless, weak, or insignificant people. For these do not possess those characteristics or goods through which we might advance our own fortunes. Much more useful is the love of rich, powerful, socially significant, and beautiful people. For they do possess the characteristics or properties that are useful to us.

The problem of impure love, then, is that it tends to seek the benefit of the lover and not that of the beloved. Its nature is to use the beloved for selfish purposes. And we can see many examples in ordinary life of this inability to love purely. Observe how many difficulties of human life result from this intent to use others for one's own benefit! Perhaps the most obvious example in our time concerns the economic power of international corporations and the great free market speculators of the world. These are able to ruin the entire economic system of weak, small nations in just a few days whenever they grab a transient chance to make great profits at the expense of others. All too often the result is that thousands of people lose not only their savings but their jobs and their very economic base for daily life. We can clearly see in such unhappy events that the core of sin is to use others for one's own benefit.

Luther's entire theological work can be viewed as an attempt to solve the problem of self-serving love. Both his view of salvation and his social-ethical writings concern the same problem. For Luther typically refuses to distinguish between the question of salvation and the question of ethics even when he does assert a difference between eternal life and the goodness of earthly life. The Reformer takes seriously the words our Lord spoke to the lawyer who asked him what one has to do to inherit eternal life: "Do this," that is, fulfill the twofold commandment of pure love, "and you may live" (Luke 10:28). Luther also takes into account the words Jesus spoke concerning the Last Judgment (Matt. 25:31-45). He is convinced that what we have done to those who in their distress have needed our love (and, therefore, have done to Christ) affects our own salvation.

Luther offers several examples of his intention to deal with the problem of pure love. His effort to build a system of social welfare with the city council of Wittenberg, his emphasis on the Golden Rule as the basis for all interhuman relations, his doctrine of two kingdoms, his critique of usury and the legal system, and his instructions for being a righteous and fair sovereign are all attempts to point out the necessity of loving God from one's whole heart and the neighbor as oneself. He was convinced that the problem of true love can be solved only through faith in God. For individuals cannot find the love that is commanded of them in themselves; it has to be given to them by God.

The title of this paper, then, already expresses Luther's answer to the problem. The believer receives through faith a pure, unselfish love from God, who is himself this love and who gives it to the believer who desires to receive him. This is also the main issue of Luther's *Large Catechism*. Its first part, which deals with the Ten Commandments, demands of us nothing other than pure love. The first commandment with its requirement of a comprehensive love of God is the central one, but it includes the love of neighbors as well. When we meditate on these commandments, however, our inability to love becomes clear to us. Therefore, we must necessarily proceed to the Creed. For the aim of the Creed is to explain how one is enabled to fulfill the law of love. Meditation on the Creed helps us to understand that God is the One who first reveals what this pure love is and that he is the source of it in us, since he donates it to us. And the Lord's Prayer instructs us as well to ask God to give us what we lack but what is nevertheless necessary for us to have, that is, pure love.

It is my aim now to examine Luther's points in the first main chapters of the *Large Catechism*. Luther notes that as we meditate through the Ten Commandments, the Creed, and the Lord's Prayer, we become the partakers of God and divine love. This participation, or "divinization" as Luther also says, involves a salvation that does not neglect the needs of earthly life. To clarify this statement, we must think the matter through in order to get to the issue of participation as Luther understands it.

2. The First Commandment: You Shall Have No Other Gods

The first commandment, "You shall have no other gods," is written as natural law at creation into the heart of all human beings. By writing his will into our hearts, the Writer — himself the source of all goodness — aims at making himself known as the Giver of goodness. For even prior to this commandment, he says: "I am the Lord, your God," that is, the source of all the goodness you need. Thus, the intention of writing these commandments into the human heart is to bring true, unselfish love into existence in this world.

Therefore, God maintains this law in our hearts in the very act of maintaining our human life. Thus, the first commandment as well as the other nine becomes an irrevocable reality in human life through God's continuous creation. Humans are aware of an object of religious worship in their very nature. Someone or something is always set forth as the god that is loved, as exemplified in their ways of paying respect and of worshiping this god.

The first commandment bears on one hand the significance of a commandment. It demands trust and faith solely in the Trinity. Luther points out: "You shall have no other gods. That is, you shall look only on me as your God. What does this mean? How is this to be understood? What does it mean to have a god?" My answer is: "A god is that to which we look for all good and in which we find refuge in all our trouble. To have a god is nothing else than to trust and believe him with our whole heart."

Luther counts fundamental trust as deciding who or what constitutes our god. Since everyone seeks refuge in something else and needs help in trouble, everyone has a god in whom he or she trusts. But this god can be something other than the triune God. Thus, Luther says, "Trust and faith alone make both God and an idol." One can trust in someone, as the first commandment requires, and still fail to trust in the true God.

Our difficulty as human beings corrupted by sin is that we fulfill the first commandment by trusting in idols. We do not even hear the promise that resides in the commandment. This promise indicates that the triune God is the source of all goodness, the one who overflows in all goodness and who wants to donate this goodness to us as a gift. Insofar as sin remains in us, we either reject that the triune God is the Giver of all goodness or else do not dare fundamentally to trust him as such. This means that we tend to understand the first commandment only as law, which we try to fulfill by means of our own strength.

Whenever one follows the commandments of the natural law, the heart begins to cling to the true object of trust and thus becomes dependent on the god in which one trusts. But this attempt to fulfill the commandments is not adequate to fulfill either the first of them or the other nine. For the law can be fulfilled only through that pure love which trusts in God with the whole heart. Therefore, Luther's explanation of every commandment in the *Small Catechism* begins with the words: "We should fear and love God. . . ." And the summary of the Ten Commandments in the *Large Catechism* repeats this demand of love: "This word, 'You shall have no other gods,' means simply, 'You shall fear, love, and trust me as your one true God.' Wherever a man's heart has such an attitude toward God, he has fulfilled this commandment and all the others. On the other hand, whoever fears and loves anything else in heaven or on earth will keep neither this nor any other."

We can see from the above, then, that the requirement to believe in God, to trust in God, and to look for our refuge in him alone is basically the same as the commandment to love God purely. We might also say, "That in which a person fundamentally and deeply trusts with the heart is in fact the one who is loved as God."

3. Love Involves Unity with Its Object

Love, according to its classic theological definition, is the power that unites the lover and the beloved to each other. Luther made this classic understanding of the nature of love his own. Both pure, unselfish, and impure, self-serving love are unifying powers.

The Reformer often argues that pure love, as well as the faith through which such love is given, is the copula that unites God and the human heart to each other. God first loves man and becomes one with the object of his love. And then this love affects those who receive it in a such way that they begin as well to love God. This mutual love forges a unifying relation between God and the receiving person, a relation that becomes ever deeper. The person thus partakes of God and thereby undergoes a thoroughgoing transformation. Love is a unifying power that tends to change the loving person into what is loved.

This idea of love as a unifying and transforming power can be heard also in the background of Luther's interpretation of the first commandment as he repeats many times that one's heart clings to the object of faith. The *Large Catechism* indeed emphasizes the idea that the love of God is a unifying power insofar as it asserts that faith and God always belong together. One's heart clings in faith to the object of faith and thus becomes one with him.

The idea that love (faith and trust) binds the heart together with that in which the heart trusts concerns also that impure love whose object of fundamental confidence is something other than the triune

God. One obvious example is our trust in money and property. Placing a whole-hearted confidence in such things, such that a sufficiency of them generates happiness and fearlessness, makes idols of them. The mistake here is not the ownership itself but the continuing compulsion to gather enough wealth to guarantee a sense of confidence for all aspects of human life. And when one achieves the possession of this object upon which all confidence is based, the result is an continuing love of that object, of what offers the sought-for security and help in life. Thus, characteristic of fundamental confidence (even when it is directed to an idol) is that it tends to unite the heart with its object of love and thus to transform the person into what is loved.

People who base their confidence for all the issues of life on the ownership of wealth and possessions orient their lives around these things. They talk about them, think about them, are worried about losing them, and assiduously guard them. We might say that such persons, because of the way that they cling to their property, in the end become nothing other than the property to which they cling. For it becomes the very means by which they exist.

The unifying power of love concerns as well all other gifts through which persons find some happiness. Luther does not deny the goodness of such gifts as great learning, wisdom, power, prestige, family, or honor; he simply observes that they can be used in a wrong or presumptuous way. And this misuse unavoidably occurs whenever a person clings to these gifts and wants to possess them or base a fundamental confidence for all the issues of life on them. Such persons understand these gifts as pertaining to their own qualities when they fix on them with their whole heart. And thus such fundamental, presumptuous, and vain confidence unites the heart with these gifts and constitutes them as gods. The final result is that such persons themselves are thrown into the focus of such misdirected acts of faith and become conformed to what they love.

4. Trust in Self and Self-love Is a Result of Sin

To place fundamental confidence in something other than the triune God is to trust in empty nothingness. God is made into an idol, and this self-serving love makes an idol of the person. Whatever form of idolatry we might consider here, the common characteristic of all of them is that God is not allowed to be God, the giver of all goodness. The goodness one should seek from God has instead been wrenched or stolen from him, preventing him from realizing his nature as the Giver.

Idolatry involves the fancy that we should expect help and consolation from creatures but not from the triune God alone. Luther describes this "core" of idolatry: "It neither cares for God nor expects good things from him sufficiently to trust that he wants to help, nor does it believe that whatever good it receives comes from God."

Another form of idolatry well known to Luther was the aim to seek help, comfort, and salvation through one's own works. This was the main point in Luther's criticism of the worship practices of the church of his time. Pure, spontaneous love was put aside in favor of blackmail and notions of reward by merit in the practices of those days. Luther's criticism was quite explicit: "This is the greatest idolatry that has been practiced up to now, and it is still prevalent in the world. Upon it all the religious orders are founded. It concerns the conscience which seeks help, comfort, and salvation in its own works and presumes to wrest heaven from God. It keeps account how often it has made endowments, fasted, celebrated mass, etc. On such things it relies and of them it boasts."

When a person seeks to merit salvation by works or achievement, nothing can be received as a gift from God. Instead, the person merely presumes that God is at once ready to give such gifts as salvation when they are earned by dint of self-approving work. Such idolatry ends up making God the servant of human beings. God is used for the person's own sake and according to human will; the individual rejects any understanding that the good comes from the true Giver, and rejects as well all love of the Giver. The final result of idolatry is that the person is made into a god, that is, he yields to self-divinization. Luther argues in the following way: "On such things it relies and of them it boasts, unwilling to receive anything as a gift from God, but desiring by itself to earn or merit everything by works of supererogation, just as if God were in our service or debt and we were his liege lords. What is this but making God into an idol — indeed, an 'apple-god' — and setting up ourselves as God?"

At the heart of false divinization is that persons use God for their own purposes. They do not love the triune God or accept that God is and wants to be the Giver in relation to those who only receive the good that he gives. Thus do they presume to be the source of all goodness in life. And thus do they divinize themselves and make themselves masters who order God to give good fortune. But such trust in self is vain and only a self-deception. To trust in oneself is to unite one's heart with nothing at all. And this act further implies that the transforming power of love, when directed by self-love, unites the heart with nothing, so that the person becomes nothing.

5. The Faith Fulfills the First Commandment, Because It Lets God Be the Giver

Self-divinization can be avoided only by faith in the triune God. True faith involves letting God be the Giver. When, especially in times of despair, we trust in God and expect all good things that we need to come from him alone, God is able to become the source of all goodness and act in accordance with his very nature. This attitude, which lets God be the Giver, is the content of true faith.

True faith is to be found within the scope of the first commandment, because it is the only means by which we can let God be God. We can trust in God, we can understand him to be the Giver, we can praise him for his gifts, and we can avoid using God for our own benefit only through faith. For true faith is to receive all goodness from God — not to imagine that we earn or merit it through good works. When true faith lets God be the Giver in life, it also receives pure love as God's gracious gift. And by receiving this love as a gift, faith fulfills the first commandment as well as all of the others. True faith, then, stands within the scope of the meaning of the commandments.

After the fall humankind became unable to believe in the triune God as the source of all goodness. The reason for this loss of capacity to believe is, as I have already argued, our sinfulness, our impure love evidenced as the use of everything for self-interest. Thus, on one hand, we require that what we are be revealed to us. And this is accomplished in the preaching of the law, which rightly drives us to despair. In pointing out our sins, the law takes away from us any possibility of trusting in ourselves and of loving ourselves. When we realize that we are nothing before God, we can no longer make of ourselves an object of selfish love.

On the other hand, we are nevertheless urged to cling to faith and trust in God in spite of the distress we experience upon seeing ourselves for what we are. For revealed also in the content of the first commandment is that God really is the overflowing eternal fountain of sheer goodness.

The preaching of the gospel that promises that the triune God will be good to us is necessary both for those who are in despair because of their sins as well as for those who are weak in their faith and need to be encouraged. The crucial point here is the content of the gospel. Faith can come into existence only if the disturbed heart has before it something so good that it can begin to trust in it. Thus, the true gospel always describes God as the pure Giver of goodness. To be God is to give and not to take. From this point of view Luther proceeds to the emphasis central for his theology: that God must become present in our life through faith if he is to give us love and salvation. This idea underlies as well his main criticism of the scholastic understanding of God and his effects in the world.

6. Faith Means that God Becomes "Most Present" in a Christian

Luther criticizes again and again the so-called Aristotelian view of God. According to this understanding, God exists and remains outside of all creation and out of human range, behind all created beings. God, the unmoved mover, put everything into motion and then settled down in complete satisfaction with his role as a mere observer of all that happens.

Luther asserts that this understanding of God is wrong. Indeed, the devil and all idolaters have made it their own. But this notion brings no joy to the Christian and need not concern the believer. True knowledge of God involves quite an opposite understanding. Luther argues: "But when knowledge is imparted about God in theology, God is known and apprehended as a God who does not remain within himself but who comes to us from outside with the purpose of being God for us."

The true trinitarian God does not isolate himself from the world within his own existence. He is according to his nature a God who comes out to meet us. This happened once when God created the world and again when he became man in his Son; and it is continuously true when Christ becomes present in a spiritual way and is born in the hearts of believers. Thus, the first sentence expressing true knowledge of God is this one: God is by his nature the God who becomes really present.

God becomes present and begins to live in us at the moment he creates true faith in us. Therefore, faith always results in union with God. Indeed, through such faith a Christian already enters into heaven. Luther argues as follows: "This is the true faith of Christ and in Christ, through which we become members of His body, of His flesh and of His bones (Eph 5:30). Therefore in Him we live, move, and have our being (Acts 17:28). Hence the speculation of the sectarians is vain when they imagine that Christ is present in us 'spiritually', that is, speculatively, but is really present in heaven. Christ and faith must be completely joined. We must simply *(simpliciter)* be in heaven; and Christ must be, live, and work in us. But He lives and works in us, not speculatively or as an idea but in the most present and effective way."

The above-quoted passages have caused great suspicion among Lutheran theologians, especially among those who have represented a so-called neo-Kantianism in this century. Luther's view of *unio cum Christo* has not been accepted in its true ontological sense or as an expression of his understanding of justification. The result of this denial is that Lutheran theology has lost some of those characteristics which are an integral part of its own doctrine of salvation, characteristics that might help Lutherans in building ecumenical contacts with other confessions.

Because of the problem of self-serving love, Luther finds it necessary to emphasize his conviction that faith implies the real presence of God in the believer. A human being can participate in God's goodness and can become loving only under the condition that God himself is present in him. The goodness that God shares with the believer belongs to God's nature. A Christian can participate, therefore, in God's essential goodness, that is, in love, only if the triune God himself becomes present through faith. Luther refers to this idea in the *Large Catechism* in the context of his explanation of the Creed, saying that the triune God gives himself to the sinner as self-giving love.

7. The Content of the Creed:
God Reveals Himself as Self-giving Love

Even if God hides himself and is unattainable to human grasp, the Creed nevertheless teaches us to know God perfectly. It describes briefly what God is by reference to his nature, what he wills, and what he does. In short, the central content of the Creed is: God is, according to his nature, self-giving love. Luther says: "In these three articles God himself has revealed and opened to us the most profound depths of his fatherly heart, his sheer, unutterable love. He created us for this very purpose, to redeem and sanctify us. Moreover, having bestowed upon us everything in heaven and on earth, he has given us his Son and his Holy Spirit, through whom he brings us to himself."

The content of revelation is that God is by his nature "sheer love," who gives himself wholly to the objects of his love. Luther generally defines God's essence and love in the same way: a love does not seek its own but gives its own to others; it gives itself, and in doing so also transforms its object. This kind of love is also God's essence, which he wants to reveal to us from "the most profound depths of his fatherly heart."

Each of the persons of the Trinity contributes to our understanding of faith as knowledge of a self-giving God. Luther points out that the Holy Spirit first teaches us to know Christ. Apart from the Holy Spirit, we would find in Christ no more than a great teacher in the history of humankind. Because of the Holy Spirit, however, we recognize in him "my Lord and my Savior" who has made us favorable in his Father's eyes. And this knowledge of Christ and of his work reveals God to be the loving Father who shows his favor and grace toward the sinner. Christ is, as Luther argues, "a mirror of the Father's heart, apart from which we see nothing but an angry and terrible Judge." Thus, it is the common task of the triune Persons to reveal God as self-giving love.

Most important, when God reveals his very essence to a sinner, he donates himself to be present in the sinner at the same time. Thus, God does not restrict what is given as a mere understanding of himself but actually gives himself to us as the triune God. In other words, all Persons of the triune God give themselves as love to the sinner.

8. God the Father Gives Himself in the Created Gifts

Concerning the first person of the Trinity, Luther describes the central content of the Creed as follows: "For here we see how the Father has given himself to us and to all his creatures, looks after us most generously in this life." Luther's insistence here is almost astonishing. The Reformer really argues that faith in God, the almighty Father, includes the idea that God the Father gives himself to us in all created goods.

The self-giving of God the Father is realized as God creates man from nothing, brings him into existence, and makes him alive. God the Father also gives himself when he continuously preserves our natural life through the goodness of creation. Everything in human life, that is, human being itself, the continuity of life, the protection of life against all kinds of destructive powers, all of the goodness of life, and even others as objects for different kinds of natural love, are expressions of God's self-giving love to humankind. He gives all of these gifts to us in order to love us and in order to make us to trust in him as pure love.

Luther's conviction that the existence of created beings is permanently dependent on God and on his continuously creative work expresses his emphasis that even as Creator, God does not separate himself from his creatures. God is present everywhere in his creatures. As a present reality he maintains the existence and the life of creatures through his own being and life. But this understanding of the omnipresence of God in no way intends a confusion of God and created beings with each other, but rather indicates a participation of created beings in God's creative life.

The idea of participation is in origin a Platonic one. Even if Luther makes it his own, he is not interested in the life that created things enjoyed in God's mind before their creation. He calls this sort of speculation pagan curiosity and denies any possibility of looking into God's mind and essence to satisfy such curiosity. Instead, Luther underlines that a created human being is able to exist only under the condition that God lives in him and makes him a partaker of God's own life. Thus, our whole existence is based on God's presence in us: we live through God, from God, and in God (cf. Acts 17:28).

Thus, Luther's idea that God the Father gives himself implies on one hand that God realizes his own life and love in creatures regardless of their belief or unbelief. On the other hand it implies that creatures participate in God's life. But even if the Christian's natural life is already a part of eternal life, this link does not yet mean that salvation is realized but is only its necessary precondition. Salvation becomes possible only when we participate in the Son and in the Holy Spirit. Luther's explanation of the first article of the Creed, therefore, ends like this: "For here we see how the Father has given himself to us and to all his creatures, looks after us most generously in this life, quite apart from showering us with indescribable gifts that last forever through his Son and the Holy Spirit, as we will hear."

9. God Donates Himself in the Son

The content of the second article of the Creed includes the same emphasis, that God gives himself to us in his Son together with all of the gifts of salvation. Luther argues: "Here we learn to know the second person of the Godhead, and we see what we receive from God over and above the temporal goods mentioned above; that is, how he has completely given himself to us, kept nothing back, but has given us everything."

Behind Luther's words can be heard the biblical notion of *kenosis,* that Christ emptied himself, took the form of a slave, and even accepted death on the cross for our sake (Phil. 2:5-8). The main point of the second part of the Creed is that God gave up his form of Godhood as he became man in Christ and donated himself to sinners. The self-giving of Christ implies that he came from heaven to help us and to redeem us from all kinds of destructive powers such as sin, the devil, death, and all evil. And beyond this notion, the self-giving of Christ implies that he takes the place of those destructive powers in our life.

When Christ gives himself to us, he indwells us and becomes one with us. Thus, redemption is something that happens not only on the cross but also in all believers whom Christ indwells through faith. Indeed, only when Christ indwells us is the redemptive work in us brought into existence. Luther describes salvation as the so-called wonderful exchange *(commercium admirabile)* through which Christ absorbs our sin and death, and, instead of them, communicates to us his own divine attributes such as righteousness, wisdom, and eternal life. Because of the indwelling Christ and his righteousness we find favor in the eyes of the Father as well. Thus, Christ is on one hand the merciful grace that protects us against God's wrath toward sin, and on the other hand the one who brings the new life in us into existence by reigning over it through his presence.

10. God the Holy Spirit Gives Himself to Us

The content of the third article of the Creed is that the Holy Spirit, too, gives himself to us with all his gifts. God gives his Spirit to us through the sacramental life of the church, in the *communio sanctorum* that is the fruit of the preaching of the word and sharing of the sacraments. The task of the Holy Spirit is to produce faith in Christ and to enable us to receive Christ with all of his gifts. To effect this aim, says Luther, the Holy Spirit first "leads us into his holy community and places us upon the bosom of the church." Second, the Holy Spirit reveals the work of Christ to us through the preaching of the word, helps us to understand God's love toward us, effects faith in us, and in this way offers and gives Christ and all the gifts of salvation to us as well.

The task of the Holy Spirit is to help Christians to find their way to Christ and to become one with Christ. On one side is Christ with all of the gifts of salvation, and on the other side is the sinner who needs Christ, salvation, and God's love but is not able alone to obtain it. The Holy Spirit, then, swings between Christ and the desiring heart. Luther describes the role of the Holy Spirit thus: "In the Word God has given the Holy Spirit to offer and apply to us the treasure of salvation. Therefore to sanctify is nothing else than to bring us to the Lord Christ to receive the goods of salvation made through Christ."

Thus, the gift itself is Christ; but the one who offers it and helps us to receive it is the Holy Spirit. In other words, the Holy Spirit brings our union with Christ into existence in us and produces in us a love for God. Furthermore, the Holy Spirit preserves us in this union of love until we are, as Luther states, "perfectly pure and holy people, full of goodness and righteousness, completely freed from sin, death, and all evil, living in new, immortal and glorified bodies." The work of the Holy Spirit continues throughout our whole life until death, when we become totally transformed into Christ and thus possess within us the complete form of Christ.

As we have seen, the threefold self-giving of God means that God reveals himself as the love that finally transforms us into God. God not only reveals his very nature to us, but he also gives himself to us as the triune God. The result is that we are made partakers of his divine nature and thus transformed into God. We can, therefore, speak about salvation as *theosis* in a genuine Lutheran sense of the word.

11. Participation and *Theosis*

The self-giving of God has the effect that a Christian becomes, as Luther says, "full of God." Luther's view of salvation includes ideas of participation in God and divinization that are usually better known from the writings of the first centuries of the church or from the Orthodox tradition. The Reformer argues quite often for a notion of *theosis* and underlines it as a central part of his doctrine of justification. Both aspects of justification, imputed righteousness as well as effective, transforming righteousness, are based on the indwelling of Christ and on our participation in him.

The effective aspect of justification involves nothing other than participation in Christ, who by giving his own Spirit as pure love constantly renews sinners and makes them also righteous and loving. The forensic aspect involves that participation in Christ through whom God's love as merciful forgiveness is extended to sinners. Thus does Christ take the still imperfect and only partially righteous sinner under his total protection. And it is only because of this latter aspect of justification that Christians are enabled to forgive their neighbors and, thus, show a similar love to them. Participation, then, to speak generally and in summary, means that the natural, created life of a Christian is permeated throughout *(perichoresis)* by the divine life of God as self-giving love.

Because this Lutheran understanding of *theosis* is not well known, the following quotation from Luther's sermon in 1525 is instructive:

> And so we are filled with "all the fullness of God." This phrase, which follows a Hebrew manner of speaking, means that we are filled in all the ways in which he fills a man. We are filled with God, and he pours into us all his gifts and grace and fills us with his Spirit, who makes us courageous. He enlightens us with his light, his life lives in us, his beatitude makes us blessed, and his love causes love to arise in us. Put briefly, he fills us in order that everything that he is and everything he can do might be in us in all its fullness, and work powerfully, so that we might be divinized throughout — not having only a small part of God, or merely some parts of him, but having all his fullness. Much has been written on the divinization of man, and ladders have been constructed by means of which man is to ascend to heaven, and many other things of this kind have been done. However, all these are merely works of a beggar. What must be done instead is to show the right and straight way to your being filled with God, so that you do not lack any part but have it all gathered together, and so that all you say, all you think and everywhere you go — in sum, all your life — is throughout divine.[1]

Luther's view of God and of his nature as self-giving love, then, leads us to the notion of the deification of a created human being. The triune God lives in the Christian, and the Christian lives, moves, and has being in the triune God. And this concept of divinization is developed in the context of Luther's response to the problem of self-serving love. We must observe, though, that this divinization means precisely our transformation into God's love such that we are God's love. Thus, the aim of salvation as participation in God and

---

1. Translated by Tuire Valkeakari in Tuomo Mannermaa, "The Presence of Christ in Faith," p. 42.

in his love is to effect in us as well the capacity to fulfill the twofold commandment of pure, unselfish love.

12. Participation in God Enables
the Pure Love of God and of the Neighbor

Luther describes the aim of God's self-giving love as he summarizes his explanation of the Creed: "Through this knowledge of God we come to love and delight in all the commandments of God because we see that God gives himself completely to us, with all his gifts and his power, in order to help us to keep the Ten Commandments: the Father gives us all creation, Christ all his works, the Holy Spirit all his gifts."

The self-giving of God first effects in us a trust in God so that we live in constant expectation of all the goodness of life that comes from him, and so that we know that he really helps us in all distress. This kind of fundamental trust in God does not come easily to us but develops through those experiences in which God shows himself to be the One who helps. We may, of course, too easily forget the goodness that is given by God, and too often as well does sin prevent us from realizing God as the one who wants to give us all goodness that is himself. For this reason God brings us in many ways into the depths of distress, where we encounter our nothingness. Such experiences break through our tendency toward self-love and make us aware of our need of God's pure love. Thus, they imply in no way that God has forsaken us. For our Lord descends even now with us into such a hell and yet dwells with us in the Father's love. Therefore, even when it seems to us that God wants only to destroy us, we are in fact always the objects of his saving love. His purpose in making us almost nothing is not to destroy us but to destroy our selfish love and to give instead his own pure love, thus effecting in us a capacity for similar love.

When Christians realize in faith that God loves them in spite of these contra-evidential experiences, they begin to return this love to God. They honor God, pray for his aid, confess him to be the Savior, worship him as the only God, and give constant praise to him for all the good gifts of life. The self-giving love of God, then, is what enables a human being to exist in God's love and at last come to love God.

Second, the self-giving of God effects in us the capacity to love our neighbors. The first three commandments and their following seven do not exclude each other. When Christians love God with the whole heart, they also love what God wills and expects from them. And it is God's will that we love our neighbors.

Even if Luther argues that, because of the self-giving of God and our participation in God's love, "there will arise a spontaneous impulse and desire gladly to do God's will," Christians still do not find it an easy task to love neighbors purely and unselfishly. God's love mediated through us is still always imperfect. Because of residual sin we always have to fight against the tendency to seek our own good instead of the good of others. Sometimes pure love involves hard work. At times we have to use our reason and all of our best abilities to discover in different situations what is the good of the neighbor.

As we can see, the Christian's understanding of the commandment to love unselfishly by no means relies on a self-evident truth. It presupposes that we have to follow Christ as the example of unselfish love. Christ lived through the Golden Rule in all of his works. He did not seek his own benefit but forsook the glory of God and became man in order to save those who are in themselves not worthy to be loved: those who are ugly, stupid, difficult, bad, and sinful.

We are called to follow this example of Christ. Whether it is a question of love between man and woman, parents and children, friends, neighbors, or some other form of natural love, the relations among people should always be based on the Golden Rule. This rule requires that we forget what benefits us and that we look to the good of the other. But our imperfection throughout earthly life causes much trouble and requires ingenuity, devotion, and steadfastness to bring the gift of God's pure love into existence in our own life. And this same imperfection engenders a continuous need to be loved by God: we need continual forgiveness of sins and the renewing presence of the triune God in us.

13. A Summary: What God Gives

Reviewing what has been said above, it seems to me that the title of this paper, "What God Gives Man Receives," refers to so many aspects of Luther's view of salvation that I cannot mention them all here. I observed first that we cannot fulfill the Ten Commandments without faith and without God. Faith is important because it alone enables us to receive God's unselfish love. When God first reveals his pure love and gives himself with all of the gifts of salvation to us, we become partakers of God and of his nature as pure love. Only under the condition of God's presence and participation do we begin to bring God's love into existence in our lives. It is actually God himself who extends through our lives his love toward all of those who need his love and want to be saved. We, like all other creatures, are the hands and all of the means of God's unselfish love.

We must take one final point into account. God really gives himself to us together with the gifts of salvation, but we are never able to possess him or his gifts as our private property or put them into our pockets. Therefore, we are continuously dependent on God and on his willingness to give us the gifts of salvation. There is no other way to love God and the neighbor than to call on God to help in all distress, honoring him because of his gifts, and giving oneself to the service of the neighbor, who needs God's love. What God gives man receives, that it may be given to the neighbor.

What does all of this say about the beginning point of this paper, Luther's great question? To find a merciful God is nothing other than to find God as pure love. But we cannot find this merciful God until we become partakers of God, who, according to his nature, is pure, self-giving love.

Natural Law and Faith: The Forgotten Foundations of Ethics in Luther's Theology

ANTTI RAUNIO

1. Introduction

It may seem odd to maintain, as the subtitle does, that natural law and faith have been forgotten in the discussion of Luther's ethical thought. One can easily find numerous books in which both natural law and faith are presented as foundations of Luther's theological ethics. The main lines of the common interpretation are as follows. It is presumed, for example, that natural law is distinct from the natural structure of creation and does not derive from it. Moreover, Christian moral activity must occur within the unchangeable orders of creation. Further, in the common interpretation faith is understood as gratitude for the imputed grace of God and as the inner freedom flowing from such grace. It gives therefore a new motivation for moral action, a motivation quite different from that required by natural law.[1] However, I will show here that these notions do not properly interpret Luther's understanding of natural law and faith.

My aim is to show that the common interpretation of the foundation of Luther's ethical thought has in fact ignored some crucial aspects of the content that Luther gives to them. I treat first the

1. Cf., e.g., James M. Gustafson, *Protestant and Roman Catholic Ethics* (Chicago, 1978), pp. 14-15.

question of how Luther understands natural law, and second his concept of faith. Both sections include a discussion with the usual Luther research. For the sake of brevity I have tried to choose some representative samples from the vast literature available.

2. Luther's Concept of Natural Law in the Research

Dualistic Interpretation of Luther's Concept of Law

One of the central problems concerning Luther's understanding of natural law is how to relate his emphasis on the unity of law to his utterances about natural law and his negative view about the condition of the fallen human. I am seeking a formula that combines these seemingly contradictory statements.

I follow here Theodor Herr's summary about the main line of German Luther research concerning Luther's thought about natural law.[2] The common approach is to view Luther as an adherent of the nominalism of the late Middle Ages. His nominalism, however, is not a mere consequent of the late-medieval discussion but also contains features of the Aristotelian-Thomist tradition. Luther has inherited from the nominalist tradition the voluntarist way of combining law and justice with the decisional volition of a personal God. This acceptance of voluntarism means as well that he abandons the ontology that characterizes the Thomistic view of natural law as grounded in the essence of God. The voluntarist starting point leads also to the separation between "is" and "ought." Insofar as we can speak about "natural law," we are no longer referring to the law of nature in the strict sense but to a divine command that we can decide

---

2. Theodor Herr, *Zur Frage nach dem Naturrecht im deutschen Protestantismus der Gegenwart*, Abhandlungen zur Socialethik 4 (Munich, 1972), pp. 39-43. Herr's description is grounded on the studies of F. X. Arnold, J. Heckel, H. Liemann, H.-H. Schrey, H. Welzel, and E. Wolf. Heckel and Wolf especially have been influential in Luther research. I have presented a more detailed analysis of the Luther research concerning natural law in my *Summe des christlichen Lebens. Die Goldene Regel als Gesetz der Liebe in der Theologie Martin Luthers von 1510 bis 1527*, Reports of the Department of Systematic Theology 13 (Helsinki, 1993), pp. 21-56.

to obey or to disobey. Natural law is grounded neither in human nature nor in any objective order of being. Luther's intention has not been to presuppose any objective structure of being upon which the natural law is grounded.

Perhaps the most important consequence of taking this voluntaristic view is a certain dualism in Luther's thought. Natural law is separated into two parts: the divine law and the human or the worldly natural law. This distinction is also considered decisive for the doctrine of the two governments. But though Luther speaks of two different laws and, respectively, two different governments, they are not in his thought totally separated. The concept of natural law is actually a misinterpretation that natural reason illegitimately draws out of the notion of divine law. Indeed, Luther's concept of natural law seems to be a *non sequitur*. His trust in natural reason and natural moral law ends up being a reliance on a corrupted thought that is unable to grasp the content of the divine law.

The common interpretation, that Luther is inconsistent on this point, reveals other difficulties as well. Luther, after all, stresses the unity of the law, summarizing the whole law in the Golden Rule. He thus abandons, for example, the distinctions among natural, written, and evangelical law.[3] We must decide whether Luther really is so inconsistent in his position or whether we should rather doubt the common dualistic interpretation of Luther's concept of natural law. Does Luther mean by "natural law" the law whose content differs from divine law and which the corrupted human reason understands and follows, or does he mean something else?

An accurate characterization of the problem would be more nuanced, but I shall try to focus on the clear points of difficulty. Unfortunately, Lutheran theology has not well clarified the founda-

---

3. WA 2, 580, 7-14: "Nec minus caute intelligenda est vulgatissima illa distinctio legis naturae, legis scriptae, legis euangelicae. Cum enim apostolus hic dicat, omnes in uno et in summa convenire, certe charitas omnis legis finis est, ut i. Timo. i. dicit. Sed et christus Matt. vij. illam legem naturae, ut vocant, 'omnia quae vultis ut faciant vobis homines, et vos facite illis' expresse eandem facit cum lege et prophetis dicens 'haec enim lex est et prophetae'. Cum autem ipse euangelium doceat, clarum est, tres has leges non tam officio quam falso sensu intelligentium differre."

tions of ethics and the Christian way of life. One reason for the diversity of interpretation concerning Luther's views on this matter is, of course, that Luther did not leave any systematic account concerning it in his theology. But there are other reasons as well. Lutheran theology has been influenced by many theological and philosophical traditions and concepts that do not reflect Luther's own thought. Thus, if we find it difficult to understand how both natural law and faith can be integral parts of Luther's ethics, we may not know exactly what he means by "natural law" and "faith." We may be cognizant of many features of his thought while having lost our hold on some crucial aspects that could make it more coherent and understandable.

Paul Althaus on Rational
Natural Law and the Law of the Cross

A scholar who tries to do justice to Luther's concept of the unity of the law is Paul Althaus in his book *The Ethics of Martin Luther.*[4] According to Althaus, Luther thinks that human beings are born with a natural knowledge of what they should and should not do. This knowledge, which is called "natural justice," the "law of nature," or the "natural law," is implanted by God in human reason. Although natural law is rational in the sense that human reason knows it, it still remains God's law and will. Althaus emphasizes that Luther makes no distinction between "natural" and "divine," or between "natural" and "revealed" law.[5]

Althaus stresses further that Luther identifies natural law with the commandment of love. Christ and natural law teach the same thing. Natural law is summarized in the Golden Rule: I ought to treat my neighbor as I would like to have him treat me. And Luther equates acting according to the Golden Rule with "Christian love."[6]

I can agree with Althaus until I come to his interpretation of Luther's *Admonition to Peace, a Reply to the Twelve Articles of the*

4. Paul Althaus, *Die Ethik Martin Luthers* (Gütersloh, 1965). I have also used the English translation, which was published in 1972.
5. Althaus, *Ethics*, pp. 32-33.
6. Althaus, *Ethics*, pp. 36-37.

Peasants in Swabia, where he seems to abandon the principle of the unity of law and to arrive at a dualistic view. Luther does speak there about "natural justice" and "Christian justice." But Althaus suggests as a solution to this hermeneutical problem that one should at least attempt to see a divergence in substance between the concepts of "natural law" and "Christian law."[7]

What makes Althaus's solution dualistic is the idea that the Golden Rule is a natural law that places humankind under a law of reciprocity. People easily understand this law and fulfill it out of an interest in peace and in ordering the common life. Rational insight is what compels them to keep this law. And this activity is possible without any real motive in love, or at least without the love of Christ. Althaus sees a difference between the action of one who does not avenge himself but rather endures injustice according to the Golden Rule and a similar act of endurance in a Christian. The Christian's action is determined by something more than the insight that one must act in this way for the sake of peace and order. When Christians endure injustice without resisting, they do so not on the basis of the natural law of reason but on the basis of the law of the cross that holds for Christ and for Christians.[8]

Althaus's solution seems at first sight to be very near what Luther intended to say, but it still raises problems. The actual result of his interpretation is that we end up with two natural laws or Golden Rules, one the natural law of reason and the other the natural law of Christian love. This interpretation is dualistic, because rational law and Christian law differ in content. If the natural law in the field of reason refers to something other than the field of Christian love, how do we move from the law of reason to the law of love?

---

7. Althaus presumes that one can in this context change "justice" to "law" without changing the meaning of the former term. It seems to me, however, that Luther uses the term "natural justice" to mean justice in the outward sense, i.e., as justice that the Worldly Government exercises by coercion against the inner will of fallen human beings. "Christian justice," then, means the free and willing activity of individuals out of love. The distinction used here does not allow one to postulate two different laws, the natural and the Christian. See WA 18, 307,5–310,18.

8. Althaus, *Ethics,* pp. 39-41.

Cargill Thompson on Luther as Continuator of the Thomistic Natural Law Tradition

Cargill Thompson's presentation of Luther's political thought was posthumously published about a decade ago.[9] It is not as well known as Althaus's work on Luther's ethics, but it is interesting because, compared to the standard interpretation, it gives in some respects a very different picture of Luther's understanding of natural law. Thompson opposes the main line of Luther research by emphasizing the continuity of the natural law tradition from the end of the Middle Ages to the end of the sixteenth and the beginning of the seventeenth century. Nevertheless, his interpretation also leads to a dualistic conclusion.

According to Thompson, Luther accepts the standard medieval view that affirms a universal moral law to which God binds all humankind, the knowledge of which God plants in our hearts. In Thompson's opinion, the differences between Luther's position and the Thomist position are minor. The first involves Luther's insistence on a clear distinction between the areas of natural law and revelation. Natural law, like reason, is limited to the temporal order: it is the law of the "worldly Kingdom" — one cannot be saved by observing it. The second involves the greater emphasis Luther places on the extent to which the human understanding of natural law was darkened by the Fall.[10]

Luther is equally traditional in his view concerning the content of natural law. In his attempts to define natural law he usually equates it either with the precepts of the Decalogue or with Christ's two commandments. The first of these was seen as summarizing the content of one of the Tables of the Law, and the second was summarized in the Golden Rule of "Doing unto others."[11]

Thompson also states clearly that natural law is limited to the temporal order and is concerned only with the external actions of a person. Luther's understanding of natural law is closely bound to his

9. W. D. J. Cargill Thompson, *The Political Thought of Martin Luther* (Sussex, 1984).

10. Thompson, *Political Thought,* p. 86.

11. Thompson, *Political Thought,* pp. 86-87.

concept of natural and secular law, following logically from it. Thompson thinks that Luther adapted the traditional concept of natural law to his doctrine of the "two governments." For Luther's concept of natural law also follows from his doctrine of the Worldly and the Spiritual Governments.

Luther does not hesitate to stress the importance of reason in the context of the natural order. The faculty of pure reason embodies the basic principles by which humans ought to rule their natural lives. When speaking of reason in this sense Luther tends to equate it, in traditional fashion, with natural law or equity.[12]

Thompson does not differentiate between two natural laws and two Golden Rules as does Althaus; but his interpretation, too, presupposes a dualism in Luther's thought: Even though he recognizes that for Luther natural law consists of the two Commandments of Love and of the Golden Rule, he insists that natural law belongs only to temporal government. This position follows from the view that in Luther's thought natural law is adapted to the idea of the "two governments." Luther, however, actually held the opposite position. The "doctrine of the two governments" is his solution to the question how natural law can be fulfilled. Another problem in his interpretation is that, according to him, Luther's position is continuous with the Thomistic natural law tradition mediated to the modern age by Richard Hooker. Even though Luther's concept of natural law was not Ockhamist in the sense in which it is often purported to be, we still err if we maintain that he belongs to the Thomistic natural law tradition.

3. Luther on Natural Law as the Foundation of Ethics

The Golden Rule as the Law of Divine Nature

That Althaus and Thompson, who give learned and often exact interpretations of Luther's understanding of natural law, nonetheless fail in their interpretations is an example of how Luther's thought is not easy to understand. And no doubt occasions for different views and scholarly disputes will arise in the future.

12. Thompson, *Political Thought*, p. 84.

I shall argue here that in understanding Luther's notion of natural law one should not distinguish between the natural law of reason and the natural law of Christian love, nor declare that natural law belongs only to the temporal government and to the social order of peace and justice.

Both Althaus and Thompson refer to the Commandment of Love and to the Golden Rule as the content of natural law. They do not pay much attention, however, to the precise meaning of natural law in Luther's thought. They do not ask how Luther understands the Commandment of Love and the Golden Rule. Thus, Althaus, like many other Luther scholars, must distinguish between two Golden Rules, and Thompson on the other hand sees only a few minor differences between the Thomistic and the Lutheran understandings of natural law.

To my knowledge, no one has recognized that natural law, that is, the Golden Rule, is from the beginning for Luther the law of divine nature, or the law of divine love. The Reformer calls it the law of pure and uncontaminated nature, which is identical to love.[13] More precisely, the distinction between a "worldly natural law" and a divine natural law of love does not belong at all to Luther's theology. For Luther natural law is always the law of divine love, and it is satisfied with nothing less than that. Our failure to understand and obey natural law does not change its original content.

The common dualistic interpretation of Luther's understanding of natural law does not hold true. He does not intend the concept of "natural law" to mean something less than the requirement of divine love, but rather stresses that the demand of divine selfless love is written in the whole of creation as well as in human hearts. His view concerning the structure of creation clarifies this matter. By "structure of creation" I do not mean just the so-called orders of creation, such as ministry, family, and political authority. We have largely forgotten or failed to take into consideration adequately that for Luther the whole creation is an "order of love." In this order nothing exists for itself but all things exist for others. The sun shines, water flows, and trees produce fruit for others and not for themselves. Nature follows this law, and the aim of natural

13. WA 1, 502, 16-26.

law is that fallen humankind, too, regains participation in this order of creation.[14]

Creation is an "order of love" because God himself continuously gives his good through creatures.[15] Thus, in spite of the sin of humankind, the whole creation reflects God's nature. "To be God is to give, not to take," is Luther's description of God. God's nature as the Giver of everything good is also the foundation of Luther's understanding of natural law.

Luther often says that the Golden Rule is written on the hearts of all people. Important here is that natural law can be written on the heart in two ways. Employing the technical language of Middle Age theology, Luther says that the law is written either *obiective* or *formaliter*.[16] Another way to say the same thing is to assert that the "letter" or the knowledge of the demand of the law is written on the heart, or that the Holy Spirit himself is present, dictating and exercising love in the heart.[17] This distinction does not imply, however, that the content of the law changes. The letter of the law is the demand of divine love, though it cannot guarantee the fulfillment of the law. On the contrary, because of the unwillingness of human beings to change, it only increases sin and hatred toward God and his law.

---

14. AWA 2, 48, 11-21; StA 1, 334,32-39; WA 1, 502,16-26. Raunio, *Summe des christlichen Lebens*, pp. 223-24. Researchers such as Bayer, Duchrow, Haikola, and Wingren have acknowledged Luther's understanding of nature as an order of self-giving love. But this acknowledgment has not led to any thoroughgoing reevaluation of Luther's natural law thought. See Oswald Bayer, *Schöpfung als Anrede. Zu einer Hermeneutik der Schöpfung*, 2nd ed. (Göttingen, 1990), p. 71; Ulrich Duchrow, *Christenheit und Weltverantwortung. Traditionsgeschichte und systematische Struktur der Zweireichelehre*, 2nd ed. (Stuttgart, 1983), p. 561; Lauri Haikola, *Usus legis*, 2nd ed. (Helsinki, 1981), p. 119.

15. See, e.g., the text in n. 24.

16. WA 57 III, 195,20–196,19.

17. WA 39 I, 370,3–371,16; 372,7-11; 372,20–373,12.

Moral Reasoning and Moral Motivation
according to the Golden Rule

What then is the concept of natural law or the Golden Rule? The most common way of understanding the rule is to consider it as a principle of reciprocity, as does Althaus. The concept of reciprocity is not very clear, however, and can be understood in different ways. It can mean that one person takes care of another while expecting the same treatment from that person. Such care-taking includes an interest in guaranteeing one's own benefit. The modern liberal social-contract tradition considers this way of motivating ethical action "rational." Another way of understanding reciprocity is to view it as the necessity to consider the benefit of the neighbor as much as one seeks one's own advantage. This interpretation signifies a balance, an equal division of benefits between people.

Both meanings of reciprocity have been attributed to Luther's understanding of the Golden Rule as natural law of reason. I think that the modern concept of rationality and of the rational moral agent, which developed at the beginning of the modern era, has greatly confused the understanding of Luther's thought about rational moral law. As far as I understand Luther, he never connected the content of the Golden Rule with rationality in the modern sense, that is, as a moral action taken in order to ensure finally one's own benefit.

Distinguishing between two aspects of the Golden Rule is helpful in understanding Luther's concept of natural law. In Luther's thought as well as in the general discussion concerning it, the rule is treated both as a principle of moral reasoning and as a requirement for a certain type of moral motivation. Different interpretations abound, however, concerning the intention of the Golden Rule in both of these aspects.

The essential feature of its application as a principle of moral reasoning is the inner exercise of setting oneself in the place of the other and seeking the good of the other.[18] Luther's interpretation of

---

18. WA 1, 502,16-20: "Idcirco omnibus in genere illa regula charitatis servande est, quam dominus Mat: vii, ponit: Quae vultis ut faciant vobis homines, et vos facite illis. quare in omni tractatu necessarium est unicuique, ut prospiciat prius quomodo secum velle agi, si esset in alterius loco, ita faciat et ipse, et tutus erit. haec vocatur lex naturae, immo est charitatis."

the rule can be comprehended only if we recognize that he applies the Golden Rule to our relations to God as well as to the relations obtaining between people.[19] And according to Luther, the correct application of the Golden Rule begins with our relation to God.[20]

This exercise can to some degree occur even without the presence of divine love, because of the knowledge of the "letter" of the law.[21] "Outward" obedience to the Golden Rule is not the realization of the love that God requires, though, because in such obedience neither the subject nor the object of love are what they should be. In relation to God this obedience implies that people do not let God be God, the substance and giver of everything good. Though they know the divine characteristics such as eternity, power, goodness and so on, they cannot ascribe these characteristics to the real living God but end up applying them to some created thing or rob God of them as they apply them to themselves.[22] When they illegitimately ascribe the divine attributes to themselves, they make themselves the subjects of goodness, that is, of love and of good works.[23]

In relation to the neighbor this kind of obedience implies that a person cannot unite with the other by giving everything possible in order to do what the other needs. One tries to achieve some self-

19. WA 56, 199,34–200,2: "Si enim hoc alteri facimus, quod volumus nobis fieri, Et nobis volumus non nisi bona, gloriosa et magna, primum hoc Deo optemus, scil. propriam voluntatem, Iudicium, gloriam et alia, que Dei sunt, a nobis arrogata cum Lucifero; secundo et proximis, quibus superesse querimus. Sint ergo nobis superiores, Et ecce totam humilitatem impleuimus tam erga Deum quam homines, i.e. totam perfectamque Iustitiam."

Cf. WA 1, 252,24-32; 259,13-18; WA 10 II, 379,13-16; 380,4-11. In his sermons on Matthew 5–7 (1530) Luther seems to change his mind about the Golden Rule as the summary of the whole divine law. But if we take account of the whole structure of Luther's thought, we can see that he does not abandon his earlier idea when he applied the Golden Rule in relation to God, namely, that of attributing all good properties to God.

20. WA 10 II, 379,13-16: "Wan wir nu das naturlich gesetz ansehen, tzo finden wyr, wie bilich und gelych alle dise gepot seyn. Dan nichts ist hie gepotten gegen gott und dem nehsten zu halten, das nit eyn iglich wolt yhm gehalten haben, wenn er got an gottis und seynes nehsten statt were."

21. WA DB 7,34.

22. WA 19, 206,7–207,13.

23. StA 2, 277,20–278,5; WA 1, 429,6-10; AWA 2, 225,7-16.

centered good from his activity as well. Luther thinks that this search for one's own good, even though it be done wholly unaware, spoils the relation to God as well as to neighbor.[24] The deepest evil in this is that by seeking good for themselves people deny the goodness of God to their neighbors.

The Golden Rule, however, is properly addressed to sinful people who already love themselves above all else and desire everything good from God as well as from others. Thus, as far as the motivation of human activity is concerned, the Golden Rule demands a total change in the direction that love must take. That is, according to the rule, people should love God and others just as much as they now love themselves.[25] They must let God be the Giver of everything good and must do those good things to others that they would want for themselves from them. In this form, as the demand of a selfless divine love, the Golden Rule is not a rule of reciprocity according to which one may seek one's own benefit.

The Golden Rule demands and instructs us in a love that is not directed just to the good, the beautiful, and the pleasant people who in some way are useful for the lover. It demands the love of those who do not seem worthy of loving. The rule commands love to every neighbor, even to those who are the most difficult and unappealing.

24. WA 10 II, 14-17; WA 10 I 1, 24,1-12; 25,12–26,4.

25. WA 56, 518,4-10: "Igitur Credo, quod isto precepto 'Sicut teipsum' Non precipiatur homo diligere se, Sed ostendatur vitiosus amor, quo diligit se de facto, q.d. Curuus es totus in te et versus in tui amorem, A quo non rectificaberis, Nisi penitus cesses te diligere et oblitus tui solum proximum diligas. Peruersitas enim est, Quod Volumus ab omnibus diligi et in omnibus querere, que nostra sunt; Rectitudo autem est. Vt si id omnibus facias, quod tibi fieri vis perverse."

WA 2, 581,2-7: "Et Christus, quando Matt. vij. dicit 'Omnia quaecunque vultis ut faciant vobis homines,' certe declarat, iam inesse eis voluntatem et amorem sui, nec praecipit ibi eandem, ut claret. Quare pro mea temeritate, ut dixi, videtur praeceptum loqui de perverso amore, quo quisque oblitus proximi ea tantum quaerit, quae sua sunt, qui tunc rectus fit, si rursum seipsum oblitus proximo tantum serviat."

WA 17 II, 102,15-18: "Nü ists eben so viel gesagt, habe deynen nehisten lieb als dich selbs, alls, was du dyr gethan willt haben etc. Denn eyn iglicher fulet, das er will geliebt und nicht gehasset seyn, so fulet und sihet er auch, das er eym andern eben dasselb schuldig ist, das heysst aber lieben den andern als sich selbs."

WA 32, 496,32–498,2; WA 40 II, 71,9–72,6.

For everyone wants to be loved, even those who are most unpleasant among us. Consequently, the Golden Rule demands a divine love that does not just discover its object but actually creates it.[26] The Golden Rule also directs people away from counting one's own benefit to the consideration of the need and benefit of others. This turn includes a change in the aim of human love, a change that happens through continuous meditation on the Golden Rule.

Continuous Meditation on the Golden Rule

Luther understands the practice of Christian ethics and love as a continuous meditation on the Golden Rule. He particularly treats this meditative aspect of natural law in his *Lectures on Paul's Epistle to the Romans* (1515/16), and he returns to this theme explicitly in his *Interpretation of the Sermon on the Mount* at the beginning of the 1530s.

Luther speaks in these works about the rumination of the Commandment of Love and of the Golden Rule. This commandment seems to him, when correctly meditated upon, to be a most demanding precept. It may seem unimportant at first sight; but when we apply it to particular cases, it teaches us the way of sanity in all things.[27] People should not trust their own reason and will in choosing works that are supposed to be relevant to the situation and good. They should compare all of their works, words, and thoughts with the Golden Rule and ask: What would you expect from your neighbor? In coming to understand this, they begin to behave in this way toward

26. WA 56, 482,28–483,10: "Vnde profundissimum Est preceptum et diligenti examine quilibet seipsum ad illud probare debet. Quia per hoc verbum 'Sicut teipsum' excluditur omnis Simulatio dilectionis. Vnde Qui diligit proximum Vel propter diuitias, gloriam, eruditionem, fauorem, potentiam, consolationem et non itidem, qui est pauper, ignobilis, indoctus, aduersarius, subiectus, asper, patet, Quod simulate diligit, Non ipsum, sed ea, que sunt illius, ad suam comoditatem, Ac per hoc non 'vt seipsum,' Quippe qui seipsum diligit, etiamsi sit pauper, insulsus et penitus nihil. quis enim tam inutilis, qui sese odiat? Et tamen Nullus tam nihil, Quin seipsum diligat et alios non ita diligat."

WA 2, 604,24-34; WA 10 I 2, 68,19–69,20; WA 20, 762,18–763,14.

27. WA 56, 483,9-18.

the other. The result of such obedience to the Golden Rule would be the end of all quarrels, spite, and disagreement. Instead all virtue, grace, sanctity, and fulfillment of the law would abound.[28]

In his interpretation of the Sermon on the Mount Luther calls the Golden Rule the sum of the preaching of the prophets as well as of Jesus himself. In this form everyone can carry this preaching with himself, meditate on it, and see it written on one's heart and in all of one's deeds as well as in the whole of one's life. When we ruminate on the Golden Rule in this way, it forms us throughout our whole life.[29] If we measure our life and deeds continuously by this rule, we should always have enough to do and can teach ourselves about what we should do.[30] If we only pay attention to the Golden Rule, we can notice how it goes through all of our deeds, words, and thoughts and how it permeates our heart, body, and soul. If we apply ourselves to meditate on the rule, it is also capable of bearing fruit. And the first fruit is that such application puts anyone to shame and arrests his or her normal activities. For the example of the love demanded comes so near as the person himself. No one can escape the model for how he or she should act in respect to others.[31]

In Luther's thought the application of the Golden Rule in concrete life is organically connected with the content and reality of the Christian faith. However, this connection does not occur in the common dualistic interpretation, which places natural law only in the worldly orders.

Before treating the role of faith, one can ask what the "worldly kingdom" has to do with divine, self-giving love. Briefly, the kingdom of the world also belongs to the order of love. God to some degree (and often quite markedly) brings people in its context to realize the demand of love, although their inner will opposes such a demand. The world is so structured that self-seeking activity must be restricted, coercing from us some degree of care for others. As mothers and fathers, fellow workers, judges, ministers, members of the cabinet, and so on, people have to take the common good into account and

28. WA 56, 484,5-11.
29. WA 32, 495,9-14.
30. WA 32, 494,13-15.
31. WA 32, 495,15-27.

sometimes even lose sight of their own good. Throughout his literary work Luther gives many examples of the ways in which the Golden Rule should be obeyed in different offices or callings.[32] The point here is not that the worldly kingdom obeys only the natural law of reason. For rulers or judges use the same Golden Rule in their office as in their private life. But in one's office one never acts from a personal motive in making decisions. Judges do not employ the Golden Rule directly as governing between themselves and other persons but employ it in judging about relations between other people or between people and institutions. According to the Golden Rule, they cannot give other people over to robbery and violence, although they can as Christians personally forgive evildoers. Thus reason, which follows the Golden Rule, should alone decide the proper penal sentences and measures to be taken in respect to crime.

4. Faith as Foundation of Christian Life

The Problem of Defining the
Role of Faith in Christian Activity

If Luther's concept of natural law is often understood as a principle of rational reciprocity, faith has been thought to lead beyond such rationality. Faith can, of course, mean different things, and indeed the concept of faith in Luther research often seems to contain aspects that are difficult to combine. I take again Paul Althaus's interpretation of Luther's ethics as an example.

Althaus naturally treats faith, when Luther is concerned, together with justification. According to Althaus, justification is both the *presupposition* of all Christian activity and the *source* of all Christian activity.[33] What does this mean, and how do these aspects relate to each other?

As the presupposition of activity, justification has both negative and positive significance for the Christian ethos. First, since fellowship

32. StA 3, 64,6-23; 70,24–71,8; WA 17 II, 101,20-27; WA 32, 495,29–496,2.
33. Althaus, *Die Ethik Martin Luthers*, p. 11.

with God is grounded entirely in God's gracious acceptance of the sinner, justification rules out all possibility of understanding human activity or the Christian ethos as a way of attaining God's approval. Salvation or fellowship with God is granted only by faith. It always precedes human action. We can relate to God only through faith and never through our own accomplishments. The activity of the Christian whose ethos is based on faith is understood as gratitude to God for the salvation freely given prior to anything we can do. Since it is obedience that is required of us, our works are nothing more than simple compliance with God's command. This means that our attitude toward God can be only that of obedience, thanksgiving, and praise.[34]

The positive significance of justification is that just as God accepts me as righteous and looks upon me with favor even though I am and remain a sinner, so God also accepts and approves my work. Empirically, what the Christian does is never so good as to be right and acceptable in the sight of God, for our sinful nature continues to contaminate everything we do. Nevertheless, the Christian's deeds are right in the sight of God, because in his grace he approves them. For he approves the person who in faith lays hold of his wondrous grace and favor. It is by virtue of this justifying "Yes" of God that the Christian is given, through faith, a good conscience about his or her works. In and of itself, in an immanent sense, the Christian lacks a good conscience but is given a good conscience in a paradoxical way: through the word of forgiveness, God's act of justification.[35]

Justification is not just the presupposition but also the basic source of Christian action. This notion is based on the truth that when an individual comes to faith, Christ enters into that person and God's Holy Spirit is given to him or her. Thus far Althaus follows Luther's own statements. But he begins to go astray when he interprets Luther's concept of the new condition of humanity. According to Althaus, justification is a completely new kind of encounter between God and humans. God now confronts humanity as the self-giving love he really is. This confrontation implies that God gains a new kind of power over the human heart. God enflames the heart with a

34. Althaus, *Die Ethik Martin Luthers*, pp. 11-13.
35. Althaus, *The Ethics of Martin Luther* (E.T. 1972), pp. 13-14.

love for God. Through this loving approach God draws people into the process of his own love.[36]

Briefly put, the process of God's love involves our first experiencing his love and then going on to love the neighbor. The Christian's action flows out of the experience of God's love. And since this action is itself love, it shares all of the characteristics of God's own love. The love, too, is spontaneous, free, voluntary, happy, and eager. It possesses a spontaneity that changes the "thou shalt" to an inner "I must." The imperative is set aside through the indicative worked by God's Holy Spirit.[37]

Again, Althaus seems in this interpretation to follow Luther's thought reliably. But Althaus's view is not without its problems. First, he does not relate the two aspects of faith and of justification to each other. In one sense justification is clearly understood as the forensic acceptance that leaves a person a sinner in himself. In another sense justification is understood in the effective sense as Christ and the Holy Spirit entering into the Christian. Even though Althaus says that the Holy Spirit works in the believer, he avoids speaking about the presence of divine love or about participating in God's being. He speaks rather about "God's new power in the heart of man." Similarly, he understands love of neighbor as following from the experience of God's love for the individual. The love of neighbor, then, shares the characteristics of divine love. Althaus does not say, however, that the love of neighbor is a participation in the divine love itself. Thus, I conclude that Althaus modifies the meaning of the concepts in a modern direction when he interprets Luther on this point.

36. Althaus, *Ethics*, pp. 18-20.

37. Althaus, *Ethics*, pp. 21-22. Here I have followed the English translation of Althaus's book, but it is perhaps too free to give the accurate content of Althaus's thought. He writes: "Wo Geist und Glaube ihr Werk tun, da hat das Handeln des Christen nichts Gemachtes, Gezwungenes mehr, sondern es geschieht mit einer inneren Notwendigkeit, für die die Naturvorgänge wie das Fruchttragen der Bäume ein Gleichnis sind. Es ist eine Spontaneität, durch welche das Soll zu einem inneren Muß des von der Liebe Gottes Ergriffenen worden ist. Die Imperativ ist hier aufgehoben in dem von Gottes Heiligem Geiste gewirkten Indikativ: die Christen tun die guten Werke von selbst, die sie tun sollen."

Faith as the Reception of Divine Love

The loving application of the Golden Rule is possible for Christians only because Christ has first fulfilled its demand and does so continuously as present in the heart of the believer through faith. Luther says that Christ has done to us what he would have wanted someone to do to him, had he been in an emergency equal to ours. This has occurred in his incarnation, passion, death, and resurrection and occurs continuously through faith. When Christ unites himself with a Christian through his faith, he acts toward him just as if Christ himself were that person. Christ takes the burden of his sin onto himself and gives his own power, righteousness, and wisdom in return.[38] This means that through Christ, who is present in faith, the Christian participates in the divine attributes.[39] The attributes are essential qualities; therefore, the Christian participates through them in the divine essence itself. Because Christ fulfills the divine law of love by setting himself in the place of the individual according to the Golden Rule, the person becomes a participant in the divine nature, which is the love that gives itself to the other.[40]

The Christian then knows through faith the loving God who becomes human in order to save him. He learns to ascribe the divine

38. WA 10 I 2, 30,30–31,24; 42,5–43,7.

39. WA 2, 491,12-19.

40. WA 10 I 1, 100,8–101,2: "erfinden teglich szo viel newer werck und lere, das wyr tzuletzt nichts mehr wissen vonn rechtem gutem leben, szo doch alle Christlich lere, werck und leben kurtz, klarlich, ubirflussig begriffen ist ynn den zweyen stucken GLAUBEN UND LIEBEN, durch wilch der mensch tzwischen Gott unnd seynem nehisten gesetzt wirt alsz eyn mittel, das da von oben empfehet und unten widder auszgibt unnd gleych eyn gefesz oder rhor wirt, durch wilchs der brun gotlicher gutter on unterlasz fliessen soll ynn andere leutt. Sihe, das sind denn recht gottformige menschen, wilche von gott empfahen allis, was er hatt, ynn Christo, und widderumb sich auch, alsz weren sie der andern gotte, mit wolthaten beweiszen; da geht denn der spruch ps. 81: Ich hab gesagt, yhr seyt Gotter und kinder des allerhochsten allesampt, Gottis kinder sind wyr durch den glawben, der unsz erben macht aller gottlichen gutter. Aber gotte synd wyr durch die liebe, die unsz gegen unszernn nehisten wolthettig macht; denn gottlich natur ist nit andersz denn eytell wolthettickeyt und, alsz hie .S. Paulus sagt, freuntlichkeyt und leutselickeyt, die yhr gutter ynn alle creatur ubirschwenglich auszschuttet teglich, wie wyr sehen."

qualities to the God who hides himself in the form of a suffering and dying man. Thus, through Christ the Christian learns to let God be the essence and subject of everything that is good, and in Christ has always the graceful, loving God nearby, present in faith.[41] Only when the Christian possesses such a God who continually gives him good things and whom he considers always the font of everything good, can he love the neighbor without searching for anything from him as reward. If faith as a divine gift is the "organ" that receives good things from God and lets God be the Giver, then love is the "substance" that always gives itself to others. Through the gift of the divine nature or love the Christian gives himself continually to God and to his neighbor.

The person is truly given to God only when he has returned his own will to God. Possessing God's own will is a divine attribute. It belongs to God, but it has been stolen from him. An essential aspect of fulfilling the Golden Rule in relation to God is, thus, the return of the stolen will back to its owner. This implies that at the same time the believer is united with the divine will, that is, with divine love.[42]

Giving oneself to God and to the neighbor is a process that does not become complete during this life. If fulfilling the Golden Rule in relation to God means returning all of the stolen attributes back to God so that he may be who he is, in relation to the neighbor it means putting oneself in the neighbor's situation in order to know what the neighbor needs and what is good for him or her. Following the Golden Rule in relation to the neighbor also mortifies selfish love.

When a Christian puts himself in the place of the neighbor and gives himself to him in love, his action is not his own work but the work of God in which the Christian takes part as a cooperator.

Luther also speaks, then, about our cooperation with God. Its proper place is the situation in which the alien justice of Christ has been infused in the Christian, and Christ dwells in his heart through faith. The infused justice is also Christ himself who dwells and works in the Christian, and the Christian cooperates with Christ. This cooperation happens in respect to three relations: the relation to

41. AWA 2, 200,3–202,14.
42. WA 10 I, 2, 405,24-36; WA 2, 581,2-20; AWA 2, 40,3–41,5; 43,21–44,3. Raunio, *Summe des christlichen Lebens*, pp. 304-9.

him/herself, to the neighbor, and to God. Cooperation with the justice of Christ means to "crucify the flesh and concupiscence," that is, to mortify selfish love and to transform the perverted will so that one no longer seeks his or her own benefit but loves the neighbor and seeks what is good for him or her. Luther stresses that those who seek the benefit of others realize love and fulfill the will of God. This means that the Christian's life becomes correct in all three of the aspects mentioned above.[43]

In cooperation with Christ's justice we follow the example of Christ and become conformed to his image. Christ has fulfilled the law by letting God be the source of everything good and by giving himself for us. Thus, the Christian participates through faith in everything that Christ is and that he has. Christ possesses divine essences such as wisdom, strength, justice, goodness, freedom, and so on. As he became a man he accepted the form of a slave. He gave the divine essences back to his Father and acted as if all of our evil were also his, thus taking our sins and our penalty onto himself. Cooperation with Christ means now that we act similarly in relation to God and to our neighbor. Although we through faith participate in the divine essences, we cannot be arrogant about them but acknowledge that they belong to God. We should live as if we did not have them and as if we were equal to those who do not have them. Christians should also relate themselves to others as if their infirmity and sin belonged to themselves.[44] This is the only way to serve people so that they do not get scared or driven away. The aim of cooperation with Christ is not to make those who possess defects to experience more profoundly their weakness and inability but to improve their life by defending and exalting them. This should be done just as we would desire that others would help us, that is, by obeying the Golden Rule.[45]

The Golden Rule also demands good deeds, which can be realized only through uniting with divine love. Such a good deed is to take on the sin of the neighbor as if it were one's own, to stand before God for him and to pray for him. And such a good deed is to let the righteousness, power, and wisdom that Christ has given to the Chris-

43. StA 1, 223,21-27.
44. StA 1, 223,28–224,6; 224,12-18; 224,25–225,4; 225,15-23.
45. StA 1, 226,17-26.

tian be in service of the neighbor as if they belonged to the Christian. Luther thinks that because of the unity of love, which God creates, these qualities actually become common qualities that the neighbor can share. Through uniting love the Christian "lives in his neighbour," as Luther says in *De libertate christiana*.[46]

Uniting Love, Community, and Diakonia

Luther's idea of divine love as uniting power leads to his understanding of the church as the "communion of love" in which everything becomes common, every member takes part in the sin and distress, the righteousness and success, of others, as if they were his own. Uniting love, insofar as it puts oneself in the other's place, is also the foundation of Christian *diakonia*.

Uniting love becomes concrete in participating in the suffering and need of others. To participate in the life of others means not only to act but also to share their suffering in an "ontological" sense. Uniting love makes the suffering of the other also one's own. And when Christians give themselves in divine love, the other is enabled to participate in that love. As members of the body of Christ, the church, Christians receive continuously both Christ and the neighbor. They receive Christ through the word and the sacraments. They also bring Christ, who is present in faith, to the neighbor. For this reason Christians can help each other both materially and spiritually.

The essence of the church is that selfless love which does not seek its own benefit. In the church both temporal and spiritual gifts become common through love.[47] Some scholars, for example Althaus, have thought that the idea of the church as communion disappears from Luther's works rather early. But even though the most comprehensive treatment of this theme was completed in 1519, Luther re-

---

46. StA 2, 304,12-16: "Concludimus itaque, Christianum hominem non viuere in seipso, sed in Christo (et) proximo suo, aut Christianum non esse, in Christo per fidem, in proximo per charitate(m), per fidem sursum rapitur supra se in deum, tutrsum per charitatem labitur infra se in proximum, manens tamen semper in deo, et charitate eius."

47. WA 6, 131,2-6.

turned to it in many later writings. Important for us is that his understanding of the "structure" of the church is also grounded precisely on his concept of the Golden Rule as natural law.

Uniting with Christ occurs through the love that is donated to the Christian through faith. In uniting love Christ and the Christian receive each other and put themselves in each other's places. When Christ unites with the Christian through word and sacrament, he acts according to the Rule of Love. He puts himself in the place of others and deals with them as if their affairs concerned him even more than they concerned them. In the *Freedom of the Christian* Luther expresses this by saying that Christ deals with us as if he were what we are. And thus Christians can receive Christ as if they were what Christ is. In this way they become conformed to Christ. This is, according to Luther, the deepest and most intimate union and can be compared to the union of food with the one who eats. The process of uniting in which Christ and the Christian receive each other is a process that lasts until human sin is totally annihilated, and the Christian has become like Christ on the Last Day.[48]

48. StA 1, 279,15-30: "dann keyn ynniger tiefer vnzuteyliger voreynigung ist vbir die voreynigu(n)g des speyß mit dem der gespeyset wirt Syntemal die speyß geht vnd wirt vorwandelt yn die natur vnd wirt eyn weßen mit de(m) gespeyßten. . . . Alßo auch wir mit Christo yn dem sacrament voreyniget werden vn(d) mit allen heyligen eyngeleybet das er sich vnßer alßo an nympt fur vnß thut vnd lest alßo were er das wir seynd was vnß antrifft auch yhn vnd mehr dan vnß antrifft Widderu(m)b wir vnß seyn alßo mugen an nehmen als weren wir das er ist als dan auch endlich geschehen wirt d(aß) wir yhm gleych formig werden. . . . Da(nn) die voreynigu(n)g machts alles gemeyn alßo lang biß das er die sund yn vnß gantz vortliget vnd yhm selbs vnß gleych mache am Jungsten tage. Alßo auch sollen wir yn vnßer nehsten vnd sie yn vnß durch dieselben lieb voreynigt werden."

WA 12, 490,9-18: "Ist es nicht grosz, das die hohe majestet fur mich trit und auch sich mir zu eigen gibt, darnach das alle heiligen fur mich tretten und stehen, nemen sich meiner an und sorgen fur mich, dienen und helffen mir, also setzet uns Got ynn die gemeinschaft Christi und aller seiner erwelten; do haben wir eyn grossen trost, da wir uns uff verlassen. Bin ich ein sünder, so steet Christus da und spricht 'Der sünder ist mein, den will ich angreiffen mit meyn heyligen fingern, wer wil dawider murren? Also fellet mein sünd hin, und ich geniesz seiner gerechtikeit. Also thuen wir Christen undereinander auch, nympt sich eyner des andern an, das einer des andern sünd unnd geprechen tregt und mit seiner frumket dienet."

Because Christ is the Head of the church he wants first to give himself to others, to make their suffering and tragedy common and to bear it for them. He does so in order to let the members of his body bear each other's misery. This act of giving himself to others fulfills the aim of uniting love: through it everything that Christ is and that he has is shared commonly with Christians.[49]

The unity between Christ and Christians is constituted by the sharing of all spiritual gifts as well as all misery and sin.[50] In this community of sharing between Christ and Christians, Christians may also enjoy Christ and each other. This mutual enjoyment includes the annihilation of selfish love and the increase of the love that seeks the common good in the context of this communion.[51] Both spiritual gifts and sin and suffering become common only through the love that leads people outside of themselves. Love sets free everything that people claim for themselves and thus do not allow to become common.

49. StA 1, 276,31-37: "Als sprech er [Christus] ich bin das heupt ich will der erst sein der sich fur euch gibt will ewr leyd und vnfall mir gemeyn machen vnd fur euch tragen auff das yhr auch widderumb mir vnd vntereynander ßo thut vnd alles last yn mir und mit mir gemeyn seyn vnnd laß euch diß sacrament des alliß zu eynem gewissen warzeiche(n) das yhr meyn nit vorgesset. Sondernn euch teglich dran vbet vnd vormanet was ich fur euch than hab vnd thu damit yhr euch stercken muget vnd auch eyner den andernn alßo trage."

50. StA 1, 274,15-18: "Dyße gemeynschafft steht darynne das alle geystlich guter Christi vnnd seyner heyligen mit geteyllet vnd gemeyn werden dem der dyß sacrament empfeht widderumb alle leyden vnd sund auch gemeyn werden vnd alßo liebe gegen liebe antzundet wirdt und voreynigt."

WA 12, 487,19-23: "Das ist, das wir eyn kuch werden mit dem Herren Christo, das wir tretten ynn die gemeynschaft seiner gueter unnd er inn die gemeynschaft unsers unglucks. Dann hie stossen zusamen sein frumket unnd mein sünd, mein schwacheit unnd sein stercke, unnd wirt also alles gemeyn, was meyn ist das wirt seyn, und was seyn ist, das hab ich auch."

51. StA 1, 284,16-23: "Ist die frucht dißes sacraments gemeynschafft vnd lieb da durch wir gesterckt werden widder tod vn(d) alles vbell. Szo das die gemeynschafft zweyerley sey Eyne d(aß) wir Christi vnnd aller heyligen genyessen Die andere das wir alle Christe(n) menschen vnßer auch lassen geniessen warynne sie vnd wir mugen das alßo die eygen nutzige liebe seyns selbs durch diß sacrament auß gerodtet eyn lasse die gemeyn nutzige liebe aller menschen vnd alßo durch der liebe vor wa(n)dlung eyn brott eyn tranck eyn leyp eym gemeyn werde das ist die rechte Christenliche bruderliche eynickeyt."

As Christians have received love and support from Christ and his church, so they in turn show love and support to Christ and Christ's own who need him. Thus, they bear all of the misery and injustice that innocent people suffer. All of this should be on their hearts in such a way that they defend the unfortunate and work and pray for them as much as they can.[52] The Christian community is not only a spiritual and inner unity, but it also realizes itself in working for all who suffer in this world.

The love of Christians continuously increases and transforms them such that they become "common" with everyone. Luther even says that through love Christians will be transformed into each other. This means that by following the Rule of Love they receive the misery and evil of others as their own and share their gifts with them. In such a love, which bears the sin and evil of others, is found the meaning of Holy Communion, and in it the "commonness" of Christians with Christ and with each other grows complete.[53] Luther

52. StA 1, 276,13-27: Wan du alßo diß sacraments genossen hast odder niessen wilt. So mustu widderumb auch mit tragen der gemeyn unfall. . . . Ja es trifft sie alles leyd vnd lieb aller heyligen auff erden. Da muß nu deyn hertz sich yn die lieb ergeben vnd lernen wie diß sacrament eyn sacrament der lieb ist vnd wie dir lieb vnd beystand geschehn widderu(m)b lieb vnd beystand ertzeygen Christo yn seynen durfftigen. Dan hie muß die leyd seyn alle vneere Christi yn seynem heyligen wort alle elend der Christenheit alle vnrecht leyden der vnschuldigen des alles zumall vbirschwencklich vill ist an allen oertern der welt hie mustu weren thun bitten vnd ßo du nit mehr kanst hertzlich mit leyden haben. Sich das heyst dan widderumb tragen Christus vnd seyner heyligen vnfall vnd widderwertickeit da geht dan der spruch Pauli. Eyner trag des andernn puerden ßo erfullet yhr Christus gepott. Sihe ßo tregstu sie alle ßo tragen sie dich widder alle vnd seynd alle ding gemeyn gutt vnd boeße." See also Ulrich Lutz, *Unio und Communio. Zum Verhältnis von Rechtfertigungslehre und Kirchenverständnis bei Martin Luther* (Paderborn, 1990), p. 259.

53. StA 1, 278,20-25: "Neyn wir mußen der andern(n) vbell widder vnßer lassen seyn wollen wir das Christ(us) vn(d) sein heylige(n) vnßer vbel solle(n) yhr lassen sein ßo wirt die gemeynschafft gantz vn(d) geschicht de(m) sacrament gnug. Da(nn) wo die lieb nit teglich wechst vn(d) den mensche(n) alßo wandelt d(aß) er gemeyn wirt yderma(nn) da ist diß sacraments frucht vn(d) bedeutu(n)g nicht."

StA 1, 279,7-12: "Widderu(m)b solle(n) wir durch die selb lieb vnß auch wandeln(n) vn(d) vnßer lassen sein aller ander Christe(n) geprechen vn(d) yhr gestalt vn(d) notdurfft an vns nehmen vnd yhr laßen seyn alles w(as) wir gutis

similarly describes the life that obeys the Golden Rule as real love. All of the gifts that flow from God through Christ to Christians become common so that the members of the church deal with others as if they were in the place of the others. Christians take the sins of their neighbors onto themselves; they labor for them and serve their neighbors as if these sins were their own. They place their faith and righteousness before God in order to cover the sins of their neighbors and to seek grace for them.[54]

The communion of love is, however, a hidden reality. It is an object of faith, so that faith sees the communion of love and receives the common help through Holy Communion.[55]

---

vormuge(n) das sie desselbe(n) genieße(n) mugen das ist recht gemeynschafft vn(d) ware bedeutu(n)g diß sacraments Alßo werde wir ynn eynander vorwandelt vn(d) gemeyn durch die liebe an wilche keyn wa(n)dell nit geschehe(n) mag."

StA 1, 281,12-19: "Darnach sich zu das du auch yderma(nn) dich er gebist gemeyn zu seyn vn(d) yhe niema(n)t yn haß odder tzorn absonderst da(nn) diß dulden. Du must der andern(n) geprechen vnd durfft dyr zu hertzen lassen gehen als weren sie dyn eygen vnd deyn vormugen dar bieten als were es yhr eygen gleych wie dir Christus ym sacrament thut D(as) heyst durch lieb yn eynander vorwandelt werden auß vielen stucken eyn brott vnd tranck werden seyn gestalt vorlassen vnd eyn gemeyne an nehmen."

Oswald Bayer, in *Promissio. Geschichte der reformatorischen Wende in Luthers Theologie* (Göttingen, 1971), p. 237, sees here a *ius talionis*–type of thinking according to which the spiritual gifts are exchanges following the principle of *do-ut-des*. This interpretation does not correspond to Luther's view. As the context shows, the concern here is the transformation of human selfish love and the aim of a common sharing with all people.

54. StA 2, 304,1-11: "En, ista regula oportet, vt quae ex deo habemus bona fluant, ex vno in alium, et comunia fiant, vt vnus quisq(ue) proximum suum induat, et erga eum sic se gerat, ac si ipse esset in loco illius. E Christo fluxerunt et fluunt in nos, qui nos sic induit, et pro nobis egit, ac si ipse esset, quod nos sumus. E nobis fluunt in eos, qui eis opus habe(n)t), adeo vt et fidem et iustitiam meam oporteat ciram deo poni, pro tegendis et depraecandis proximi peccatis, quae super me accipiam, et ita in eis laborem et seruiam, ac si mea propria essent, sic enim Christus nobis fecit. Haec est enim vera charitas synceraque Christianae vitae regula, Ibi autem vera et syncaera est, vbi vera et syncera fides est. Hinc Ap(osto)lus 1. Cor. 13. Charitati tribuit, quod non quaerit, quae sua sunt."

55. WA 6, 130,26-132, 24; StA 1, 280,32-38: "das su begerest hertzlich/diß sacraments vn(d) seyner bedeutung/vnd nit dran zweyffelest/wye das sacrament deutet/so geschech dyr. Das ist/das du gewiß seyest/Christus vnd alle heyligen

Concluding Remarks

The conclusion that Luther did not think, as he has often been interpreted, in a dualistic way leads to a new understanding of several aspects of Lutheran theology. First, it means that Lutheran theology does not after all presuppose a distinction between "nature" and "spirit." Christian spiritual life is not something "higher" than human nature, but has as its aim to fulfill the natural order of self-giving love. The Golden Rule, which is written in the hearts of all human beings, is natural law in the sense that it reflects the "essence" of all creation. Creation reveals the essence of God as self-giving love. Natural law also demands the very love that is God's own nature. For this reason the common dualistic understanding of law does not correspond to Luther's idea.

Luther emphasizes, of course, that human beings are indeed determined by self-interest and seek their own benefit. The content of the natural law is not based on this self-interest, though, nor even on any moderate form of self-interest. On the contrary, Luther's fundamental idea is actually that natural law demands a change of motivation in human activity. And this change involves our whole way of existing as human beings. The change actually begins when divine love comes to dwell in the Christian through Christ and the Holy Spirit.

Second, Luther's idea of the Golden Rule as natural law, if understood as the commandment that we put ourselves in the place of our neighbor, proves to be a critique of the modern liberal notion of the concept of rational self-interest. The Golden Rule does not confirm that seeking one's own benefit is rational but rather directs the person who tries to follow it to take into account the concrete situation of others, their need and good, as the starting point of moral reasoning.

Third, understood in its theological meaning, the Golden Rule

---

treten zu dir/mit allen yhren tugenden/leyden vnd gnaden/mit dir tzu leben/thun/lassen/leyden vn(d) sterben/vn(d) wollen gantz deyn sein alle dingk mit dir gemeyn haben/wyrstu dyssen glauben woll vben vnd stercken/ßo wirstu empfinden/wie eyn fro(e)lich reych/hochtzeytlich mall vnd woll leben/dir deyn gott/auff dem Altar bereytt hat."

connects moral activity with the right service of God. For the God who makes self-giving love possible and who realizes it is the God who first gave himself. This is why the Golden Rule contains the demand to let God be God, the Source and Giver of everything good. In this sense natural law requires a faith that receives God's material and spiritual gifts while always regarding them as given by God. Luther's understanding of natural law and faith is also an integral part of his theology of love.

This demand of divine love becomes more and more concrete in our everyday relations to other people, and, as natural law, also makes a direct connection between our existential situation and our relation to God, that is, to the source of everything good. This understanding of love challenges Lutheran theology to new reflection on the theological foundations of Christian mission and diaconal work.

Fourth, we fulfill the demand of natural law through participation in the divine love, and not just as a consequence of a new self-understanding or of an experience of God's love. The self-giving God is in his essence present in the hearts of Christians and transforms them into the likeness of Christ's image. This conformity with Christ implies participation in both the divine and the human natures of Christ. Christians do not treat others as "Gods" but as "Christs," who take the sin, weakness, and distress of others upon themselves as if these were their own. This divine love constitutes the communion of Christians where both the gifts of God and the sin of the people are held in common. In this spiritual communion the requirement of natural law is fulfilled in its deepest sense, as giving oneself to the other. During this life such love does not become perfect. Its transforming presence has just begun its work. For this reason the communion of love is not an object of sense knowledge but an object of faith. As an object of faith it is an existing reality; it participates in self-giving and unites ever more with divine love. Thus, Luther's thinking on natural law and faith leads to the most discussed theme of ecumenical theology: the church as *koinonia*.

Bibliography

Works of Martin Luther

(StA = Studienausgabe, WA = Weimarer Ausgabe)

Divi Pauli apostoli ad Romanos epistola. 1515-1516.	WA 56.
Divi Pauli Apostoli ad Hebreos epistola. 1517-1518.	WA 57 III.
Eine kurze erklätung der 10 Gebote. 1518.	WA 1, 250-56.
Decem praecepta Wittenbergensi praedicata populo 1518.	WA 1, 398-521.
Sermo de duplici iustitia. 1518.	StA 1, 221-29.
Auslegung und Deutung des heiligen Vaterunsers.	WA 9, 123-59.
In epistolam Pauli ad Galatas M. Lutheri commentarius. 1519.	WA 2, 443-618.
Eyn Sermon von dem Hochwirdigen Sakrament des Heyligen Waren Leychnams Christi. Vnd von den Bruderschaften.	StA 1, 272-87.
Operationes F. Martini L. in psalmos, wittebergibus theologiae studiosis pronuntiatae. 1519.	AWA 2, 1-648.
Operationes in psalmos. 1519-1521	WA 5.
Tractatus de libertate Christiana. 1520	StA 2, 264-309.
Das Magnificat verdeutschet und ausgelegt. 1521	StA 1, 314-64.
Adventspostille. Das Evangelium am ersten sontag des Advents. Matth. 21,1-9. 1522.	WA 10 I 2, 21-26.
Weihnachtspostille. Epistel Pauli in der Frühchristmesse, Tit 3,4-7. 1522	WA 10 I 1, 95-128.
Betbüchlein. 1522	WA 10 II, 375-482.
Predigten des Jahres 1522. Luk. 15,1-10.	WA 10 III, 217-22.
Von weltlicher Oberkeit, wie weit man ihr Gehorsam schuldig sei. 1523	StA 3, 31-71.
Ein Sermon D. M. Lutheri am Gründonnerstag. 1523	WA 12, 476-93.
Ermahnung zum Frieden auf die zwölf Artikel der Bauernschaft in Schwaben. 1525	WA 18, 291-334.
Fastenpostille. Röm. 13,8ff. 1525	WA 17 II, 88-104.
Der Prophet Jona ausgelegt. 1526	WA 19, 185-251.
Vorlesung über den 1. Johannesbrief. 1527	WA 20, 592-801.
Wochenpredigten über Matth. 5–7. 1530-32.	WA 32, 299-544.
In epistolam S. Pauli ad Galatas Commentarius	

ex praelectione D. Martini Lutheri (1531)
collectus 1535. WA 40 I, 1-688.
WA 40 II, 1-184.

Die erste Disputation gegen die Antinomer.
18. Dezember 1537. WA 39 I, 360-417.
Das Neue Testament. Der Römerbrief. 1522/46 WA DB 7, 27-.

Literature

Althaus, Paul
1967   *Die Ethik Martin Luthers.* Gütersloh.
1981   *Die Theologie Martin Luthers.* Gütersloh.
Bayer, Oswald
1971   *Promissio. Geschichte der reformatorischen Wende in Luthers Theologie.* Göttingen.
1990   *Schöpfung als Anrede. Zu einer Hermeneutik der Schöpfung.* 2. erw. Aufl. Göttingen.
Duchrow, Ulrich
1983   *Christenheit und Weltverantwortung. Traditionsgeschichte und systematische Struktur der Zweireichelehre.* 2. Aufl. Stuttgart.
Gustafson, James M.
1978   *Protestant and Roman Catholic Ethics.* Chicago.
Haikola, Lauri
1981   *Usus legis.* 2. Aufl. Helsinki.
Herr, Theodor
1972   *Zur Frage nach dem Naturrecht im deutschen Protestantismus der Gegenwart.* Abhandlungen zur Sozialethik 4. Munich, Paderborn, Vienna.
Lutz, Ulrich
1990   *Unio und Communio. Zum Verhältnis von Rechtfertigungslehre und Kirchenverständnis bei Martin Luther.* Paderborn.
Raunio, Antti
1993   *Summe des christlichen Lebens. Die Goldene Regel als Gesetz der Liebe in der Theologie Martin Luthers von 1510 bis 1527.* Reports of the Department of Systematic Theology XIII. Helsinki.
Thompson, W. D. J. Cargill
1984   *The Political Thought of Martin Luther.* Sussex.

Response to Antti Raunio,
"Natural Law and Faith"

WILLIAM H. LAZARETH

We are all deeply grateful for Professor Raunio's lucid and provocative presentation on the theological foundations of Luther's ethics. Allow me to highlight what I consider to be the main point and its contemporary importance.

Raunio deals with Luther's interpretation of faith's understanding of natural law as summarized for Christians and non-Christians alike in the universal "Golden Rule": "In everything do to others as you would have them do to you; for this is the law and the prophets" (Matt. 7:12).

The author contrasts Luther's concern for the unity of God's law with those of his interpreters who represent what is called "the common approach to Luther's thought concerning natural law." The latter view closely relates the Reformer's ethic to the Nominalism of the late Middle Ages as well as to the residual influence of Thomistic metaphysical thought.

Raunio charges that this latter approach as developed by such varied scholars as Paul Althaus and Cargill Thompson leads to the erroneous claim of dualistic inconsistencies in Luther. Althaus interprets Luther dualistically, as holding two natural laws or Golden Rules that differ in their content, one based on rational law and the other grounded in Christian love. Thompson also views Luther dualistically, as limiting natural law solely to temporal government, in close affinity with the Thomistic natural law tradition.

In opposition, Professor Raunio argues that Luther did not separate a natural law of reason from an evangelical law of love. Nor did he limit natural law to temporal government and the social order of peace and justice. Raunio contends rather that "natural law" (also called the "Golden Rule" or "Christian love") is "from the beginning for Luther the law of divine nature, or the law of divine love." Indeed, the divine command of selfless love is written in the whole of creation, as well as in human hearts (Rom. 2:15), since for Luther all of creation is an order of God's love.

While acknowledging that some other antidualistic Luther interpreters such as Bayer, Duchrow, Haikola, and Wingren have also depicted the Reformer's understanding of nature as an order of self-giving love, the author laments that their acknowledgment has not in fact led subsequently to any "thoroughgoing reevaluation of Luther's unified natural law thought." Hence, Raunio's programmatic subtitle: "The Forgotten Foundations of Ethics in Luther's Theology."

In support of this thesis, Professor Raunio rightly points out that Luther "never connected the content of [natural law] with rationality in the modern sense [of calculated self-interest], that is, as a moral action taken in order to ensure finally one's own benefit." Luther interpreted the biblical command, "You shall love your neighbor as yourself," to indict and limit, rather than to endorse and extend, the human self-love of sinful creatures. Raunio therefore wisely adds, "The letter of the law is the demand of divine love, though it cannot guarantee the fulfillment of the law. On the contrary, because of the unwillingness of human beings to change, it only increases sin and hatred toward God and his law."

Here I provide some of my own additional substantiation from Luther's 1535 *Galatians Commentary*:

> Satan's hatred for truly good works is evident also from this: All men have a certain natural knowledge implanted in their minds (Rom. 2:14-15), by which they know naturally that one should do to others what he wants done to himself (Matt. 7:12). This principle and others like it, which we call the law of nature, are the foundations of human law and of all good works. Nevertheless, human reason is so corrupted and blinded by the malice of the devil that it does not understand this inborn knowledge or even if it has been

admonished by the Word of God, it deliberately neglects and despises it. So great is the power of Satan!

Thus under the papacy people used to perform those foolish and meaningless works, neither commanded nor demanded by God, with the utmost pleasure, diligence, and zeal, and at great cost. We recognize this same zeal for meaningless things in the sectarians of our day and in their disciples, especially in the Anabaptists. But in our churches, where the true doctrine of good works is set forth with great diligence, it is amazing how much sluggishness and lack of concern prevails. The more we exhort and arouse our people to do good works, to practice love toward one another, and to get rid of their concern for the stomach, the more lazy and listless they become for any practice of godliness. . . . For in the justified there remain remnants of sin, which deter and dissuade them both from faith and from truly good works. (WA 40:2, 66-67; LW 27:53-54)

This is all predicated, of course, on Luther's radical view both of the inherent "governing sin" of the unredeemed, as well as the persisting "governed sin" of the redeemed. In short, so-called natural law has become wholly "un-natural" for all sinners this side of the primal fall. Hence the need for the ongoing struggle for the faithful Christian's daily renewal and "truly good works" through the presence, gifts, and exhortations of the indwelling Spirit of Christ.

However, Luther's 1530 *Sermons on Matthew 5–7* prompt Raunio to acknowledge (with qualification) that Luther "seems to change his mind" there about any unified Golden Rule as the "summary of the whole divine law." Christian love once again appears to be dualistically divorced from natural law for disciples living "in but not of" this world. After all, in the Sermon on the Mount, it is the same Christ who in continuity declares, "I have not come to abolish the law or the prophets but to fulfill them" (Matt. 5:17; 7:12), and yet who also makes the repeatedly discontinuous claims, "You have heard it said . . . but I say to you . . ." (Matt. 7:21-48).

It was precisely this tension-filled eschatological radicality, along with such sin-responsive biblical passages as Genesis 9, Exodus 21, Romans 13, and 1 Peter 2, that forced Luther gradually to make his major ethical mid-course corrective. Historically, it was in meeting the challenges of the chaotic mid-1520s that Luther increasingly complemented — *not replaced* — his earlier dualistic and eschatological

Augustinian model (the "two kingdoms" of God *or* Satan) with his later dialectical and historical Pauline model (the "twofold reign" of the one Triune God through Christ *and* Caesar, against Satan).

As Luther's former model eternally normed salvation *(coram deo)*, so his latter model ethically normed service *(coram hominibus)*. Both were constituted and sustained by dynamic christocentric inter-penetration. The crucified and risen Christ, working both for us *and* in us, regenerates *and* renews Christians to grow faithfully in grace and to cooperate lovingly with both God and neighbors in struggles for peace and justice in society.

Nevertheless, much of traditional Lutheranism betrayed Luther's biblical and ethical development (thwarted, to be sure, by his own pessimistic apocalypticism and linguistic inconsistencies). Lutherans, too, frequently became socially quietistic by virtually identifying Luther's later Christ *and* Caesar dialectic ("twofold reign") with his earlier God *or* Satan dualism ("two kingdoms"). That disastrously weakened any positive role for natural law's "civil righteousness" (the law's *usus politicus*), and practically left the public sector to the devil.

So it is salutary indeed to have Professor Raunio claim here that "the 'doctrine of the two governments' is his [Luther's] solution to the question concerning how the natural law can be fulfilled." Further-more, and this is also crucial for the Lutheran sanctification/*theosis* discussion with Eastern Orthodoxy, it is precisely the indwelling Spirit of the risen Christ in the effectively — and *not solely forensically* — justified Christian that is decisive for generating Luther's mature ethic. To view justification as a "legal fiction" that results in ethical Quietism is to be rejected as unbiblical and therefore un-Lutheran. It is for further documenting this badly needed corrective among Lutherans that we should be grateful for the author's splendid research. "Where there is forgiveness of sin, there is life."

Luther and Metaphysics: What Is the Structure of Being according to Luther?

SAMMELI JUNTUNEN

1. Can We Relate the Question of Ontology to Luther?

The title of this paper is very daring, even reckless. Luther, after all, wrote little about such questions as "What is the ontological structure of the world?" What interests him is something else, themes like sin, salvation, Christ, Trinity, and the sacraments. Thus, those who write about Luther's ontology have to reconstruct Luther's line of thought from scattered writings that do not explicitly deal with ontological issues.[1] Such an enterprise cannot be very reliable.

The lack of explicit material about ontology in Luther's vast literary production gives rise to the suspicion that Luther's thinking is in its foundations antimetaphysical and antiontological. Such a view envisions faith as a relation to God, not as something that could be characterized as *being*, with the result that all ontological questions in theology arise as corrupted questions. Such an understanding of Luther's thought is essentially involved in the so-called personalist Luther-interpretation (Gerhard Ebeling, Wilfried Joest).

---

1. The fact that Luther doesn't write much about ontological questions doesn't mean that they would be unfamiliar to him. He knew his Aristotle quite well and had read and thought about other metaphysical systems as well. See WA 6, 458:18-25; WA 59, 424:5-14, 425:11–426:10.

According to Ebeling and Joest, Luther's theology replaces an Aristotelian substance-metaphysics with a relational ontology.[2] Thus, even when he uses the same concepts as did the scholastics before him (e.g., *forma, substantia, materia*), he gives them a completely new meaning that can be used to describe an existentialist worldview.[3] And this view is something totally different from that of the previous substance-metaphysics.[4] But, as Risto Saarinen has shown, the notion that Luther's thought is antimetaphysical or antiontological was common in Luther-interpretation even before Ebeling. According to Saarinen, the neo-Kantian division between *Geist* and *Natur* is one of the major explanations of the so-called antimetaphysical character of Luther's thinking as seen in "neo-Protestant" Luther-scholarship (Albrecht Ritschl, Wilhelm Herrmann) or in the Luther-interpretation of the Luther-renaissance (Karl Holl, Erich Vogelsang, Reinhold Seeberg, Erich Seeberg). In these interpretations faith is for Luther a reality referring to "Geist" and

---

2. See, e.g., G. Ebeling, *Lutherstudien*, vol. 1 (Tübingen: Mohr, 1971), pp. 156-57, 173; Ebeling, *Lutherstudien*, vol. 2, *Disputation de homine. Text und Traditionshintergrund* (Tübingen: Mohr, 1989), pp. 460-61; Ebeling, *Lutherstudien*, vol. 2, *Disputatio de homine. Die philosophische Definition des Menschen. Kommentar zu These 1-19* (Tübingen: Mohr, 1982), p. 268.

3. See G. Ebeling, *Lutherstudien*, vol. 3, *Begriffsuntersuchungen — Textinterpretationen — Wirkungsgeschichtliches* (Tübingen: Mohr, 1985), p. 327; W. Joest, *Ontologie der Person bei Luther* (Göttingen: Vandenhoeck & Ruprecht, 1967), p. 134.

4. I think that Ebeling and Joest see only two possibilities when describing Luther's ontology and its relation to medieval thinking: either a static and non-personal substance-metaphysic or a relational-existentialist ontology, which is personal and dynamic. Recent Finnish Luther-scholarship has in some sense tried to find a third way and has stated that even when Luther's thought is not grounded in a static substance-metaphysic, neither is it based altogether on external relations. The notion of being *(esse)* is important for it. J. Forsberg (1984, 63, 68-69, 74-75, 77) states that for Luther faith means the presence of a new *"Seinswirklichkeit"* in the believer, which is not to be interpreted merely as a new relation to God. Earlier *Mannermaa* (1989, 21, 26-36 [first published in Finnish in 1979]) used the term *"real-ontisch"* to stress that the ontological presence of Christ is important for the Reformer's notion of faith. In a later article (*Mannermaa* 1993) he combines the *"real-ontisch"* aspects of Luther's ontology with the dynamic aspects of the Reformer's understanding of being.

thus can be articulated by ethical or relational concepts and not through ontological *"Seins-Aussagen."*[5]

Luther is actually in some sense "antimetaphysical," but not along the lines of thought just described. The reason for the anti-metaphysical character of his theology is not refusal of the concept of being, but a certain understanding of love, which is fundamental for his theology.

For Luther God is in his essence a pure, giving love whose motive is not to get good for himself, but to give good to that which lacks it in itself. God's love is creative; it never finds its object as something preexistent. Rather, it turns to that which is nothing and is in itself needy in order to create it and make it existent and good through loving it. This divine love *(amor dei)* is opposite in its motive and direction to natural human love *(amor hominis),* which directs itself to the good, which the lover can get for him/herself. The *amor hominis* is an egoistic love in which the lover "seeks his/her own (good)."[6]

According to Luther, a person's love, its motive and direction, determines his or her whole existence. In a *homo naturalis* everything — including religion, ethics, and the use of reason — has as its principle of life and action the egoistic *amor hominis*. One does not notice or understand things that are not beautiful, wise, elegant, or in some other way good for one, such that one could benefit from them. The *novus homo* who has received Christ and the divine *amor dei* through faith as a new principle of life, on the other hand, seeks as the object of love those beings to whom he or she can give non-self-centered good.[7]

---

5. See *Saarinen* 1989, 28, 41, 67-68, 77-78, 93-94. Another important reason for the interpretation of the neo-Protestant Luther-scholars and those of the Luther-renaissance that Luther's thinking is antimetaphysical, Saarinen (1989, e.g., 230-31, 103) found in the so-called "transzendentale Wirkungsdenken," according to which God can be present in the world only in his actual effects (especially on the will and the conscience of the believer), which are to be differentiated categorically from his being.

6. WA 1, 365:2-18, WA 56, 361:6-24, 362:28–363:7, 356:18–357:11, WA 4, 269:25-26; *Mannermaa* 1989, 108-29; *Juntunen* 1996, 262-66.

7. See WA 7, 547:1-32, WA 10.3, 187:15–188:3; 180:1-14; *Juntunen* 1996, 320-24, 363-69; *Raunio* 1993, 313-17 and the previous footnote.

Luther's criticism of metaphysics is understandable on the grounds that in his view the *amor hominis* is the motivating principle of human philosophy.[8] A person may believe that he is seeking God or the highest good *(summum bonum)* in his metaphysical thought. Actually one is not seeking God, but oneself and one's own good, which he wants to reach through being wise in his own eyes and in the eyes of the neighbor. The metaphysician finds the *summum bonum,* but this is not God; it is the *summum bonum* in respect to *amor hominis,* that is, the ability to set oneself as God, as someone who is ultimately wise and possesses the final truth. His own egoistic person as a metaphysician is the object that he is actually seeking when he is seeking the *summum bonum.*[9]

The metaphysician's failure to find God does not result from God's not being the *summum bonum* or the *summum ens.* As far as I understand Luther, he does not deny the analogy of being and goodness between God and the world.[10] God himself is the *summum bonum* as such, but people cannot understand this (or spiritually benefit from the analogy of being), because the *amor hominis* so completely determines their life, senses, and intellect.[11] As mentioned, the good and the lovable for *amor hominis* are only those things that the lover can use as a medium for self-promotion. The real God refuses to be made into a medium for human egoism, because he loves people and wants to save them. This supposes that the former principle of life, the *amor hominis,* is destroyed when a new principle, Christ, is given through faith to the person.[12] The *homo naturalis* can in no way accept a God who works against everything understood to be good and noble. To the *homo naturalis* God is the enemy.[13] The real God seems to be the opposite of all goodness and being and not the *summum bonum.*[14]

8. See WA 1, 365:1-8, 361:32–363:14, 364:4-6; *Mannermaa* 1989, 129; *Kopperi* 1993, 73, 85-86.

9. See WA 59, 409:1–410:12, WA 1, 361:32-33; *Mannermaa* 1989, 132-233; *Raunio* 1993, 167; *Kopperi* 1993, 73.

10. See WA 56, 76:25-27, 198:21-24.

11. See WA 56, 393:21-25, 372:30–376:6; *Juntunen* 1996, 329-31.

12. See *Mannermaa* 1989, 136-39; *Juntunen* 1996, 246-56, 277-93.

13. WA 31.1, 249:16–250:2; *Mannermaa* 1989, 141.

14. WA 56, 362:31–363:2, 392:28–393:3; *Juntunen* 1996, 324-29.

The antimetaphysical element of Luther's theology is also a result of the very important role that he gives to the concept of love in his theology, in respect to the *amor hominis* and to the divine *amor dei*. The reason he speaks against the use of metaphysics is not that he believes that the concept of being should be abandoned in theology. It is rather that, according to him, the practice of metaphysics is based on *amor hominis*.

Still, Luther does not altogether reject metaphysical thinking. Even as a philosophical discipline practiced without faith it may be relatively good and come to formally right conclusions. According to Luther some pagan philosophers have understood with partial correctness many things about the formal metaphysical relation between God and the world, in a way similar to that in which the truth of Scripture speaks of these things.[15] Thus, metaphysics is not absolutely and formally wrong. It is partially good in a formal sense.[16]

Yet it is very important to notice that, according to Luther, even the partial formal goodness of metaphysics does not imply that the concrete practice of metaphysics would be anything more than a complete "spiritual adultery" and egoistic self-divinization.[17] *Amor hominis*, which functions as the motive of all philosophizing, causes us to have recourse to the partial good of formal metaphysical knowledge in a totally corrupt way and to a wrong end, that is, in making oneself into one's own God.[18]

As we know, the only way to God for Luther is through Christ and his cross and not through metaphysics. God wants to reveal

15. Siehe WA 10.1.1, 195:13–196:14, WA 59, 424:5-14, 425:11–426:10, WA 56, 177:11-15, WA 43, 240:22-30.

16. This can be noted, e.g., in the fact that for Luther the metaphysical scheme of Platonic philosophy with its different ontological *hypostases* is in some sense better than the Aristotelian one-dimensional scheme, because it can be more easily used in understanding such theologically important themes as the dependence of the world on God or the immanence of the Transcendent in the world. *Kopperi* 1993, 83-84; WA 59, 424:5-14, 425:11–426:10; *Juntunen* 1996, 43-44, footnote 14.

17. WA 59, 410:10-12; *Juntunen* 1996, 44, footnote 14.

18. WA 56, 177:6-18, 361:6-17; *Mannermaa* 1989, 131-33; *Raunio* 1993, 165-68.

himself only in opposition to that which the philosophical under-standing can estimate as good or wise, that is, in the cross and in suffering.[19] In the wretchedness of his self-revelation and in the an-guish that is inevitably present in the faith of everyone who believes in him, God destroys *amor hominis* in the believer at the same time that he gives Christ as the new principle of spiritual being *(opus alienum — opus proprium)*. This continuous destruction of *amor hominis* has as one of its results that a Christian under the *opus alienum* is at least in some sense able to employ philosophical under-standing about such matters as the metaphysical relation of the world to God as an *ancilla theologiae,* a servant of faith.[20] Because the *amor hominis* is continuously destroyed, it cannot lead the formally good metaphysical knowledge to a false end with such completeness as it does in philosophy practiced without faith.[21] The purification of the reason from the *amor hominis* in the life lived as an object of the *opus alienum dei* has as one of its results for Luther that the Augustin-ian *ordo charitatis*–scheme[22] is abandoned as a basic line of thought.[23] Another thing that has to be clearly noted, according to Luther, is that before any philosophical wisdom can become a true servant of faith, when philosophical concepts are taken in the service of theology they have to be "bathed": they receive a new meaning that may be somewhat different from their normal meaning as part of a philo-sophical system.[24]

19. *Mannermaa* 1989, 133-37.

20. See WA 39.2, 24:20-26, WA 1, 355:1-5, WAT 3, 104:24-27.

21. See WA 59, 409:3-21; *Kopperi* 1993, 78-79, 83-86.

22. I.e., that one should love more those things which are higher in the hierarchical order of being than those which are lower. Also: that one can and should direct one's essentially good but accidentally perverted natural love away from loving creatures to loving God as the *summum bonum*.

23. See *Raunio* 1993, 353-54; *Juntunen* 1996, 327-31.

24. See WA 39.1, 228:14–229:21.

When taken in the service of theology, philosophical concepts become "*nova vocabula*" (WA 39.2, 94:17-26, 103:5-11, 105:4-7, 19:7-9). This means that when they are used in theology, not all of the connotations and lines of thought implied in their normal system are acceptable. The meaning of the "*nova vocabula*" is determined by a totally other and truer worldview (though less evident to the senses) than what their normal context (philosophy based on

Luther's notion of faith does possess some understanding of the structure of being.[25] As noted, Luther says that a Christian can employ some degree of metaphysical understanding when trying to gain this understanding in faith.[26] Still, I think that the role of philosophical metaphysics is very limited in Luther's thinking. His understanding of the structure of being is above all *theological* — it is a matter about which one knows something through the Scriptures and through the intellect, which assumes *(apprehensio)* the divine Word.[27] Thus, I will not speak about "Luther and Metaphysics" but about the kind of understanding of the structure of being that belongs to Luther's theology. Such a question about Luther's theological ontology is very difficult to answer, but it is a legitimate one and relevant for Luther's theology. As I have tried to show, the antimetaphysical aspect of Luther's thought is a result of his understanding of love but not an indication that he would abandon the use of the concept *esse* in the *proprium* of theology.

---

natural reason) can offer, i.e., by a theology based on divine truths apprehended by a divinely illumined intellect. This is why, e.g., the syllogism "*Omnis homo est creatura. Christus est homo. Ergo Christus est creatura*" is true in philosophy, but not in theology. Philosophy doesn't recognize a "*homo*" who is not a "*creatura.*" Christian theology does, because the Word of God and its *apprehensio* in faith have opened a new understanding of reality, according to which the concept "*homo*" comprehends an entity, i.e. Christ, who is not a "*creatura.*" The word "*homo*" is also a "*novum vocabulum*" when compared with what "*homo*" means in philosophy (see *White* 1994, 328-48).

This "bathing of words" (together with the notion of the possible formal goodness of a metaphysical system and the notion of the "egoistic nature" of a philosophy practiced without faith) makes the question of the relationship of theology and philosophy in Luther's thinking a *very* difficult but important theme for understanding the Reformer. Luckily there are already three good works treating this subject: *Työrinoja* 1987, *Kirjavainen* 1987, and *White* 1994. It is a pity that the *Kirjavainen* and *Työrinoja* works are short articles and that *White* uses such rude language against the scholars he opposes that they probably will not read his work and benefit from it.

25. See *Metzke* 1961, 164; *Joest* 1967, 15; *Malter* 1980, 2-3, 7, 244. Note that the ideas of Joest and Malter concerning what is the structure of being for Luther are very different from mine.

26. See footnote 16.

27. See WA 39.2, 5:35-40, WA 6, 511:25-39; *Juntunen* 1996, 394, footnote 184; *Kirjavainen* 1987, 243.

In my recently published dissertation "Der Begriff des Nichts bei Luther in den Jahren von 1510 bis 1523," my task was to analyze Luther's use of the concept "nothing."[28] When I analyzed the lines of thought connected with this theme, I had to reconstruct a part of Luther's theological ontology. I'd like to present this reconstruction here. In doing so I am aware that I am walking on thin ice. I'll try to proceed carefully.

2. The Areas of *esse gratiae* and *esse naturae*

In reconstructing Luther's understanding of being, we must first state that the Reformer distinguishes between natural being *(esse naturae)* and the "being of grace" *(esse gratiae)*. This distinction is very important in his first *Commentary on the Psalter* (*Dictata super psalterium*, 1513-1515) and is also present in later works.[29] Luther means by *esse naturae* the natural being of a human being in all of its aspects (body, reason, senses, reproduction, etc.). *Esse gratiae* is the spiritual being of a Christian in the church. Luther uses the expression "*creatio nova*" to express the birth of this spiritual reality. In *creatio nova* God creates anew the person (who has without this new creation only the *esse naturae*, which is in itself good, but deeply corrupted by sin) and makes this person a part of the "new, spiritual world," that is, the church.[30]

According to the standard interpretation, which has been predominant especially among German Luther-scholars of the "personalist" interpretation of Luther (Ebeling, Joest, zur Mühlen) since the 1950s, this distinction between *esse naturae* and *esse gratiae* is one between two modes of existentialist self-understanding. For Ebeling persons are *spiritualis* insofar as they have a relationship to

---

28. The Reformer uses this concept surprisingly often. He says, e.g., that persons are *"nihil coram deo,"* or that they have to be brought back into nothingness *(redactio ad nihilum/annihilatio)* in faith.

29. See WA 3, 321:14-17, 429:19-28, 354:23-25, WA 4, 600:22–601:6, WA 18, 752:3–753:5, 785:26-38; *Juntunen* 1996, 155-56.

30. WA 4, 127:4-7, 450:33-35, 189:11-25, 444:26-32, WA 3, 154:24-28; *Juntunen* 1996, 155-57.

God as the constitutive element of their self-understanding (existence *coram deo*), and *carnalis* insofar as they understand themselves on the basis of a relation to the world *(coram mundo)*.[31] This interpretation is linked with the claim that existence in faith does not mean for Luther a *being (Sein)*. Rather, it is a *becoming (Werden)*.[32] Faith is an "actualistic" happening *(aktuales Geschehen)* in relation to God, who stands opposite the believing person. Because faith is an "actualistic" and external relation, it lacks internal being; that is, it lacks *forma*. A Christian is always on the way to his spiritual *forma*, which is not yet present in him, because he does not receive it until the eschatological fulfillment.[33] The spiritual *forma* can be present only in the sense that the Christian bases her existence on faith in God's promises, which do not became an internal intrinsic reality until the *eschaton*. According to Ebeling a new relational and existentialist ontology is needed to describe such an understanding of faith.[34]

Ebeling's interpretation as far as I understand it, and which I hope I have not simplified too much here, is incorrect. It is not totally incorrect, however, because Luther's understanding of being really is in some sense existential (e.g., in its emphasis on *affectus*),[35] non-

31. *Ebeling* 1971, 20-21, 25-29, 30-31, 218-19. A similar interpretation can be found in *zur Mühlen* 1972, 92, 266.

32. *Joest* 1967, 323, 351; *Ebeling* 1964, 228.

33. *Ebeling* 1985, 327-28; *Ebeling* 1971, 35, 62.

34. See *Ebeling* 1985, 54, 327-28; *Ebeling* 1989, 87-88, 505-6, 460-61; *Ebeling* 1982, 267, 268.

35. By "existential" I mean something that is experienced in the innermost part of a person. By "existentialist" I mean something connected with a certain philosophical tradition that emphasizes the self-understanding as a fundamental category of the being of a person. Luther's theology is *existential* because it emphasizes that the truths of faith are experienced in the *affectus* of the innermost being of the person. (We note that for Luther an *affectus* means much more than an "emotion" means in modern thought. For him the *affectus* of faith presupposes the presence of God's Spirit in the spiritual center of a person that regulates the whole being of the person. This is why the profound change in the *affectus* caused by the Word means for Luther the spiritual annihilation of the person and his/her recreation (see *Juntunen* 1996, 233-37, especially footnote 267). Luther's thinking is not *existentialist* because it doesn't create the new personal understanding as an exclusive category.

static, dynamic, relational, and extrinsic.[36] But it is incorrect insofar as it claims that these characteristics deny the intrinsic aspect of being, which, according to Luther, belongs to the natural aspect as well as to the spiritual being of a person.

3. Being (Both *esse naturae* and *esse gratiae*) as a Result of Continuous Creation

That Luther's understanding of being is in some sense a relational and extrinsic one is clearly seen in his claim that both *esse naturae* and *esse gratiae* are ontologically dependent on God. In respect to both of these types of being, humankind is *ex se* totally nothing *(nihil/Nichts)*.[37] This nothingness, which extends to all created being, does not mean that creatures do not exist. It means rather that they are not *ens per se* but *ens per aliud,* that is, through God.

To this total ontological dependence of the created being on God belongs the notion of creation as a continuous process *(creatio continua).* Luther seems to be influenced in this notion by the thought of William of Ockham. Ockham did not accept the traditional view concerning the mediating role of the created natural *ordo* and substantial forms in the coming into being and remaining in being of new creatures. The earlier tradition distinguished between *conservatio* and *creatio,* but for Ockham all *conservation* is actually a continuous creation. The *creatio ex nihilo* continues through every moment of the existence of the created individual. It is the continuous, direct, and in this sense "actualistic" dependence of the in-

36. This whole presentation is actually an interpretation of what the extrinsic and intrinsic characteristics of being are for Luther. That is why I can't yet define what I mean by these concepts. In order to make this presentation more understandable to the reader, I can say at this point that the extrinsic character of being refers to the openness of a being toward something that is in some sense outside of it. By the intrinsic character I mean those aspects of being that are in some sense inside that which is.

37. In this use of the concept *nihil* as an expression of the ontological dependence of the world on God Luther follows an old tradition, which leads all the way (through, e.g., Staupitz, Tauler, Eckhart, Bonaventure, and Bernhard) back to Augustine and in some sense even to Plato. See *Juntunen* 1996, 405.

dividual (as such, without any mediating ontological principles such as *essentia, forma substantialis,* or the *ordo naturae*) on God's *potentia absoluta.*[38]

Luther's notion of being is clearly connected with this Ockhamistic *creatio continua.* According to him creation has not occurred only once. God always creates all things.[39] Above every created individual (as both *esse naturae* and *esse gratiae*) hangs the same nothingness out of which God once created the world and still creates it. In this sense it is legitimate to speak about the actualizing, nonstatic understanding of being in the Reformer. For Luther being is not a static being-in-itself. Being is a matter of continuous reception of being from God. Human beings exist only because they receive God's gifts from outside themselves, such as life, being *(esse),* reason, intellect, nourishment, and clothing.[40]

Important here is that Luther (in quite another way than the Ockhamist tradition, to which the reality of grace is always something accidental in the human substance) extends the scope of the *creatio*

38. *Ockham,* Report., 2, qu4 (OT 5, 65:15-19); qu3-4 (OT 5, 75:18-22), Quodl., 7, qu2, ad2 (OT 9, 706:72-78), Quaest. variae, 3 (OT 8, 85:468-70); *Leff* 1975, 462.

39. WA 9, 66:29-33: "Unde conservare videtur majus esse quam creare. Quia multi incipiunt, sed pauci perseverant. Est enim conservatio semper nova inceptio. Est autem conservare idem quod continue creare. Et conservatio est continuata creatio, unde adhuc hodie creat deus Heb. 1. 'portans omnia' u."; WA 1, 563:6-13: "Impossibile est ulla perseverantia creaturae, nisi assidue accipiat magis ac magis: inde enim dicunt acuti quidam, quod conservatio rei sit eius continuata creatio. Sed creare est semper novum facere, ut etiam patet in rivulis, radiis, calore, frigore, maxime dum sunt extra suum principium. Quare et spirituali calori id est amori dei, in animabus opus est continuata conservatio (donec absorbeantur in suum principium divinum) ac per hoc et augmentum, etiam si verum esset, quod essent perfectae, licet extra deum esse nec pervenisse et esse perfectum sint contraria"; WA 43, 233:22-25: "Iudaei dicunt creatum esse sexta die cum aliis animalibus et divina ordinatione conservatum ad illud tempus usque. Nos Christiani scimus, quod apud Deum idem est creare et conservare"; *Löfgren* 1960, 37-45.

40. WA 3, 429:19-22: "Nam cum singulis diebus et horis beneficia dei acceperis scilicet vitam, esse, sensum, intellectum, insuper victum et amictum et ministerium solis, coeli et terre et omnium elementorum multis nimis varietatibus, manifestum est quod acceptis gratias debes."

continua into the *esse gratiae*. Christians are comparable to the Son of God, who is continuously born of the Father. In a similar way we must at all times be born, renewed, and generated *(nasci, novari, generari)*.[41] The *esse gratiae* of a person, like the *esse naturae*, is a continuous reception of the gifts of God, namely, the *dona gratiae*, the *"sacramenta et bona ecclesiae"* in which Christ himself is present[42] and is given to the Christian. Through these sacramental gifts (i.e., through Christ, who is given in them) the Christian continuously receives life, reason, being, and nourishment on the level of spiritual existence.[43] Through these gifts individuals, who in themselves are

41. WA 4, 365:14-25: "Si enim filii dei sumus, semper oportet esse in generatione. Unde dicitur: 'Qui natus est ex deo, non peccat', sed generatio dei conservat eum. Sicut enim in deo filius semper et abeterno et ineternum nascitur: ita et nos semper oportet nasci, novari, generari. Illam enim generationem omnis mutatio creature significat anagogice, et hanc tropologice, et Ecclesie allegorice. Sic in scriptura dicitur de nobis, quod sumus infantes quasi modo geniti semper. Et ps. 71. 'florebunt sicut fenum terre'. Impii et carnales etiam comparantur feno, sed arescenti: nos florenti et non arenti, illi arenti et non florenti. Sed florere non potest, nisi continue novum fiat et crescat. Ergo si florentia feni nobis comparatur, non oportet nos marcescere, sed semper florere, semper ire de virtute in virtutem, de claritate in claritatem, ex fide in fidem. . . ." See also *Mannermaa* (1993, 11), who constructs on the basis of WA 1, 26-27 a theological ontology in Luther's thinking. "Von diesem Seinsverständnis her, nach dem der *actus producendi verbum* das Sein Gottes und in dem *esse divinum verbum* ist, entwirft Luther dann den knappen Grundriß einer allgemeinen Ontologie des geschaffenen Seins. Das leitende Prinzip liegt darin, daß alle Grundebenen des Seienden die *processio verbi* in Gott stufenweise vertreten. . . . Alle diese Seinstufen spiegeln je auf ihre Weise das Hervorgehen des Wortes innerhalb der Heiligen Trinität wieder."

42. WA 3, 303:20-26: ". . . Nomen domini non dat sanctis bonum aliud quam est ipsummet: sed ipsummet est bonum eorum. Et sic dat seipsum et ita non dat, sed est bonum et tota beatitudo sanctorum. Nam sicut dicitur 'deus dat sanctis seipsum', quod valet 'Deus est bonum sanctorum suorum', ita etiam nomen eius dat seipsum illis, i.e. est bonum eorum. Est autem nomen dei ipse Christus filius dei, verbum quo se dicit et nomen quo se nominat ipsum in eternitate"; WA 3, 105:32-35: ". . . Dominus pars hereditatis mee, id est Spes et merces mea, et passionis mee, non est quid carnale et temporale, sed ipse dominusmet, id est spiritualia [quia dominus non habetur nisi in et cum spiritualibus bonis]."

43. WA 3, 429:24-28: "Secundo in gratuitis perceptis, scilicet sacramentis et bonis Ecclesie: que non minus tibi ministrat, quam totus mundus, cum ipsa sit

nothing before God, become "something" on the spiritual level of existence *(aliquid coram deo).*[44]

I think that his notion of the *creatio continua* makes at least partly understandable Luther's criticism in his early writings of the use of the terms *substantia* and *quidditas* in theology.[45] For him a creature is not *ens per se,* as he learned in the nominalist studybooks of natural philosophy. The extrinsic character, which belongs to every created being (i.e., its continuous dependence on the gifts of God, which it must receive in itself from outside of itself in order to remain in existence), makes it impossible for Luther to consider a creature as *substantia* or as *quidditas,* as something that has its principles of existence *(ens per se).*

That the being of the world is constituted in reception is understandable, because the one who stands metaphysically opposite to the world, God, is in his essence pure giving. His divinity consists in his free, unselfish love.[46] Even though the world is very deeply distorted by the sin of humankind, we can still see that the foundation of created being is the divine *agape*-love: according to Luther, all creatures except the human naturally follow the principle of *agape.*[47]

4. Being as a Reality with an Extrinsic and an Intrinsic Aspect

I said previously that Ebeling's notion of the actualizing and relational character of Luther's ontology is in some sense correct. Still, he errs in stating that the implication of this dynamic character is that Luther denies the intrinsic character of being altogether, that he claims that the

---

mundus quidam intellectualis. Igitur vitam, sensum, esse, intelligere, victum et amictum in spiritualibus, ministerium solis iustitie, coeli et terre et omnium que sunt in Ecclesia bonorum accipis sine intermissione."

44. WA 3, 43:18-20: "Vides igitur, quod propheta exquisitissime agnoscit accepta dona Dei, que, ut dixi, omnia sub iustitia continentur et misericordia, saltem spiritualia, quibus homo coram Deo aliquid sit."

45. See WA 3, 419:25-38; *Juntunen* 1996, 187-89, 416-26.

46. See WA 3, 102:31-32, 349:35-39, WA 4, 269:25-30, 278:7, 15-35.

47. See WA 4, 593:4-9, WA 56, 177:25-31, WA 2, 581:2-9, AWA 2, 48:11-21; *Raunio* 1993, 129-30, 163-64, 222-26.

"Werde-Charakter" of existence makes impossible a *"Seins-Charakter."*
One can see the incorrectness of this view in Luther's first *Commentary
on the Psalter* (*Dictata super psalterium,* 1513-1515), where he more
or less explicitly discusses the ontological nature of God's actions in the
world. He divides these actions into two categories.[48] The first is God's

48. WA 3, 154:3-13: "Distinguit propheta hic opera Iudeorum et opera
manuum eorum. Similiter et opera dei et opera manuum eius. . . . Opera Dei
sunt, que Deus vult a nobis fieri et sunt secundum deum [Gal. 5 opera spiritus
et fructus], ut Ezre 4 'Urgerent opus domini', Ioh. 6 'Quid faciemus, ut operemur
opera dei?' Et sic more philosophorum opera dei sunt opera cause secunde volita
a causa prima precipue hominum. Opera manuum autem dei sunt creature ipse
seu facture, ut more philosophorum ipse cause secunde: talia enim solus Deus
facit, ut sunt opera creationis, iustificationis, redemptionis, scilicet quando facit
creaturas, sanctos et beatos"; 155:38–156:14: "Et recte dicit 'opera' et 'opera
manuum'. Quia opera manuum sunt, que manu fieri solent, ut figuralia et
artificiata et effecta seu facta, opera autem etiam aliorum organorum sunt, ut
oculorum, pedum. Quare sola manuum opera exprimunt factibilia. Alia autem
sunt agibilia. Sic similiter ad deum eodem modo. Opera dei sunt agibilia vel acta
ipsa, opera autem manuum sunt factilia seu facta [infra ps. 63]. Quia deus omnia
facit et cum omnibus agit, et opera eius sunt usus factorum, quia illis utitur in
operibus suis, in factis autem nullo utitur. Sicut et homo factis utitur ad operan-
dum. Et aliud est agere et facere in homine. . . . Est et alia doctrina illorum, quia
acta transeunt et sunt nullius existentie, facta autem prestant, unde recte Ecclesia
et Incarnatio Christi sunt facta dei, et opera eorum seu acta eius sunt opera dei,
ut supra 'Annunciaverunt opera dei et facta eius intellexerunt' "; WA 3, 368:14-
16: "Aliter quoque intelligi possunt opera ad modum, quo supra ps. 27. expositum
est, ut opera dei sint acta in Christo et Ecclesia: facta autem sint ipse Christus et
Ecclesia tanquam cause secunde operum dei"; WA 4, 189:1-25: "Sepissime dictum
est de operibus dei, quomodo sint duplicia, scilicet facta et acta. Sed per acta
proveniunt facta. Et primum de Christo, cuius opus actionis fuit euangelisare:
sed opus factionis fuit Ecclesia, quam constituit per opus actionis sue. . . . Quare
notandum, quod duplex est mundus seu creatura: Visibilis, quem prius fecit et
deinde cum illo egit et operatur. Hic enim prius est factura quam operatio. Nam
cum omni creatura agit, qui facit eam. Nam et hec opera creature recte 'opera
domini' dicuntur, sicut ipsa quoque est opus manuum eius. Invisibilis, intelligibilis
per fidem Ecclesia, que vocatur novum celum et nova terra. Et hic sunt facture
dei Apostoli, prophete, doctores, 1. Corin. 12, sicut partes integrales huius mundi
et opera manuum eius seu facta, que fecit. Sed opera seu acta, quibus ista fecit,
sunt opera virtutum et maxime predicationis. Quia verbum dei est instrumentum,
quo operans effecit istam facturam, sicut ait: 'Verbo domini coeli firmati sunt
&c.' Sicut et prima creatio verbo dei facta est velut medio actionis"; WA 4,

acta: these are acts that God, the *actus primus* of all that happens in creation, produces through creatures. Creatures are only *causae secundae* of their works, since they are in their existence and in their causal power totally dependent on God's desire that they exist and that he works as the *causa prima* of their actions. These *acta dei,* which God causes through creatures, are "actualistic" events: They are without intrinsic being and duration *(acta transeunt et sunt nullius existentiae).*[49] One such an event could be, for example, scoring the puck in the upper right corner of the goal, which God, the *causa prima* of all events, causes to happen through a *causa secunda,* Teemu Selänne.

The second category is God's *facta:* God's creation of a *factum,* an existing thing, which possesses some intrinsic being and duration *(facta praestant),*[50] even though it is nonetheless totally dependent on God's continuous causal sustenance. To this ontological category describing God's actions in the world also belongs Teemu Selänne, because he is an existing creature, a "thing," and not just an *actus,* like the event, in which he as God's *causa secunda* and cooperator shoots the puck past the goalie.

My theme, however, is not ice hockey but Luther's claim that

444:26-32: "Opera dei sunt duplicia: primo facta seu creata, secundo operationes in illis factis: sicut differunt agere et facere, agibilia et factibilia, acta et facta, actus et facture. Et si versus loquitur de primo et visibili mundo, tunc sensus est, quod in illis actis et factis mystice intellexerit acta et facta novi et spiritualis mundi, que est Ecclesia. Cuius facture sunt singuli fideles creati in Christo Ephes. 2 et Iacob. 1. Actus autem et opera sunt eorum virtutes et merita, que Christus in illis operatur."

Against my interpretation the accusation can be raised that it is based on a relatively early text and would therefore not be relevant to the theology of Luther's later "reformatory" theology. Against this accusation I can only say that the modern standard interpretations of Luther's ontology that are opposed to mine are also very much based on the *Dictata* (I mean the interpretations of *Ebeling* and *Joest*).

It is interesting to note that Luther knows a similar ontological division in a much later text. In a letter from 1543 to a pastor called Wolferinus he discusses the question whether the sacraments are *actiones* (i.e., actualistic events) or *factiones* (i.e., more durable and stable ontological realities) (see WA Br 10, 338-39, 341, footnote 8, 340:16-22; *Jolkkonen* 1996, 22-23).

49. WA 3, 156:11-14 (see previous footnote).
50. WA 3, 156:11-14 (see footnote 48).

persons are in both their natural and spiritual existence *factura* and not *actus*.[51] This point already proves that the existentialist Luther-interpretation concerning the dynamic and nonstatic nature of spiritual existence (i.e., *"nicht Sein, sondern Werden"*)[52] is incorrect. Essential to understanding the continuous flow of God's spiritual gifts to the Christian is that, even when this flow is continuous and thus dynamic and nonstatic, God actually creates something through these sacramental gifts (i.e., through Christ, who is the hidden content of these gifts).[53] This "something" has an ontological status beyond that of a mere happening *(actus)*: it is a *factum gratiae*. The continuous flow of God's spiritual gift causes being *(esse gratiae)*, which is ontologically totally dependent on God and his continuous creating activity but which still has a certain intrinsic moment in its ontological structure. I will discuss later what is this intrinsic moment of being in the *esse gratiae*. It is enough to note here that for Luther it clearly cannot be anything like the scholastic idea of habitual grace.

That Luther views Christians as having in their spiritual existence a degree of intrinsic being (i.e., *"auch Sein und nicht nur Werden"*) is clear from his claim that the ontological axiom *"agere sequitur esse"* is correct not only in the natural but also in the spiritual realm of existence.[54] Just as that which possesses *esse* on the natural level of existence can on this basis *do* something *(agere)*, so one who possesses *esse in spiritualibus*, that is, who is united by faith to Christ and has received him as the principle of spiritual being, does deeds *in spiritualibus* (i.e., prays, loves other people and helps them, praises

51. See footnote 48. From it can be seen that for Luther there are not only two kinds of *facta*, namely, *facta gratiae* and *facta naturae*, but also a third kind, *facta gloriae*, which he understands as the mode of existence of the saints in heaven. I don't treat this third mode of existence in this paper, because already enough disagreement can be found in the present state of Luther-scholarship concerning the levels of *facta naturae* and *facta gratiae* alone. Another reason for leaving the *facta gloriae* out of discussion is that this theme doesn't have as much ecumenical relevance as a correct understanding of the modes of *facta naturae* and *facta gratiae*; I think the *facta gloriae* have already solved all their ecumenical disagreements.

52. See footnotes 32-33.

53. See footnote 42.

54. WA 56, 117:25-29, 442:2-9, WA 1, 226:8-9; *Peura* 1994, 144; *Juntunen* 1996, 299-301.

God, etc.).[55] Luther's *agere in spiritu* follows in an "ontological" and spontaneous way from *esse in spiritu,* because the continuous reception of the *dona gratiae* creates a being who also possesses some intrinsic features, such as the capacity to act by virtue of being. Faith is not only an existential relation to something, which stays outside the believer, but is a relation that causes a principle *(forma)* of spiritual being *(esse)* and spiritual action *(agere)* to be received *inside* the believer, as a new spiritual reality.[56] The presence of this spiritual *forma* produces a spiritual existence that is not only a "becoming" *(Werden)* in extrinsic relation to God, but also a "being" *(Sein)*.

Earlier I said that Ebeling's claim concerning the relational character of Luther's ontology is partially correct. It is correct in the sense that Luther (like every theologian whose thinking is based on the notion of *creatio*)[57] does believe that all beings exist through a relation of creatureliness to God, who constitutes their existence. Yet Ebeling has not adequately thought through the nature of this relation.[58] Before one claims that Luther's ontology is relational, one should consider carefully what kind of relation one means.

An important issue in the medieval discussion about the nature of *relatio* concerned whether relations are completely mind-dependent *(relatio rationis)* or rather have some sort of extramental reality *(relatio realis)*. A second issue involved the question how such an extramental reality might exist. Can relations be reduced to the things that stand in relation with one another? Or are they their accidents? According to Henninger, all medievals agreed that real relations exist independently of the mind. The question under debate concerned the nature of their existence. And most agreed that a real relation bears

55. See the previous footnote and *Raunio* 1993, 315-17.
56. About the thought *"Christus forma fidei,"* see WA 40.1, 228:27–229:32; *Mannermaa* 1989, 20, 35-39.
57. See *Schönberger* 1994, 47.
58. This is very understandable. Medieval theologians, learned fellows like Albert the Great, Henry of Ghent, and Aegidius Romanus, said that the *relatio* is a very difficult thing to understand (*Schönberger* 1994, 47). I can't say that I have understood it, neither the medieval discussion nor the *relatio* of Luther's theology. The following simple thoughts are based on what I could grasp from *Henninger's* (1989) and *Schönberger's* (1994) excellent works about the medieval *relatio*-discussion.

two aspects of being: (1) its "being-in" *(esse-in)* and (2) its "being-toward" *(esse-ad)*.[59]

Expressed in medieval terminology, then, Ebeling seems to have in mind the notion of a relation that bears primarily the *esse-ad* aspect and very little if any *esse-in* aspect. For him external relations, not substances, constitute the world.[60] If spiritual existence in relation to God has any *esse in,* it can be characterized only as a new existential mode of being (the new self-understanding claimed through the forgiveness of God).[61]

59. See *Henninger* 1989, 3-7, 12, 174-84.

In Aquinas's thinking both aspects of these are mutually important. Characteristic for his theory about relations (as for many other theories of the *via antiqua*) is that the *esse-in* was thought to be an accident inhering in a thing that stands in relation (*Henninger* 1989, 175-76, 13-17, 19-23). In later theories this notion became untenable, e.g., because the relation of being created, which constitutes the existence of all creatures, cannot be understood as an accident: for this relation does not involve just an accident of a creature but the creature in itself, in its essence, who receives existence from God (*Schönberger* 1994, 87, 92-94, 97). The extrinsic aspect of the *relatio,* the *esse-ad,* took a more predominant role; and the *esse-in* was understood as a *modus* of the existence of the whole *relatum* and not as something inhering in it (see *Henninger* 1989, 177-81, 53, 128).

60. See footnote 2.

61. The emphasis in Ebeling's Luther-interpretation on the extrinsic aspect of relations and on the new mode of existential self-understanding as the only "intrinsic aspect" in the relation of the believer to God might bring to mind a certain development in the medieval *relatio*-discussion: the *esse-ad* of a real relation became increasingly important and the *esse-in* was interpreted as a *modus* of the being of the whole *relatum* (i.e., of the individual substance), not as something inhering in it (see footnote 59).

It is interesting that Ockham and other thinkers who emphasize the *esse-ad* of *relatio* and interpret the *esse-in* as a *modus* of the existence of the *relatum* do *not* have an ontology that is based on relations, such as that which Joest and Ebeling claim to have found in Luther's thought. E.g., for Ockham the individual substances and not their relations are what constitute the world. Relations are not ontological entities. Relative terms are connotations that signify substances (*Henninger* 1989, 128). The ontological status that is given to relations in these theories is very different from that which the Luther-interpretations of Joest and Ebeling give to them. Accordingly, Joest and Ebeling are correct in writing that the relational ontology that they claim to have found in Luther's theology is very different from all that preceded it (see *Ebeling* 1971, 24; *Joest* 1967, 36).

Luther's notion of the concept of *relatio* has not so far been studied. I think that Luther has not been very explicit on this subject, thus making it a very difficult theme to explore.[62] Still, I dare say that Ebeling's presupposition that Luther employs a primarily extrinsic *(esse-ad)* notion of *relatio* in his theological ontology is not correct. Certainly for Luther the person's natural relation to God (i.e., created-ness) as well as one's spiritual relation to God (i.e., the *esse gratiae*) both have extrinsic *(esse-ad)* and intrinsic *(esse-in)* aspects. By the *esse-ad* aspect I refer to the continuous need of the person to be made *nihil ex se,*[63] to be made open and empty toward God in order to receive both the natural and the spiritual gifts of God which together raise the person into existence before God.

We must pay attention as well to the *esse-in* aspect of the relation. Certainly Luther would deny that this aspect of one's relation to God is accidental.[64] The relation in question is that of being created, and it gives to persons more than mere accidents; it gives them all that they are or ever can be. This is true not only of the *esse naturae* but also of the *esse gratiae*. In both of these God creates, and in both he gives more than mere accidents. He gives *esse* and he makes *facturae,* namely, the *facturae gratiae* and the *facturae naturae*. Even in the area of *esse gratiae* the *esse-in* aspect of the relation to God does not imply mere accident in the human subject. It refers to a completely new being and not just to something accidental.

The intrinsic aspect of being in Luther's theology is clarified as we turn to the question about being as participation.

62. According to my understanding, a study of this theme, together with studies of the notions of *affectus* and *substantia,* and one that explores whether the Reformer has a general ontology based on the notion of participation, would at this point be most important contributions for the future evolution of Luther-scholarship.

63. See *Juntunen,* 1996, 407-9.

64. As previously noted (footnote 59), it was commonplace already much before Luther to deny that the *esse-in* of a relation is an accident inhering in the *relata*.

5. Being as Participation in God

Common in the theological metaphysics of the classical period and of the Middle Ages was the position that created, contingent *esse* is a limited form of participation in the primary and absolute *esse* of God.[65] This idea was often linked with the supposition that contingent and created being can exist only "within" the divine *esse*, in its presence. The difference between God and the created world cannot be a spatial difference. An *ens* can exist only within the range of *esse*, by having a share of *esse*.[66] God did not create the world outside of his divine reality, because outside of him, of *esse* in the proper sense of the word, is absolutely nothing, the *nihil negativum*. God in creation "called the world out of nothingness into being," to participate in his being. This is why the difference between God and created reality cannot be spatial. It is a metaphysical difference between an original and independent reality *(esse per se)* and the metaphysically lower, contingent reality *(ens per aliud)*.[67]

William of Ockham rejected altogether this ontology based on the notion of participation. Ockham does not seek "behind" the concrete individual substance to find any principle of being such as *esse* or *essentia*. Rather, he denies ontological meaning to such terms. Both *esse* and *essentia* are terms that signify the same individual

---

65. *Augustine,* De gen. ad litt., 8, 26, 48 (PL 34, 391-92), De civ. dei, 12, 2 (PL 41, 350), Sermo 7, 7 (PL 38, 66-67), En. in ps. 101, sermo 2, 10 (PL 37, 1311); *Bernhard of Clairvaux,* De considerat., 5, 14 (3, 478:22–479:2), De div., s. 4, 2 (6.1, 95); *Bonaventura,* In sent., 1, ds37, p1, ar1, qu1 (1, 639); *Thomas Aquinas,* S. theol., 1, qu8, ar1, co (Busa, 2, 194); *Meister Eckhart,* LW 4, 207:11–208:11; *Juntunen* 1996, 175-79.

66. *Kremer* (1969, 29, 47-48) gives, e.g., the following examples: *Augustine:* Conf. IV, 12, 18; I, 2, 2; VII, 11, 17; VII, 15, 21; XI, ii, 13; En. in ps. 113, 1, 14 (CChr.SL 40, 1640f.); 122, 4 (CChr.SL 40, 1816:1–1817:46); De gen. ad litt. IV, 18; VII, 26, 268:17-20; *Ambrosius:* De fide I, 16, 106 (PL 16, 552 D–552 A); *Hieronymus:* In Isaiam XVIII, 66, 1 (PL 24, 652 A); Comm. in Epist. ad Ephes. I, 2 (PL 26, 472f.); *Hilarius of Poitiers:* De Trin. II, 6 (PL 10, 55); *Bernhard of Clairvaux:* De consid. V, 6 (PL 182, 796 C, D); *Bonaventura:* 1 Sent. 36 dub. IV; II 22a; De pot. Dei III, 16, ad 24; *Meister Eckhart:* LW II, 372:10f.; LW II, 328:7f.; LW II, 459:1f.

67. See *Juntunen* 1996, 175-80.

substance viewed according to different connotations.[68] The creation cannot therefore be described as God effusing to creation the *esse commune,* nor does the existence that the creature receives imply a certain kind, limited by the *essentia,* of participation in God's unlimited *esse.* For Ockham no ontological principles of existence lurk behind the concrete individual substance. God's absolute will alone is able to bring into existence the individual substance as such. To say that an individual is created does not signify the being of anything other than the individual and God, who wills it to be.[69] The notion of participation loses its meaning, as does the idea that God's presence is required in a creature in order for it to exist. That God wants something to be does not mean that he has to be present in it. According to Ockham God's will can act from a distance to cause a being,[70] which was impossible according to the older view based on the notion of participation.[71]

When we think that Luther received an Ockhamist methodological education of which he approves even later in his theological career,[72] it seems impossible that he could base his idea of being on the notion of participation, that he could think that the existence of a creature consists in a certain kind, limited by the *essentia,* of participation in the absolute *esse,* God.

We should understand, however, that Ockhamist ontology (according to which only individual substances and their accidents are real), based on the theory of *suppositio,*[73] could not make a total breakthrough in all areas of theology. Luther's teachers Jodocus Trutvetter and Bartholomaus Usingen, who wanted to renew teaching at the University of Erfurt and bring it into line with orthodox Ockhamist tradition, were actually themselves Ockhamist only in their logic. When they treated themes like creation or the existence of creatures in their natural philosophy, they could imply the concept of *participatio* in a way that was contradictory to Ockham's basic

---

68. *Leff* 1975, 166-67.
69. *Ockham,* Quodl., 7, qu1 (OT 9, 703:1–704:27); *Leff* 1975, 463-64.
70. See *Ockham,* Ord., 1, ds37, qu.un, resp. (OT 2, 566:16-18, 568:12-13).
71. See, e.g., *Thomas Aquinas,* S.theol., 1, qu8, ar1, co (Busa, 2, 194).
72. See *White* 1994, 26-32.
73. See, e.g., *Leff* 1975, 135, 139, 149.

intentions.[74] The education which Luther received can be called Ock-hamist only in a limited sense. That his teachers did not pay much attention to contradiction between the use of the *suppositio* theory and the ontological use of the concept of participation leads one to think that Luther might have understood created being as participation in God, though as a good "terminist" he should not have done so.[75]

Some basic lines of thought in Luther's theology seem to indicate that for him the existence of created being in general implies participation in God. One such line of thought is his emphasis on the omnipresence of God, that is, his presence in each being at the basis of its existence.[76] The whole created world is for Luther a mask and

74. See *Trutvetter*, SITP, Lib1, cap1, a6: "Nam hoc ipsum dum eternaliter in se ipso absque omni mutabilitate consisteret quatenus bonitatem suam extra se diffunderet, sub consonanti quadam differentia res differenter suam perfectionem participantes producturum ex tempore (dum nihil extra se fuisset) creavit de nihilo (: sive post nihil in esse prodire iussit) . . ."; SITP, lb8, tr1, z5: "Naturalissimum operum in viventibus est quecumque perfecta sunt: non orbata et generationem spontaneam non habentia facere alterum tale quale ipsum est: ut animal quoddam animal et planta plantam: quetenus ipsi esse divino et immortali participient secundum illud quod possunt"; *Usingen*, PPN, fo 121: ". . . et quia essentia dei est similitudo omnium rerum in hoc quod est idea omnium aliarum rerum ideo cognoscens se simul cognoscit omnia que relucent in eo. Et quia omnis res habet ideam in mente divina secundum illos ideo secundum illam cognoscitur a deo. Et ponunt illi multas ideas in mente divina indistincta tamen menti divine. Sed ad illum sensum quod res multipliciter imitantur deum secundum diversos gradus perfectionis quos deus continet per excellentiam et est una perfectio quam differenter participant creature secundum quam differentiam nominatur multe idee. Et sic asinus habet aliam ideam in mente divina quam homo scilicet alia ratione cognoscitur producendus vel productus quia secundum alium gradum perfectionis."

75. I think the reason that the concept of participation was not altogether abandoned with the acceptance of Ockhamist *suppositio*-theory was that this theory, in destroying the traditional conceptual tools of theology, did not yield any new possibilities to treat such theologically important themes as the presence of the Transcendent in creation or the ontological dependence of the *already existent* being of God. It is even more understandable that the *participatio*-metaphysics was used even after Ockham when we keep in mind that one could find this way of thinking in the texts of authors who were considered authoritative, such as Augustine.

76. See, e.g., WA 3, 407:22-29, WA 4, 255:19-23, WA 23, 133-36, 138; *Juntunen* 1996, 184-86.

a hiding place of God. In it not only the lovely things, like birds, but also every kernel of wheat under the dirt and the dung speaks about its creator.[77] Of note also is Luther's praise of the concept of *participatio* in the philosophical portion of the Heidelberg disputation[78] and his moderately cautious acceptance of the traditional view concerning the preexistence of created beings as ideas of the divine Logos *(esse virtuale)*.[79] These might indicate that for Luther all created being implies participation in God.

Still, I think that this question concerning participation and *esse naturae* in general should be left open until someone makes a

77. WA 37, 119:27-32, WA 4, 643:11-18.

78. WA 59, 425:11–426:10: "Imitatio numerorum in rebus ingeniose asseritur a Pythagora, sed ingeniosius participatio idearum a Platone. . . . Secunda pars patet ex Platone in Parmenide, ubi pulcherrima disputatione primum exuit illud unum et ideam, donec omnia ei auferat et ipsum nihil esse relinquat. Rursum illud idem induit omnibus, donec nihil relinquitur, in quo non sit illud unum, et nihil sit, quod non imposito uno sit. Et sic est extra omnia et tamen intra omnia, quomodo et beatus Augustinus libro 1 De vera religione disputat. Ista autem participatio et separatio unius seu ideae magis potest intelligi quam dici, imo numeri intelligi quam vere est." See *Juntunen* 1996, 43-44, footnote 14, 190, footnote 114.

79. WA 10.1.1, 199:17–200:18: "Sihe, disser vorstand ist eynfelltig und besserlich, wie S. Paulus die lere des Euangelii pflegt tzu nennen doctrinam pietatis, eyn lere, die den menschen gnadenreych machet. Aber der ander vorstand, den auch die heyden haben, das alle creatur ynn got leben, macht woll subtile schwetzer, ist auch finster und schwere, leret aber nichts von der gnade, macht auch keyn gnadreiche menschen, darumb die schrifft sich seyn alss eynss furwitzigen eusserett. Wie man nu Christus wort aussslegt, da er sagt: Ich bynn das leben, allso soll man ditz auch aussslegen, gar nichts von dem leben der creaturn ynn gott auff philosophisch, ssondern widderumb wie Gott ynn unss lebe und seyniss lebens unss teylhafftig mache, das wyr durch yhn, von yhm, und ynn yhm leben; denn das ist auch nit tzu leugnen, das durch yhn auch das naturlich leben besteht, das auch die unglewbigen von ihm haben, alss Paulus sagt Act. 17: Wyr leben ynn yhm und schweben ynn yhm und wessen ynn yhm und sind seyner artt. Ja, das naturlich leben ist eyn stuck vom ewigen leben und eyn anfang, aber es nympt durch den todt seyn end, darumb, das es nit erkennet und ehret den, von dem es herkompt, dieselb sund schneydet es ab, das es muss sterben ewiglich. Widderumb die da glewben und erkennen den, von dem sie leben, sterben nymmermehr, ssondernn das naturlich leben wirt gestreckt ynss ewige leben"; *Juntunen* 1996, 267-71, 352-53.

thorough investigation into this neglected aspect of the Reformer's thought. On the other hand, as far as spiritual existence — the *esse gratiae* — is in question, clearly this *esse* means for Luther participation in God through Christ. According to Luther a Christian is "in Christ"; the Christian exists in him through participation in him. One is righteous because one is posited in Christ.[80]

I have treated Luther's ontology previously by beginning from his idea of continuous creation, which occurs analogically in both *esse naturae* and *esse gratiae*. I have also stated that in both of these types of being, the relation of being created (naturally and spiritually) has both aspects of *esse-ad* and *esse-in*. The *esse-ad* aspect refers to how in both *esse naturae* and *esse gratiae* a person is continuously *nihil ex se* and needs to receive God's creative love in order to remain in existence. The *esse-in* aspect refers to how the result of this creative love is ontologically something more than an event, namely a *factura (factura naturae, factura gratiae)*. Both of these aspects, the extrinsic *(esse-ad)* and the intrinsic *(esse-in)*, in respect to the relation of the person to God, can be viewed alternatively from the standpoint of Luther's claim that the *esse gratiae* of a person is realized as participation in God.

Precisely this *participatio*-nature of *esse gratiae* enables Luther to deny effectively that spiritual reality is something accidental in the

---

80. In other words, because Christ gives himself to him in faith to his righteousness *(favor* and *donum)*. See, e.g., WA 3, 46:17-25: "Quoniam Christus est caput omnium sanctorum, fons omnium, origo omnium rivulorum, ex quo participant omnes, et de plenitudine eius omnes accipiunt. . . . Ac sicut omnes sui sancti fluunt ex ipso velut rivuli, ita Scriptura conformiter sese habens et ita representans ipsum cum suis sanctis, primo fontali sensu de ipso loquitur. Deinde eundem sensum derivat in rivulos (id est particulares expositiones) participative de sanctis loquens eadem verba. Si enim in gratia cum eo participant, et hereditant omnia ex ipso"; WA 3, 56:32-37: "Differunt sperare in domino et in dominum: Quia sperare in domino est in Christo deo nostro esse et participare ei ac sic in ipso existendo sperare in Dominum. In ipso enim et cum ipso et per ipsum audemus sperare et omne opus offerre. Quia sine ipso nihil possumus facere. Quantumvis ergo sis sanctus et iustus, cave, unquam per te vel in tua iustitia speres in dominum"; WA 3, 210:33: "Econtra bonum est quod iustus est: quia in Christum positus est"; WA 56, 233:30-33; *Peura* 1994; *Mannermaa* 1996, 383-91.

human subject. But it also enables him to hold the thought that the spiritual reality is an *esse*, a reality of a *factura gratiae*. Spiritual reality can never be an accident such that a person might control or modify it, for example, in making oneself a better person per se; for this *esse* is realized in the person as a participation in something, something present in the person that still has its own substantial reality. In such participation the person always stays spiritually *nihil ex se*, having *esse gratiae* only when and insofar as he or she participates in Christ. *Esse* in the proper sense of the word is not something that comes from the one who participates; it is something that is derived from him in whom one participates.[81]

The concept of participation clarifies that the spiritual relation to God also has the *esse-in* aspect: that which is participated in has to be present in that which participates. Luther speaks about this point frequently. For him the indwelling of Christ in the believer through his Spirit is not a matter of the sanctification of the believer in the sense that in it something would be added to what is the most important thing — justification — in which the spiritual existence is given. No, for Luther the spiritual existence *(esse gratiae)* is *eo ipso* the participation of a person in Christ, who gives himself to individuals as their righteousness and all anyone spiritually is and ever can be.[82] I think the motto of a Coptic monk of our time, "My teacher is Jesus Christ, my food is Jesus Christ, the source of my actions is Jesus Christ," can very well serve as a pointer to the "Luther before Lutheranism," to whom the medium of spiritual existence was not the event of "forensic justification" but the divine person of Christ. Through his incarnation, death, resurrection, and ascension he has made it possible through the word and the sacraments to be himself the spiritual existence for a human being and to clarify that he (as his Father's Logos) has always been the source of the natural being of humankind as well.

81. *Juntunen* 1996, 313-320, 406, 196-199.
82. See, e.g., WA 40.1, 228:27–229:32, WA 56, 233:30-33; *Mannermaa* 1989, 37-38.

6. Two Major Differences between the Structures of *esse naturae* and of *esse gratiae*

I have written many words about the new spiritual reality that Luther himself could not describe with human words.[83] Even if my efforts are in vain, I would like to say two things that can be expressed when we take as a point of departure Luther's claim that *esse gratiae* is participation in Christ.

First, the notion of participation clarifies that even when the *esse naturae* and the *esse gratiae* are analogical,[84] they are not univocal; that is, many important differences obtain between them, despite some similarities. In *esse gratiae* the incarnated God himself is the actual content of the *dona gratiae,* through which this *esse* is given. The *esse gratiae* is a participation in Christ, who comes into a very intense union with the believer[85] but who nonetheless remains

---

83. Luther's metaphors concerning what the new spiritual reality in faith is are always partial and describe only a small aspect of it at one time. When the concepts used in these metaphors tell something about this reality, they at the same time connote many other lines of thought that are to be denied. That Christ is the spiritual *forma* of the Christian, e.g., expresses that Christ is present in believers and causes their entire spiritual existence and is not just an accident in them, just as the *forma substantialis* of each being causes its whole existence according to the normal use of the scheme, where the concept of *forma* appears. But at the same time, though expressing what for Luther are essential aspects of spiritual reality, this metaphor connotes many unacceptable lines of thought, such as that Christ becomes a real part of the very essence of the human person. This is, of course, not true for Luther because Christ, as a divine person who (even when being also totally human) has created the believer, cannot be something that is part of that essence. The possibilities of human language can be stretched a little further by making use of another metaphor: Believers have two substances, the human substance and that which is united with it (though not mingled with it) as a substantial reality in it, i.e., Christ's substance (*Peura* 1994, 228, 238-43). But this metaphor fails because it can bring to mind some sort of schizophrenic reality that is not Luther's idea.

84. In both, e.g., the result of God's continuous creating activity is a *factura* and not just an event *(actus);* and in both types the axiom *"agere sequitur esse"* is relevant.

85. Luther says, e.g., that in faith some sort of *communicatio idiomatum* is forged with Christ and the Christian. The Christian receives the divine and

his own substantial reality without becoming part of the essence of the believer or being reduced to an accident in this essence. In the *esse naturae* God is also present in his *dona naturalia,* but not in the same way as he is in the *dona spiritualia.* The *dona naturalia* do make God present in such a strong way in those who receive them, as in those who receive the *dona gratiae.* If we are to interpret the *esse naturae* in Luther's theology as a participation in God's being, clearly, this participation is mediated in a way that does not cause the divine *esse* to be united with the created *esse.*[86]

Second, another difference between these types of being can be noted through the concept of participation. It can be expressed in the following way: The claim that the axiom *"agere sequitur esse"* is equally true in both *esse naturae* and *esse gratiae* is not altogether correct. One has a smaller role in the actions of the *esse gratiae* than in those of the *esse naturae,* where one is a *causa secunda.* Even in *esse naturae* the person is totally dependent on God, but here God's effect causes a *factura,* whose principle of action is the created human essence. In the realm of *esse gratiae* the principle of action does not belong to the created essence of the believer but is a participation in the uncreated reality of Christ's person. Persons are also agents in a stronger sense in their *esse naturae* than in their *esse gratiae.*[87] This does not mean that the axiom *"agere sequitur esse"* is not true in the *esse gratiae.* Luther understands the participation of the believer in Christ as something so "ontologically intense" that the actions which Christ works in a Christian can be considered the actions of this Christian in question

---

good attributes of Christ, such as righteousness, wisdom, and happiness; and Christ at the same time bears the sinful attributes of the Christian. Because of the intensity and reality of this *communicatio idiomatum,* Luther doesn't shun the idea that the Christian is made divine in the *unio cum Christo,* something more than just a human being *(mehr als ein Mensch).* See *Peura* 1994, 301-2.

86. See *Juntunen* 1996, 198-99.

87. See WA 4, 241:20-23: "Quod autem opus creature tribuit deo, indicat, quod de nova creatura loquitur, in qua omnia operatur deus ipse, ut Isaie 43. 'Omnia opera nostra in nobis tu operatus es domine'. Et Iohan. 14. 'Sine me nihil potestis facere'. Sic ergo 'opus eius' dicitur, quia nos ex ipso illud operamur"; WA 4, 241:15-16: ". . . creatura est opus domini, et tamen etiam creatura habet opus suum proprium"; *Juntunen* 1996, 172-74, 200.

himself.[88] Luther refers to such a possibility of spontaneous action springing up from the reality of a new spiritual being when he speaks about the *"agere sequitur esse in spiritualibus."* Christ does not work in a Christian only as an extrinsic "power" *(Macht),*[89] but also as the principle of spiritual being and spiritual action who gives himself to the Christian in such a way that Christ becomes intrinsic in the Christian. It is understandable, then, that Luther can speak about the *cooperatio* of the believer with God in the spiritual realm of existence and, at the same time, claim that a person is always spiritually *nihil ex se.*[90]

Bibliography

Authors of the Middle Ages (Selected)

Bartholomaeus of Usingen

PPN   Parvulus philosophia naturalis. — Wolfgang Stöckel. Leipzig, in vigilia S. Matthiae 1499. Bibliothek Wolfenbüttel.

Jodocus Trutvetter

STP   Summa in totam physicen: hoc est philosophiam naturalem conformiter siquidem vere sophie: que est theologia per Jodocum Jsennchensis. Maler. Effordie 1514. Bibliothek Wolfenbüttel.

Martin Luther

AWA   Archiv zur Weimarer Ausgabe der Werke Martin Luthers. Texte und Untersuchungen. Hrsg. und bearbeitet von Gerhard Hammer und Manfred Biersack. Köln, Wien 1981-.

WA   D. Martin Luthers Werke. Kritische Gesamtausgabe. Weimar 1883-.

WABr   D. Martin Luthers Werke. Kritische Gesamtausgabe. Briefwechsel. Weimar 1930-

WAT   D. Martin Luthers Tischreden. Weimar 1912.

88. WA 3, 257:10-14: "Ergo opera, que feci et que mihi foecit, narrabo ad honorem regis. . . . Vel opera mea, i.e. opera Christi, que per participationem etiam mea sunt, dicam, quod non sint mea sed Regi. Ergo ei dicam et accepta referam."

89. See *Joest* 1967, 258-59.

90. See *Juntunen* 1996, 305-17, 341-47.

William Ockham

Ord.   Scriptum in primum Sententiarum (Ordinatio). — Guillelmi de
              Ockham, Opera Philosophica et Theologica. Cura Instituti Fran-
              ciscani Universitatis S. Bonaventurae. Opera Theologica, Bd.
              1-4. Ed. Gedeon Gá l, Stephanus Brown, Girardus I. Etzkorn et
              Franciscus E. Kelley. St. Bonaventure, N.Y. 1967-1979.

Quodl.   Quodlibeta Septem. — Opera Theologica, Bd. 9. Ed. Joseph C.
              Wey. St. Bonaventure, N.Y. 1980.

Quaest.   Quaestiones variae. — Opera Theologica, Bd. 8. Ed. Girardus I.
variae   Etzkorn, Franciscus E. Kelley et Josephus C. Wey. St. Bonaven-
              ture, N.Y. 1984.

Report., 2   Quaestiones in librum secundum Sententiarum (Reportatio). —
              Opera Theologica, Bd. 5. Ed. Gedeon Gá l et Rega Wood. St
              Bonaventure, N.Y. 1981.

Modern Authors

Ebeling, G.

1964   Luther. Einführung in sein Denken.

1971   Lutherstudien. Bd. I. Mohr. Tübingen.

1977   Lutherstudien. Bd. II. Disputatio de homine. Erster Teil. Text und
        Traditionshintergrund. Mohr. Tübingen.

1982   Lutherstudien. Bd. II. Disputatio de homine. Zweiter Teil. Die philo-
        sophische Definition des Menschen. Kommentar zu These 1-19.
        Mohr. Tübingen.

1985   Lutherstudien. Bd. III. Begriffsuntersuchungen — Textinterpreta-
        tionen — Wirkungsgeschichtliches. Mohr. Tübingen.

1989   Lutherstudien. Bd. II. Disputatio de homine. Dritter Teil. Die theo-
        logische Definition des Menschen. Kommentar zu These 20-40.
        Mohr. Tübingen.

Forsberg, J.

1984   Das Abrahambild in der Theologie Luthers. Pater fidei sanctissimus.
        Veröffentlichungen des Instituts für Europäische Geschichte Mainz.
        Abteilung Religionsgeschichte, Bd. 117. Steiner. Stuttgart.

Henninger, M. G.

1989   Relations. Medieval Theories 1250-1325. Clarendon Press. Oxford.

Joest, W.

1967 Ontologie der Person bei Luther. Vandenhoeck & Ruprecht. Göttingen.

Juntunen, S.

1996 Der Begriff des Nichts bei Luther in den Jahren von 1510 bis 1523. Schriften der Luther-Agricola-Gesellschaft, Bd. 36. Helsinki.

Jolkkonen, J.

1996 Kristuksen verta viemäriin? (Christ's blood into the drain?) — TA 1/1996, 18-27.

Kirjavainen, H.

1987 Die Spezifizierung der Glaubensgegenstände bei Luther im Licht der spätmittelalterlichen Semantik. In: Thesaurus Lutheri. Auf der Suche nach neuen Paradigmen der Luther-Forschung. Hrsg. von T. Mannermaa, A. Ghiselli, und S. Peura. Veröffentlichungen der finnischen theologischen Literaturgesellschaft, Bd. 153 in Zusammenarbeit mit der Luther-Agricola-Gesellschaft (Schrift A 24). Helsinki. Pg. 237-257.

Kopperi, K.

1993 Luthers theologische Zielsetzung in den philosophischen Thesen der Heidelberger Disputation. In: Nordiskt forum för studiet av Luther och luthersk teologi 1. Referate des ersten Forums für das Studium von Luther und lutherischer Theologie in Helsinki 21.-24.11.1991. Hrsg. von Tuomo Mannermaa mit Petri Järveläinen und Kari Kopperi. Schriften der Luther-Agricola-Gesellschaft, Bd. 28. Helsinki. Pg. 67-103.

Kremer, K.

1969 Gott und Welt in der klassischen Metaphysik. Stuttgart.

Leff, G.

1975 William of Ockham. The metamorphosis of scholastic discourse. Manchester University Press. Manchester.

Löfgren, D.

1960 Die Theologie der Schöpfung bei Luther. Forschungen zur Kirchen- und Dogmengeschichte, Bd. 10. Göttingen.

Malter, R.

1980 Das reformatorische Denken und die Philosophie. Luthers Entwurf einer transzendental-praktischen Metaphysik. Conscientia, Bd. 9. Bouvier. Bonn.

Mannermaa, T.

1989   Der im Glauben gegenwärtige Christus. Rechtfertigung und Vergottung. Zum ökumenischen Dialog. Arbeiten zur Geschichte und Theologie des Luthertums. Neue Folge, 8. Lutherisches Verlagshaus GmbH. Hannover.

1993   Hat Luther eine trinitarische Ontologie? In: Luther und Ontologie. Das Sein Christi als strukturierendes Prinzip der Theologie Luthers. Hrsg. von A. Ghiselli, K. Kopperi, und R. Vinke. Luther-Agricola-Gesellschaft, Helsinki und Martin-Luther-Verlag, Erlangen. Pg. 9-27.

1996   Über die Unmöglichkeit, gegen Texte Luthers zu systematisieren. Antwort an Gunther Wenz. In: Unio. Gott und Mensch in der nachreformatorischen Theologie. Hrsg von M. Repo und R. Vinke. Suomalaisen Teologisen Kirjallisuusseuran julkaisuja, 200 (Schriften der Luther-Agricola-Gesellschaft, 35). Helsinki. Pg. 381-91.

Metzke, E.

1961   Coincidentia oppositorum. Gesammelte Studien zur Philosophiegeschichte. Hrsg. von K. Gründer. Witten.

Peura, S.

1994   Mehr als ein Mensch? Die Vergöttlichung als Thema der Theologie Martin Luthers von 1513 bis 1519. Veröffentlichungen des Instituts für Europäische Geschichte Mainz. Abteilung Religionsgeschichte, Bd. 152. Verlag Philipp von Zabern. Mainz.

Raunio, A.

1993   Summe des christlichen Lebens. Die "Goldene Regel" als Gesetz der Liebe in der Theologie Martin Luthers von 1510 bis 1527. Reports from the Department of Systematic Theology, University of Helsinki, Bd. 13. Helsinki.

Saarinen, R.

1989   Gottes Wirken auf uns. Die transzendentale Deutung des Gegenwart-Christi-Motivs in der Lutherforschung. Veröffentlichungen des Instituts für Europäische Geschichte Mainz. Abteilung Religionsgeschichte, Bd. 137. Steiner. Wiesbaden.

Schönberger, R.

1994   Relation als Vergleich. Die Relationstheorie des Johannes Buridan im Kontext seines Denkens und der Scholastik. Studien und Texte zur Geistesgeschichte des Mittelalters, Bd. 43. E. J. Brill. Leiden–New York–Köln.

Työrinoja, R.

1987   Nova vocabula et nova lingua. Luther's Conception of Doctrinal Formulas. In: Thesaurus Lutheri. Auf der Suche nach neuen Paradigmen der Luther-Forschung. Hrsg. von T. Mannermaa, A. Ghiselli, und S. Peura. Veröffentlichungen der finnischen theologischen Literaturgesellschaft, Bd. 153 in Zusammenarbeit mit der Luther-Agricola-Gesellschaft (Schrift A 24). Helsinki. Pg. 221-36.

White, G.

1994   Luther as Nominalist. A Study of the Logical Methods Used in Martin Luther's Disputations in the Light of Their Medieval Background. Schriften der Luther-Agricola-Gesellschaft, Bd. 30. Helsinki.

zur Mühlen, K.-H.

1972   Nos extra nos. Luthers Theologie zwischen Mystik und Scholastik. Beiträge zur historischen Theologie, Bd. 46. Tübingen.

Response to Sammeli Juntunen, *"Luther and Metaphysics"*

DENNIS BIELFELDT

When searching for a dissertation topic for George Forell at the University of Iowa about ten years ago, I noticed a lack of secondary sources dealing with explicitly philosophical issues in Martin Luther's thought. I had just read Ulrich Asendorf's *Luther und Hegel* and was interested in Luther's ontology and semantics.[1] Unfortunately, I discovered little helpful literature at the time — although I can remember excitedly checking out Wilfried Joest's *Ontologie der Person bei Luther,* thinking that I would now know Luther's thinking on being.[2]

Lamentably, Joest's philosophically interesting and theologically suggestive analysis did not assist me in understanding the ontology of the historical Luther. Neither did the work of the great Luther interpreter, Gerhard Ebeling. From the standpoint of semantics, it seemed that although both men could plausibly model the *existential empowerment* aspect of Luther's theological language, they failed to pay sufficient attention to that language's *propositional content.* Considered from the point of view of ontology, while their existential-

---

1. Ulrich Asendorf, *Luther und Hegel* (Weisbaden: Franz Steiner Verlag, 1982).

2. Wilfried Joest, *Ontologie der Person bei Luther* (Göttingen: Vandenhoeck & Ruprecht, 1967).

hermeneutical starting points made sense of the believer's own onto-logical situation *coram deo,* their methods were inadequate when it came to grasping something Luther presupposed: the *in se* character of the ontology of the divine and its relation to the created order.

It was during these early days of my Luther study that I became convinced of the following positions:

1. Luther was not an irrationalist, but rather had a high regard for the powers of human reason. In fact, he was remarkably adept at logic and linguistic analysis.[3]
2. The so-called existentialist interpretation of Luther could not be sustained in the face of the Luther texts, for it failed to take seriously Luther's assumption that there was a definite ontologi-cal contour to the divine order, and the relationship between that order and the created realm. (I tried at that time to under-stand the theological order in Luther as an inversion of the ontological, an inversion that nonetheless presupposed the onto-logical.)[4]
3. The distinction between philosophy and theology was much more subtle and nuanced than most Luther interpreters had allowed, and semantic issues were crucially important in under-standing it.

I remember Forell telling me then that I must become acquainted with the Finnish school of Luther research, for I would discover kindred spirits there.

Unfortunately, I never got around to reading the Finns seriously until Risto Saarinen gave me a copy of *Thesaurus Lutheri* at the 1988 Luther congress in Oslo.[5] My immediate reaction was positive, for I

---

3. See Graham White, *Luther as Nominalist: A Study of the Logical Methods Used in Martin Luther's Disputations in the Light of Their Medieval Background* (Helsinki: Luther-Agricola-Society, 1994).

4. See Dennis Bielfeldt, "Luther, Metaphor, and Theological Language," *Modern Theology* 6 (January 1990): 121-35.

5. T. Mannermaa, A. Ghiselli, and S. Peura, eds., *Thesaurus Lutheri: Auf der Suche nach neuen Paradigmen der Luther-Forschung* (Helsinki: Luther-Agricola Gesellschaft, 1987).

was both stimulated by the new questions being asked, and exhilarated by the fact that many of the Luther passages I had found intriguing in the late disputations the Finns also recognized as significant. I soon realized that my own research was neither as groundbreaking nor as profound as I had hoped.

I have read a fair amount of Finnish scholarship over the past seven years and have learned much from it. But interestingly enough, the more of their work I have studied, the less sure I have become about the truth of some of my own early opinions about Luther's semantics and ontology, opinions that, I think, are generally quite in harmony with strands within the Finnish project. Perhaps this is due to an inclination in their work that I also sense in myself: the desire to "systematize" Luther.

The Finns are adept at discovering key passages (often from the early Luther), and ingenious in interpreting them in support of a comprehensive systematic theological vision built around deification. While this certainly has its theological benefits (especially for ecumenical work), I sometimes am disquieted by the thought that the results of their research may reflect their own presuppositions almost as much as the findings of the neo-Kantian Luther scholars obviously reflected theirs. I hope this is not the case.

Sammeli Juntunen's excellent paper and his published dissertation, *Der Begriff des Nichts bei Luther in den Jahren von 1510 bis 1523,* are examples of the kind of theologically stimulating and ecumenically fertile Finnish scholarship that now leave me just a bit uneasy. On the positive side, I can agree with all of the following:

1. Luther's own ontology does not conform to that which has been foisted upon him by Ebeling and Joest. Their understandings of Luther's comprehension of being are anachronistic, for they discover post-Gadamerian sophistication in a pre-Cartesian thinker. The problem has been the existence of certain neo-Kantian presuppositions that have precluded scholars from bringing Luther's own ontology into clear focus.
2. The antimetaphysical element in Luther's theology is due to a rejection of how *homo naturalis* employs metaphysics for purposes of self-aggrandizement. Luther asserts no general denial of ontology.

163

3. Luther holds to the Ockhamist notion of *creatio continua,* and thus denies any mediation by an *essentia, forma substantialis,* or *ordo naturae.* The Thomistic distinction between the divine *conservatio* and *creatio* collapses.

4. There is, for Luther, both an *esse-in* and *esse-ad* aspect to particular ontic regions; for example, both are required to understand the process of justification. However, Luther's denial of the category of created or "habitual" grace *(gratia gratum faciens)* requires the *esse-in* to be conceived as a presencing of *gratia increata.*

5. For Luther, a Christian is *nihil* before God because the human being is fully dependent upon God. In contrast to Ockham, a human being is not an *ens per se,* but rather an *ens per participatum* in the sense that the ground of its being lies outside itself.

6. God allows the believer to "descend into nothing" in order to cleanse her of the *amor hominis.* In the *opus alienum* of God, human beings are led into *Anfechtung* such that an annihilation of the old is accomplished, and a new "justified" being can take its place. There is, however, no complete eradication of concupiscence.

My uneasiness about Juntunen's work relates to concerns such as these:

1. The textual evidence for a general ontology in which reality has both an extrinsic and an intrinsic, nonsubstantial aspect appears to rest principally upon the distinction Luther draws in the 1513-1515 *Dictata super Psalterium* between God's *acta* and his *facta.* (While Luther's criticism of *substantia* recognizes that created beings have no *ens per se,* the Reformer nonetheless allows being to have an intrinsic aspect, a *factum dei* present in that being's natural and spiritual relationship to God.) But I am not sure that the five passages cited in the *Dictata* (two from the scholia to Psalm 28:4-5, one from Psalm 64:9, one from Psalm 104:23, and a glossa from Psalm 143) are sufficient to establish this distinction in Luther.

2. The preference Luther expresses for Plato over Aristotle in the *Heidelberg Disputation* is made to carry too much weight in

suggesting that all of created, natural being *(esse naturae)* itself participates in God. That the created order has its ground outside itself does not entail a "participation" in that ground. In fairness, Juntunen does indicate that there may not be enough evidence to support this suggestion.[6]

3. Shed of its existentialistic connotations, the distinction between *esse gratiae* and *esse naturae* seems to suggest a rather strong dualism. While Juntunen claims that his interpretation should no more be dismissed because it is based on early, "pre-Reformation" texts than the alternate interpretation of Ebeling, one must mention an asymmetry. Ebeling believes his view fits the mature Luther, and that it can already be found in the *Dictata;* Juntunen claims that his view nicely fits the *Dictata,* and that it can be extended into the mature Luther. When in doubt assume the thinker's mature position.

4. A final point concerns the Finnish penchant to place the category of *participation* at the conceptual center of their project. While Luther undoubtedly employs the notion, it seems to me that it must nonetheless be ontologically distinguished from the relation of being *present in*. It is not that the infinite can be predicated of the substance of the finite, but rather that the infinite is present in, permeating the substance of the finite in a nonaccidental way. The gift of Christ's person is present in the subject such that there is in the Christian an ontic unity of subjects. Perhaps *perichoresis* is the better image because it does not suggest that the finite person participates in the substance of the infinite.[7] We say, after all, that Christ's body

6. In *Der Begriff des Nichts bei Luther,* Juntunen devotes 110 pages to a survey of the notion of "nothing" in representative thinkers from Parmenides through Johannes von Staupitz. While at times, in both the paper and the book, he cautiously backs away from the claim that men and women enjoy a type of natural created participation in God, he nonetheless at other times strongly suggests participation, and devotes considerable effort to making it plausible. For instance, he writes: "Unseres Erachtens setzt Luthers Denkmodell, nach dem Gott im *esse naturae* anwesend ist, weil er die Existenz des Geschaffenen mit der Gegenwart seines Wesens wirkt, voraus, dass das *esse naturae* eine Teilhabe an Gott bedeutet" (p. 186).

7. This is not to suggest that the Finns don't use this notion as well. See,

is *present in* the bread, not that the bread *participates* in Christ's body.

None of what I say is meant to detract from the creativity and integrity of Sammeli Juntunen's work. It is clearly an example of the fascinating kind of scholarship that can emerge in a period of creative tension when a new paradigm is struggling to assert itself. It is good to have new, global questions asked of Luther, for they challenge our own presuppositions and allow us to read the Reformer with new eyes.

My caution in regard to Juntunen's project pertains to the sheer size of the Luther corpus, and the difficult task of synthesizing into a systematic position key passages sprinkled throughout these texts. It is so easy for those with a systematic-dogmatic approach to purchase Luther's theological consistency at the expense of the texts' own theological tensions, ambiguities, and imprecision. Given the *strukturierenden Idee* of deification, it is not surprising to find Juntunen finding in Luther an ontology in which divinization plays the central role.[8]

---

e.g., Risto Saarinen, "Die Teilhabe an Gott bei Luther und in der finnischen Lutherforschung," in *Luther und Ontologie,* ed. Ghiselli, Kopperi, and Vinke (Helsinki: Luther-Agricola Gesellschaft, 1993), pp. 175ff.

8. Recently, Klaus Schwarzwaller has raised five critical questions about the Finnish deification project in his "Verantwortung des Glaubens," in *Freiheit als Liebe bei Martin Luther,* ed. Dennis Bielfeldt and Klaus Schwarzwaller (Frankfurt: Peter Lang, 1995), pp. 146ff.: (1) Since the texts do not explicitly recognize divinization as their "organizing center," is it not possible that the interpreter's own projection is responsible for finding it there? (2) Are the Finns sometimes guilty of an interpretation of passages that contradicts the "immanent dynamic" of the texts themselves? (3) Do the Finns sometimes confuse the relation of identity with that of biconditionality, and a "logical identity" with a "doxological" one? (4) Do the Finns sometimes interpret Luther's idiomatic expressions too literally? For instance, "Greta gives herself in love to Hans" would not normally be interpreted as "Greta gives to Hans her being," or "Greta participates in the being of Hans." (5) Is it theologically justified to employ a univocal category of being when talking about God and the world? Whatever might be thought about the strength of these questions — I find (1) and (4) quite powerful — it is obvious that the Finns must give more attention to the task of defending their methodological starting point.

Salvation in the Lutheran-Orthodox Dialogue: A Comparative Perspective

RISTO SAARINEN

At its eighth meeting in Limassol, Cyprus, in August 1995, the Lutheran-Orthodox Joint Commission adopted a common statement called "Understanding of Salvation in the Light of the Ecumenical Councils."[1] This is the first soteriological statement during the fifteen years of dialogue at the world level.[2] But it was of course preceded by a number of regional common statements. In 1992, the results of the American Lutheran–Orthodox dialogue from 1983 to 1989 were published.[3] Among the many dialogues of the Evangelical Church of Germany (EKD), the fifth round of conversations with the Romanian Orthodox Church (1988) was fruitful in that it produced the document "Justification and Glorification (Theosis) of the Human Person through Jesus Christ."[4]

1. In the following this hitherto unpublished document is quoted according to its numbered paragraphs.
2. The earlier documents have been published as a booklet: *Lutheran-Orthodox Dialogue: Agreed Statements 1985-1989* (Geneva: LWF, 1992). To be added is the Statement of the 1993 Sandbjerg Consultation published in *LWF Today* 5 (1993): 10-11.
3. John Meyendorff and Robert Tobias, eds., *Salvation in Christ: A Lutheran-Orthodox Dialogue* (Minneapolis: Augsburg, 1992).
4. Recently published as *Rechtfertigung und Verherrlichung (Theosis) des Menschen durch Jesus Christus*, EKD-Studienheft 23 [hereinafter *RV*] (Hermanns-

Already in the 1970s the Finnish Lutheran Church, however, in its conversations with the Russian Orthodox Church, adopted a number of soteriological statements that compare the Lutheran doctrine of justification with the Orthodox view of deification *(theosis)*. Especially after the English publication of the results of the Finnish-Russian dialogue,[5] other regional conversations have made both explicit and implicit use of them. In the following survey of the above-mentioned Lutheran-Orthodox statements, I will begin with a presentation of the Finnish-Russian dialogue and then proceed to other regional dialogues and, finally, to the new document of the Joint Commission.

Soteriology in the Finnish-Russian Dialogue

During the ten conversations between the two churches, from 1970 to 1995, significant soteriological statements were adopted in Kiev (1977), Turku (1980), and Järvenpää (1992). The best known and most influential of these have been the theses on "Salvation as Justification and Deification," drafted in Kiev in 1977. The preamble to the theses claims that "Until recently, there has been a predominant opinion that the Lutheran and Orthodox doctrines of salvation greatly differ from each other. In the conversations, however, it has become evident that both these important aspects of salvation discussed in

---

burg: Missionshandlung Hermannsburg, 1995), pp. 29-33. All dialogues of the EKD have been published in the series "EKD-Studienhefte." The most recent overall bibliographical survey is Heinz Joachim Held, "40 Jahre Begegnungen EKD-Orthodoxie," *Materialdienst des Konfessionskundlichen Instituts Bensheim* 3 (1995): 47-54.

5. Hannu Kamppuri, ed., *Dialogue between Neighbours* (Helsinki: Luther-Agricola Gesellschaft, 1986; hereinafter *DBN*). Later conversations have appeared in English in the series "Documents of the Evangelical Lutheran Church of Finland," published by the Foreign Office of the Finnish Church. Minutes of the taped conversations are available in Finnish and Russian in the Foreign Office; they are in the following referred to as *Minutes*. For an overview, see Risto Saarinen, "25 Jahre theologische Gespräche zwischen Evangelisch-Lutherischer Kirche Finnlands und Moskauer Patriarchat," *Ökumenische Rundschau* 4 (1995).

the conversations have a strong New Testament basis and there is great unanimity with regard to them both."[6]

According to the Kiev common theses, justification of the human person takes place in baptism; baptism further initiates the process of deification, which is described as participation in divine life. The old Adam remains, however, even after baptism. Repentance and obedience to the commandments of God are therefore a necessary part of this process.[7] In this sense the doctrine of deification covers the idea of a Christian's life as righteous and sinful at the same time.

Given this, the Christian life can be described as follows: "When the Christian has been justified, he takes a new road leading to deification. The church understands it to be a process of growing in holiness or coming closer and closer to God. 'But we all, with open face beholding as in a mirror the glory of the Lord, are changed into the same image from glory to glory, even as by the Spirit of the Lord' (2 Cor. 3:18). Deification takes place under the influence of the grace of the Holy Spirit by a deep and sincere faith, together with hope and permeated by love (1 Cor. 13:13)."[8]

The churches further make two other common statements that may, from a Lutheran viewpoint, appear somewhat risky. First, they claim that the faith of parents and godparents plays a substitutionary role in infant baptism.[9] Second, concerning free will in salvation, the Kiev document says that "Grace never does violence to a man's personal will, but exerts its influence through it and with it. Every one has the opportunity to refuse consent to God's will or, by the help of the Holy Spirit, to consent to it."[10]

This formulation was afterward much discussed among Finnish theologians. Some found it more or less semi-Pelagian,[11] but others

6. *DBN*, p. 73.
7. *DBN*, p. 74.
8. *DBN*, p. 75.
9. *DBN*, p. 75.
10. *DBN*, p. 76.
11. Fredric Cleve, "Samtalen mellan Finlands och Rysslands kyrka," *Nordisk ekumenisk årsbok 1978-1979*, p. 84. Karl Christian Felmy, "Die orthodox-lutherischen Gespräche in Europa," *Ökumenische Rundschau* (1980), p. 514, says diplomatically that with this formulation the Finnish Lutherans have "met the concerns [Anliegen] of Orthodox synergism."

claimed that it only refutes a "quietist" view, according to which the Christian would be no more active in the process of salvation than is a stone or a log of wood.[12] Tuomo Mannermaa, who actually suggested the final formulation in Kiev, later defended it, saying, "The wording 'everyone has the possibility to refuse consent to God's will' can be understood in the light of the fact that the Orthodox in our conversations evidently speak of free will and of the freedom of human person in a strongly ontological sense. That is, they are in constant doubt that we conceive the human person as a stone or plant or animal which does not possess any freedom whatsoever. For them, freedom belongs to the constitution of human beings."[13]

The issue of synergism has a wider ecumenical significance because it plays a role in the Catholic-Lutheran dialogue. The recent discussion on the lifting of doctrinal condemnations between those churches offers parallels to the Lutheran-Orthodox discussions in Kiev in 1977.[14] In view of the Catholic-Lutheran convergences reached on this point one would think that the solution of Kiev may today be more easily acceptable for the Lutherans.

The real stumbling block for many, however, has not been synergism but rather the very idea that the Lutheran doctrine of justification can be compared adequately with the idea of deification of the human person. Whereas at least some Catholic theologians can hold that "the Roman Catholic Church has always taught the deification of man through God's grace,"[15] Protestants have during the last one hundred years constantly claimed that this ambivalent notion inevitably belongs to the abominable *theologia gloriae*.[16]

---

12. Referring to *Solida declaratio* II,59, the Finnish Archbishop Martti Simojoki (Kiev 1977 minutes, p. 87) pointed out that Lutherans do not teach such quietism although they consider the will to be "bound."

13. Minutes of Finnish-Russian preparatory seminars, April 17, 1979, p. 22.

14. See Karl Lehmann and Wolfhart Pannenberg, eds., *The Condemnations of the Reformation Era: Do They Still Divide?* (Minneapolis: Fortress, 1989), esp. p. 46. The issue of free will is also dealt with in the American Lutheran–Orthodox dialogue; see *Salvation in Christ*, pp. 28-30.

15. Miguel Garijo-Guembe, "Schwesterkirchen im Dialog," *Catholica* (1994): 279-93, here p. 285.

16. Cf. Georg Kretschmar, "Die Rezeption der orthodoxen Vergöttlichungslehre in der protestantischen Theologie," *Luther und Theosis* (Helsinki:

Although the reception of the idea of deification often has been criticized, especially in Germany,[17] some professional ecumenists have viewed it positively. Heinz Joachim Held, for example, says of justification as a lifelong process: "Perhaps one can here really draw, as one of the Kiev common theses does, a connecting line between the understanding of justification of the sinner through God's work in the theology of the Reformation and the view of the Orthodox church concerning the salvatory action of God upon human beings called 'deification.'"[18]

On the other hand, the Orthodox still often experience that the notion of deification is simply unacceptable for Protestants. During the ninth Finnish-Russian conversations in Järvenpää in 1992, Vladimir Sorokin described the situation, saying, "I participated in a dialogue with German Lutherans, and there the word 'deification' had to be deleted from the text. It was totally incomprehensible for the German Lutherans."[19]

But on what theological grounds, then, do the Finnish Lutherans consider that a convergence between the two notions can be established? The main arguments can be found in the paper delivered by Tuomo Mannermaa in Kiev. This paper, later enlarged to a book and published in German as a study in Luther's theology,[20] has been extensively discussed in Reformation research. I have surveyed this discussion elsewhere;[21] here it suffices to say that Mannermaa con-

---

Luther-Agricola Gesellschaft, 1990), pp. 61-80; and Simo Puera, *Mehr als ein Mensch? Die Vergöttlichung als Thema der Theologie Martin Luthers von 1513 bis 1519* (Mainz: Philipp von Zabern, 1994), pp. 9-45.

17. In a later Finnish-Russian preparatory seminar (minutes, October 24, 1990, p. 7), Tuomo Mannermaa tells of a German professor who remarked to him: "Immer wenn Sie, Herr Mannermaa, über Theosis reden, bekomme ich Magenschmerzen!"

18. Heinz Joachim Held, "Glaube und Liebe in der Erlangung des Heils," *Das Heil in Christus und die Heilung der Welt,* EKD-Studienheft 20 (Hermannsburg: Missionsverlag Hermannsburg, 1985), p. 53.

19. Järvenpää 1992 minutes, p. 60.

20. *Der im Glauben gegenwärtige Christus* (Hannover: Lutherisches Verlagshaus, 1989).

21. Risto Saarinen, "The Presence of God in Luther's Theology," *Lutheran Quarterly* (1994): 3-13.

siders Luther's motif of "Christ present in faith" *(in ipsa fide Christus adest),* as elaborated especially in his *Commentary on Galatians,* a "real-ontic" theological idea that approaches the Orthodox view of deification. With his students Mannermaa has also published several studies on the influence of patristic theology on Luther and the Reformation.[22]

In later Finnish-Russian conversations, the theology of love and the idea of participation in the divine life carry further the basic convergence between justification and deification. The theses of the next conversations in Turku (1980) were titled "Faith and Love as Elements of Salvation." The salvific participation is described as follows: "When we become members of his church in holy baptism, and when we believe in him, the Son of God, who came into the world to save sinners, we participate in his divine life. When we receive Christ through his holy Word and holy sacraments, we become — in the different wordings of our distinct traditions — God's children (Rom. 8:14-17), justification (Rom. 3:24) and reconciliation (2 Cor. 5:18) are bestowed upon us, and we are deified (1 John 3:2)."[23]

According to the Turku (1980) theses, the Christian's love has "a decisive role in salvation." It is a "response to the love of God" that manifests itself as faithfulness to God and love for one's neighbors.[24] The present Christ exercises a sort of sanative function in this process: "The more man extends the love he has received from God to his neighbors, the more Christ is formed in him (Gal. 4:19, Eph. 3:17-19) and the more effectively he can withstand evil. In this effort to attain sanctification man, however, always remains imperfect (Matt. 5:48, Phil. 3:12-14) and always needs renewed penitence and forgiveness of sins."[25]

---

22. In addition to the bibliographical notes in Saarinen, "Presence of God," see the two recent volumes in the series "Veröffentlichungen der Luther-Akademie Ratzeburg," namely *Luther und die trinitarische Tradition* (Erlangen: Martin Luther Verlag, 1994) and *Der Heilige Geist: ökumenische und reformatorische Untersuchungen* (Erlangen: Martin Luther Verlag, 1995).

23. *DBN,* p. 87.

24. *DBN,* p. 88.

25. *DBN,* p. 88.

In his address delivered in Turku in 1980 Tuomo Mannermaa more extensively elaborated this theology of the Christian life as participation in Christ. He there aimed at showing that for Luther the Christ present in faith is the *forma fidei,* the realization or concrete manifestation of faith. Whereas Catholic theology considers love as such a *forma,* Luther regards Christ himself as the link between faith and good works.[26] The relation between one's extending love and growing in Christ in the above-quoted statement is therefore not a causal link but a parallel and mutual development.

The ecclesial context of salvation has a primary importance for Orthodox theology. Already in the Leningrad (1983) conversations the first ecclesiological attempts were made. But in my view it was only in the theses of Järvenpää (1992) that the ecclesial dimension became consistently integrated into this view of salvation. The theses proceed from the biblical view that Christ has promised to be with his church always (Matt. 28:20). The encounter with Christ in the church further opens up a trinitarian perspective:

> In Christ we encounter the triune God. It is in his Son that God the Father reveals his infinite and incomprehensible love to us, and it is through the revelation and illumination by the Holy Spirit that we can learn to know the Son of God.
>
> Salvation is not only an event of the past but also a present reality in the church and in the lives of the faithful. The saving presence of Christ and the Holy Spirit is realized in proclaiming the gospel, in administering the sacraments and in worship. It is in and through them that God unites us with himself and gives us his gifts. He creates in us the true apostolic faith, in which we participate in the triune God and the salvation that is in him. This faith is effective as love (Gal. 5:6, 1 John 4:19).[27]

Deification is not explicitly mentioned here, but such expressions as "presence of Christ," "union with God," and "participation in the Triune God" once again underline the realistic character of salvation. One may also note in passing that the trinitarian perspective employed

26. Published in German in Mannermaa, *Der im Glauben,* pp. 95-105.
27. Järvenpää 1992, *Documents of the Evangelical Lutheran Church of Finland* 5 (1993): 15.

here offers connections with the recent ecclesiology of communion discussed in worldwide ecumenism.[28]

Salvation in the Dialogues of the Evangelical Church of Germany

The Evangelical Church of Germany (EKD) has conducted extensive dialogues with the Patriarchates of Moscow and Constantinople and with the Romanian Orthodox Church. In addition to the EKD-Romanian dialogue, some achievements of the dialogue with Moscow should be mentioned here.

The fifth EKD-Russian conversations in 1971 in particular were able to draft common theses concerning salvation. Behind this convergence one may see the influence of Professor Georg Kretschmar's background paper. Kretschmar argues on the one hand that the Orthodox view of deification does not contain any "physical-material-istic," "collective," or "automatic" implications concerning the salvatory process. On the other hand he regards Luther's idea of the Christian's growing similarity *(conformitas, Gleichförmigkeit)* with Christ as a teaching of a transformation that approaches Orthodox thinking.[29]

Although the common theses do not go this far, the EKD in them adopts a view of salvation that employs sanative terminology. Consider, for example: "Through the intimate communion with the risen Christ the Christian receives the gifts of grace which strengthen his faith and encourage him to respond to the love of God which heals his will, contributes to his moral perfection and prepares him for eternal life."[30]

---

28. See, e.g., Thomas Best and Günther Gassmann, eds., *On the Way to Fuller Koinonia* (Geneva: WCC Publications, 1994) and Lutheran–Roman Catholic Joint Commission, *Church and Justification* (Geneva: LWF and Pontifical Council for Promoting Christian Unity, 1994), esp. pp. 35-59.

29. Georg Kretschmar, "Kreuz und Auferstehung in der Sicht von Athanasius und Luther," *Der auferstandene Christus und das Heil der Welt*, EKD-Studienheft 7 [hereinafter *Heil*] (Witten: Luther-Verlag, 1972), pp. 40-82, here pp. 52-54, 65-67, 250.

30. *Heil*, p. 22.

The theses clearly affirm effective justification, but at the same time they emphasize the hiddenness of the reality of the new life. One may also note a christological concentration; of the crucified and risen Lord it is said that "he calls human persons into faith and renews them from within; in particular through the unavoidable bearing of the cross he encloses Christians in his death and resurrection. But this change of the human person remains hidden, although the living faith of Christians constantly finds its expression in their external behavior (1 Cor. 6:20). Therefore the victory of Christ over death and the gift of new life are now hidden and they can be experienced only in faith."[31]

Although these views share much with the Finnish-Russian dialogue, the notion of deification is avoided in this and other contemporary dialogue documents of the EKD. This state of affairs changes, however, in the conversations with the Romanian Orthodox Church during the 1980s. The notion of deification was briefly surveyed already in 1985,[32] but in 1988 an important common statement on salvation was adopted. In its beginning both the Lutheran doctrine of justification and the Orthodox view are outlined.

Concerning the Orthodox view, a distinction is made between deification in a proper sense, which denotes the final perfection of our communion with God, and deification in a wider sense, which covers the whole process of sanctification. This wider sense also includes justification, which is afterward "crowned by glorification" (cf. Rom. 8:30).[33] In the document the notion of glorification is understood as synonymous with deification; both the proper and the wider sense are then included.

The Lutheran view is outlined as follows: "In evangelical theology, the word 'justification' normally covers the whole way of salvation [*Heilsweg*] between God and baptized believers. This terminology can also be found in the Apostle St. Paul (e.g. Romans 5:18-19)."[34]

The common statement further declares that both partners agree with the goal of salvation:

31. *Heil*, p. 20.
32. *Das Heil in Christus*, esp. pp. 17-18.
33. *RV*, p. 30.
34. *RV*, p. 30.

We have a consensus about the goal of the road to fulfilment promised by God to God's people. The goal is participation in God's glory in communion with the crucified, risen and exalted Lord, by the power of the Holy Spirit. Although the word "deification" is normally not employed in evangelical spirituality, what it refers to [*die Sache*] is not unknown. Especially the hymns of Christmas time written during the Reformation sing of deification in agreement with the fathers of the Old Church. We also affirm together that participation in the divine nature (2 Peter 1:4) does not abolish the essential difference between Creator and creature.[35]

The theses also outline the relation between faith and love in salvation. As in the Finnish-Russian conversations, Luther's own language is referred to when the difficult issue of cooperation is discussed:

We affirm together that God is not at work in the human person mechanically, but that God wants to win the human heart and therefore calls for the person's faith, love and in this sense also good works. We do not disagree on such a "synergy of love" which affirms that God's love through Christ's cross and resurrection makes us free to love God and our neighbors and even the whole creation. We further teach that this love is also the very root of Christian social responsibility for the world. The Reformation did not describe the redemption of the sinner only as justification, but also as a bond of love, employing the picture of engagement between man and woman.[36]

The document admits, however, that the problem of *synergeia* is not completely solved. It further holds that in spite of the above-quoted convergences no common language concerning salvation has been established.[37]

The presence of God and our "being in Christ" are affirmed in a way that resembles the Finnish-Russian formulations: "Justification and the new life belong intimately together. Sanctification (deification) begins in the Holy Spirit in whom the Triune God is present and at

35. *RV,* p. 30.
36. *RV,* p. 31.
37. *RV,* p. 31.

work in the faithful Christian. . . . The Christian must and may remain 'in Christ,' who himself fights in us against sin and so lets us already now, under the cross, participate in his resurrection and glorification."[38]

In sum, we see that the topic of deification is not "totally incomprehensible" for the German Lutherans, as Professor Sorokin in our above-quoted statement had experienced. The EKD here clearly affirms "the issue" of deification, although its terminological absence is no doubt a fact in modern Protestant spirituality. As to the theological preparatory work of this statement, Georg Kretschmar's background paper once again plays a central role.[39]

The American Common Statement

The American Lutheran–Orthodox *Common Statement* quite extensively refers to the Finnish-Russian dialogue,[40] whereas the dialogues of the EKD are not quoted. Since I basically agree with what Simo Peura has written in his review essay on this document,[41] I will here only make some short comparisons with earlier dialogues.

As Peura rightly points out, a main problem in the document is the claim that "for Lutherans 'justification' and 'sanctification' are two distinct theological categories, one designating God's declaration of righteousness, the other the gradual process of growth in the Christian life."[42] As both the Finnish Lutheran Church and the EKD in their dialogues understand justification to cover the whole salvation process of which sanctification is one aspect, the terminological preconditions of the American dialogue are somewhat different.

A minor point pertains to the elaboration of 2 Peter 1:4, a central verse of the Orthodox theology of deification, of which the *Common Statement* says that it "has no such importance in Lutheran thinking or

---

38. *RV,* p. 31.

39. Kretschmar, "Rechtfertigung und Vergottung," *RV,* pp. 160-79.

40. *Salvation in Christ,* p. 23; see also pp. 59-60, 79.

41. Simo Peura, "A Review Essay on Salvation in Christ," *Pro Ecclesia* 2 (1993): 364-71.

42. *Salvation in Christ,* p. 19.

spirituality."[43] This is not quite accurate. Martin Schmidt has shown that this very verse had an especially wide currency in Pietism; Georg Kretschmar's recent studies underline the vivid impact of the same idea, for example, in the Christmas hymns of the Reformation.[44]

In spite of these remarks, however, I think that the American document in principle covers much of the same ground as the other regional Lutheran Orthodox documents. As in the EKD-Romanian statement, both churches affirm "that the ultimate goal of salvation is communion with the living God." Concerning free will and *synergeia,* the Lutheran side arrives at a certain positive understanding of the hermeneutical importance of free will in order to refute deterministic or quietist consequences. Pantheistic conclusions are avoided by saying that through deification "human beings are introduced into a personal relationship of participation in God's life."[45] Generally speaking, the christological concentration of the *Common Statement* in regard to both justification and sanctification connects its results with those of the Finnish-Russian and the EKD-Romanian dialogues.

A First Attempt at the World Level: Limassol 1995

Although the regional documents no doubt are a valuable resource, one cannot apply their results without further considerations at the global level. Since the Lutheran delegation is appointed by the Lutheran World Federation, it only includes persons from its member churches. The role of the EKD thus remains somewhat unclear. A greater practical problem, however, is that the Church of Greece is not a partner in any of the regional documents mentioned above. Moreover, the long dialogue between the EKD and the Patriarchate of Constantinople has not been able to produce any common theses on salvation.[46]

---

43. *Salvation in Christ,* p. 20.

44. Martin Schmidt, "Teilnahme an der göttlichen Natur," in his *Wiedergeburt und neuer Mensch* (Witten: Luther Verlag, 1969), pp. 238-98; Kretschmar, "Rechtfertigung und Vergottung," esp. pp. 164-65.

45. *Salvation in Christ,* pp. 24, 29-30.

46. The documentation has been published in the series "EKD-Studienhefte."

Since at the global level the Orthodox delegation consists of the members of the Orthodox churches in communion with the Ecumenical Patriarch, and since the role of Greek theologians is therefore quite strong, the statements of regional dialogues outside of Greece have only a limited significance. A careful reconsideration of all the central issues is needed. During the first twelve years of its work (1981-1993), the Joint Commission worked mainly with the problem of Scripture and tradition. After that, the Limassol statement is the first attempt at a common expression of soteriology at the global level.

The statement first describes extensively the doctrines of the Seven Ecumenical Councils. In doing so it follows the practice of the earlier dialogue results of the Joint Commission, in which it was concluded that the doctrines of these councils are authoritative for both confessions.[47]

The second part of the document is titled "Justification and Glorification as Descriptions of Salvation"; in it we find the first attempts toward convergence. Salvation is described in terms of the victory of Christ over sin: ". . . salvation in both the Old and New Testaments is our liberation from slavery to sin, the devil and death, and our participation in the life of Christ, who destroyed death by death and gives life to those in the tomb. In this context justification *(dikaiosis)* is liberation from the dominion of the devil and the restoration of our communion with God. Those who are justified are glorified (Rom. 8:30) in the Body of Christ" (para. 6).

In the EKD-Romanian dialogue, "glorification" *(Verherrlichung)* is understood as synonymous with deification. In my view, the same is true in the Limassol Statement, although the identification of the two notions is not entirely unproblematic. The use of Romans 8:30 establishes a biblical link between justification and glorification; this link enables the dialogue partners to employ both notions together.

The document then continues: "By baptism and participation in the other mysteries (sacraments) of the church, the faithful are raised to a new life of righteousness in Christ, together with all the prophets and saints of the Old and New Testaments. God gives them, in the Holy Spirit, the power to pass through purification and illumination

47. So, e.g., Sandbjerg (1993): 11.

of the heart and arrive 'with all the saints' (Eph. 3:18) at glorification (Mt. 17:2; Jn. 17:22; 2 Cor. 3:18; 2 Pet. 1:4)" (para. 6).

The use of the triad purification-illumination-glorification here is new for Lutherans. In view of the regional dialogues, this vocabulary is not the only way to express the Orthodox doctrine, but in the Limassol Statement the Orthodox position is defined (para. 8) in terms of exactly these three notions. "Illumination" is there identified with justification.

The biblical verses added to clarify the notion of glorification in paragraph 6 above reflect primarily the Orthodox understanding of the concept. On the one hand they lay out the New Testament roots of the idea of glorification, but on the other hand they are open to different interpretations. As to the Lutheran understanding of this idea, one must keep in mind the regional dialogues in which the Lutherans have been able to affirm the "issue" of deification in spite of terminological problems. This affirmation is here repeated.

The Lutheran description of salvation (para. 9), while affirming *sola fide* and the forensic declaration of righteousness, also employs the notions of participation and the presence of Christ in faith, which in regional dialogues have offered useful convergences: "Justification is a real participation in Christ, true God and true human being. In the church, the believer by faith participates in Christ and all his gifts, and so has a share in the divine life. The presence of Christ in faith genuinely effects the righteousness of Christ in us and leads believers to the sanctification of their lives" (para. 9). While sanctification is admitted, it is in this paragraph considered an aspect and effect of justification rather than a distinct reality.

While the Lutheran side is thus offering connections to the language employed at the regional dialogues, the common affirmations remain rather vague. In addition to the above-quoted paragraph 6, both sides only affirm together (para. 10) a general importance of the ecumenical councils that "provide guidelines for the purification and illumination of the heart to glorification in Christ for the salvation and justification of humanity." This statement is hardly more than an additive list of salvific notions. The last paragraph (11) says that these notions need to be explored further.

Conclusions

Compared with the important convergences reached in the regional dialogues, the new document of the Lutheran-Orthodox Joint Commission remains very general. One must keep in mind, however, that during its twenty-five years of dialogue with the Ecumenical Patriarchate (1969-1994), the EKD was never able to draft any common doctrinal statements with Constantinople. The Lutheran World Federation has at least succeeded in doing this. Another positive feature from the Lutheran perspective is that the description of justification (para. 9) is very unambiguous and at the same time compatible with the results of the regional dialogues and with dialogues with other confessions.[48]

Perhaps the rationale to be drawn from this short comparison of some recent statements is that much of the most important theological and ecumenical work is done at the regional level. Regional dialogues can take initiatives and develop new approaches to the dividing issues, whereas the dialogue at the world level often does not have the same amount of intellectual and spiritual flexibility. In the case of the Lutheran-Orthodox dialogue on salvation a number of important convergences have been discovered and mutually shared in the regional dialogues. In the course of time they may be elaborated, modified, and received in the global dialogue as well.

48. The above-mentioned Lutheran–Roman Catholic document *Church and Justification* in particular employs the language of participation in its characterization of salvation.

Contributors

DENNIS BIELFELDT, Associate Professor of Philosophy and Religion, South Dakota University, Brookings, South Dakota.

CARL E. BRAATEN, Director, Center for Catholic and Evangelical Theology; Co-Editor, *Pro Ecclesia*.

ROBERT W. JENSON, Center of Theological Inquiry, Princeton, New Jersey; Associate Director, Center for Catholic and Evangelical Theology; Co-Editor, *Pro Ecclesia*.

SAMMELI JUNTUNEN, Assistant for Ecumenics, Department of Systematic Theology, University of Helsinki, Finland.

WILLIAM H. LAZARETH, Bishop Emeritus, Metropolitan Synod of New York, Evangelical Lutheran Church in America.

TUOMO MANNERMAA, Professor of Ecumenics, Department of Systematic Theology, University of Helsinki, Finland.

SIMO PUERA, Director of Institute for Advanced Training, Järvenpää, Finland; Docent of Ecumenics, University of Helsinki, Finland.

ANTTI RAUNIO, Assistant for Systematic Theology, Department of Systematic Theology, University of Helsinki, Finland.

RISTO SAARINEN, Research Professor, Institute for Ecumenical Research, Strasbourg, France.